RESERVOIR YEAR

Praise for *Reservoir Year: A Walker's Book of Days*

"Nina Shengold's beautifully calibrated rhythm of language conveys all the rhythm of the walking—the quiet, graceful stride along with lively, animated steps, the contemplative solitary strolls and those shared with companions. But she offers us as well the rhythm of the infinitesimal and the grand; of the expected and the unexpected; of the abstract and the real. Shengold suggests what it is to be an attentive human being, which is why accompanying her on these reservoir walks is as restorative as the walks themselves."

—Akiko Busch, author of *How to Disappear: Notes on Invisibility in a Time of Transparency*

"Nina Shengold's memoir explores a reservoir of feelings. Accompanied by her elegant, unpretentious prose, the reader comes upon surprises: a bear, an eagle feather, a crimson forest. Filled to the brim with subtle revelations, of sun-washed illuminations but also the poignant history; a drowned town lies below the shimmering surface. Expect to be moved, and then overcome by the tenderness and variety of Shengold's emotional literary palette."

—Laura Shaine Cunningham, author of *Sleeping Arrangements* and *A Place in the Country*

"It's hard to imagine an investigation of place as precise and simultaneously as ebullient as Shengold's. *Reservoir Year* is a slow-cooker in a world of microwaves: if its joys don't convince you to decelerate and attend your own life a bit more, something is wrong. This is nature writing of the highest and most delightful order, a treat to read in great gulps or daily, the way Shengold lived it."

—David Van Biema, coauthor, *The Prayer Wheel: A Daily Guide to Renewing Your Faith with a Rediscovered Spiritual Practice*

"Nina Shengold's *Reservoir Year* is a book of beauty, pleasure, pathos, and wonderful good humor. Her *Walker's Book of Days* along the Ashokan Reservoir is both a lyrical form of devotion as well as halcyon cry to wake up and notice the life around us. With eyes like a Zen master, the author turns the ordinary into the extraordinary, boredom shifts into awe, and duty becomes unstoppable passion. Nina Shengold shows us how the simple act of paying attention in our tech-addled and divisive world offers restoration, sanity, and inspiration. A most timely and superb book!"

—Gail Straub, activist and author, *The Ashokan Way: Landscape's Path into Consciousness*

Reservoir Year

A Walker's Book of Days

NINA SHENGOLD

Map and Line Drawings by Will Lytle

Hand-Colored Linocuts by Carol Zaloom

Syracuse University Press

All Rights Reserved

First Edition 2020

20 21 22 23 24 25   7 6 5 4 3 2

∞ The paper used in this publication meets the minimum requirements of the
American National Standard for Information Sciences—Permanence of Paper for
Printed Library Materials, ANSI Z39.48-1992.

For a listing of books published and distributed by Syracuse University Press,
visit https://press.syr.edu.

ISBN: 978-0-8156-3696-0 (hardcover)
    978-0-8156-1124-0 (paperback)
    978-0-8156-5507-7 (e-book)

Library of Congress Cataloging-in-Publication Data

Names: Shengold, Nina, author.

Title: Reservoir year : a walker's book of days / Nina Shengold.

Description: First edition. | Syracuse, New York : Syracuse University Press, [2020] |
    Summary: "On the brink of her sixtieth birthday, Shengold embarks on a challenge:
    to take the same walk along the banks of the Ashokan Reservoir, in New York's
    Catskill Mountain region, every day for a year and find something new every
    time"— Provided by publisher.

Identifiers: LCCN 2020006850 (print) | LCCN 2020006851 (ebook) |
    ISBN 9780815636960 (hardback) | ISBN 9780815611240 (paperback) |
    ISBN 9780815655077 (ebook)

Subjects: LCSH: Walking—New York (State)—Ashokan Reservoir. | Walking—
    Philosophy. | Ashokan Reservoir (N.Y.)

Classification: LCC GV199.42.N652 A757 2020 (print) | LCC GV199.42.N652 A757
    2020 (ebook) | DDC 796.5109747—dc23

LC record available at https://lccn.loc.gov/2020006850

LC ebook record available at https://lccn.loc.gov/2020006851

Manufactured in the United States of America

to Leonard and Margaret Shengold
my trailblazers

The place to observe nature is where you are; the walk to take today is the walk you took yesterday. You will not find just the same things: both the observed and the observer have changed.

—John Burroughs, *Signs and Seasons*

Contents

Preamble

I LIVE IN THE FOOTHILLS of the Catskills, four miles from the glorious Ashokan Reservoir. For a year, I walked by its side every day, in all kinds of weather, from predawn to starlight.

My usual path is a former roadbed on top of the reservoir's main dam. There's a small parking lot near the village of Olivebridge rimmed by wildflowers, hardwoods, and pines. You pass through a row of traffic barrier columns and take a few strides to the edge of the trees, and the world opens up: a panoramic vista of water, mountains, and sky. People stop in their tracks and gasp. I once heard an awestruck child cry out, "Is that the *ocean*? Mom! What *is* this place??"

It's a good question. I spent a year trying to answer it, day after day after day. I was poised to turn sixty, a birthday that can't help but rattle the ribcage. My daughter Maya was at college in Vermont and I missed her bright energy daily; my parents were dwindling into their nineties. And my dog had died.

Chris was my first dog, a not-so-golden retriever mix we adopted when Maya was a first grader with puppy lust. Having a dog ensures that you spend time outdoors every day, however you're feeling, whatever the weather gets up to. And that lifts your spirits, whether you like it or not. It's not just the endorphins from exercise, but the subtle pleasures of noticing seasonal changes. What new flower has opened today? Look at the frost on that leaf. Are the robins back yet? It's a daily unfolding of wonder, a pause in a day that is otherwise crowded with too much to do.

For thirteen years, we took the same walk every day, at first circling the block in a three-mile loop, later a mile to the end of the road and back, and finally a stop-and-go shuffle on a flat stretch of road in front of my house. I couldn't bear to walk my block dogless, so I stopped walking. Of course I gained weight, and felt trapped and depressed, but months passed before I got a clue.

It took two of my brother David's friends, visiting from Saint Petersburg, Russia, to open my eyes. When I asked what they'd enjoyed most on their trip to America, Sergei didn't hesitate. The Ashokan Reservoir, where David had taken them that afternoon. Such magnificence!

I was flooded with shame. The Ashokan is practically in my backyard, and I hadn't walked there for months. Twelve miles long and a mile across, divided into unequal halves by a multiarched weir bridge across its wasp waist, the reservoir is an ideal reflecting pool for the Catskill High Peaks. The vast expanse of water allows a long-distance view of a densely forested range that could otherwise be seen only from above. The Ashokan is a different kind of gorgeous in every season, in every kind of weather and light. But its beauty is built on a paradox. Beneath its great bowl lie the ruins of twelve communities uprooted by the city of New York in an arrogant turn-of-the-century land grab that impounded the Esopus Creek to bring mountain water to an urban island that had outgrown its water supply.

Between 1907 and 1916, more than two thousand people were evicted from land their families had farmed for generations. Trees were chopped down, stumps grubbed, buildings burned, cemeteries exhumed. African American and immigrant laborers died in labor camp brawls and industrial accidents. When the thousand-foot dam was complete and the water began to rise, it flooded a valley once filled with farm fields and country stores, gristmills and blacksmith shops, bluestone quarries and railroad tracks, churches and graveyards. Though this grim history is detailed in such books as Bob Steuding's *The Last of the Handmade Dams* and Diane Galusha's *Liquid Assets: A History of New York City's Water System*, most of the people who visit the scenic location have little idea of what came before.

Along New York State Routes 28 and 28A, the two roads that encircle the reservoir, a series of brown highway department signs commemorates the Former Sites of Ashokan, Ashton, Boiceville, Brodhead, Brown's Station, Glenford, Olive, Olive Bridge, Shokan, Stony Hollow, West Hurley,

West Shokan. The names toll like church bells, bemoaning a past so completely erased that even official signs disagree on exactly how many hamlets and towns were destroyed or uprooted to higher ground.

The name "Ashokan" comes from an Algonkian word variously translated as "place of many fish" and "to cross the creek" (another erasure of history; the Esopus Indians were displaced by European colonists long before their descendants were displaced by the dam). Jay Ungar's haunting fiddle tune "Ashokan Farewell" was featured in Ken Burns's Civil War documentary series and widely recorded. Its plaintive blend of uplift and lament is an ideal soundtrack for this place of great natural beauty and manmade sorrow. It's a landscape that gets in your bones.

After Sergei pronounced the Ashokan "magnificent," I took a walk there one September evening, went home, and wrote about it. Then I did it again. I've always been moved by art that revisits the same subject again and again over time: Monet's water lilies and studies of Rouen Cathedral, Nicholas Nixon's photo series of four sisters aging. Could I do that with words?

More to the point, could I do it at all? What about weather, and travel, and getting sick? What about willpower?

I am not a person of discipline. New Year's resolutions head south before Groundhog Day; diets disintegrate; writing regimens of so many words per day dead-end the first time I don't make my quota. As soon as I made the decision to walk every day for a year, I felt a familiar shiver of doom. But the thought of it wouldn't let go. Reluctant or eager, I had to keep going. I got obsessed.

My intent was to write about what I observed—to be camera, not subject—but my daily walks conjured all the back roads that had brought me to this one. As a kid growing up in an orderly New Jersey suburb, my favorite book was Jean Craighead George's *My Side of the Mountain*, about a teenage boy who lives off the land in the Catskills, sleeping inside a hollow tree and training a peregrine falcon to hunt. I wanted to *be* Sam Gribley, girl version. I hungered for life in the wild.

At twenty-two, I took a radical swerve from my urban career goals and spent a year living out of a backpack with no fixed plan, wandering through the Pacific Northwest and north to Alaska. In my thirties,

I bought an old farmhouse in the Catskills and became a single mother, forging a warming fire of creative connections with my new community.

Who would I be at age sixty? I was going to find out, come hell or high water.

When I told people what I was doing, their first response was nearly always "Are you taking pictures?" It was often asked anxiously, as if the experience wouldn't exist if it weren't recorded in pixels.

"Nope," I would tell them. "I'm doing it old school." I didn't even take paper and pen on my walks; I wanted to train myself to experience things with my senses and carry them back in my mind, to hunt and gather unarmed. There's a kind of surrender in this, trusting the sieve of memory to strain wheat from chaff. In a world where we stare at computer screens for hours every day and carry our cell phones and digital cameras wherever we go, it's good to remember that we *are* recording devices: our eyes, ears, and noses, our tongues and our skin take things in, and it's good to be fully awake when it happens. When a bald eagle flies over your head, you don't want to miss it because you're hunched over your notebook.

My daily walks ranged from a quick half mile out and back to five miles or more. Sometimes I went off road, exploring the many access points for fishing and hunting along the reservoir's forty-four miles of shoreline. (Since I wasn't fishing or hunting, this wasn't exactly approved "Recreational Use," but I improvised.)

I walked sometimes with family and friends, more often alone. As a freelance writer-editor-teacher, I could start or end my workday at the Ashokan, or take a lunch break between marathon sits at my desk. I could—and did—go out walking after midnight. From September 2015 to September 2016, I structured my comings and goings around reservoir walks, rerouting both day-to-day errands and overnight trips. If I had to travel, I stopped at the Ashokan on my way to or from the train station or airport. I commuted daily from a residential writing workshop across the Hudson and irritated my relatives by driving home and back—a round trip of more than five hundred miles—midway through a family reunion.

This is how an obsession takes hold. It's not a decision to strap on the harness, but a slow-dawning realization that you've got a bit between your teeth and an unshakable weight on your back spurring you on. I had no way to predict what would happen during my reservoir year. I only knew where I had to be to find out.

It wasn't a wilderness retreat on some remote mountaintop, or even Thoreau's Walden Pond (down the railroad track from his parents' house, where the apostle of solitude often ate lunch). The Ashokan walkway—what locals call "walking the dam"—is a paved former road frequented by hikers, exercise walkers, runners, bicyclists, rollerbladers, skateboarders, tourists with iPhones, and wildlife photographers staking out calendar shots of the resident eagles. I'm far from the only regular, and the human ecology interested me as much as the minks and mergansers. If you live nearby and frequent "the res," you may find yourself (or some version thereof; certain names and identifying details have been changed) in this book. My apologies for any misguided assumptions.

What I set out to do was go back to the same place again and again and find something new every time, to check in with the daily rhythms and cycles of nature, and sometimes to glimpse the sublime. Come along for the walk.

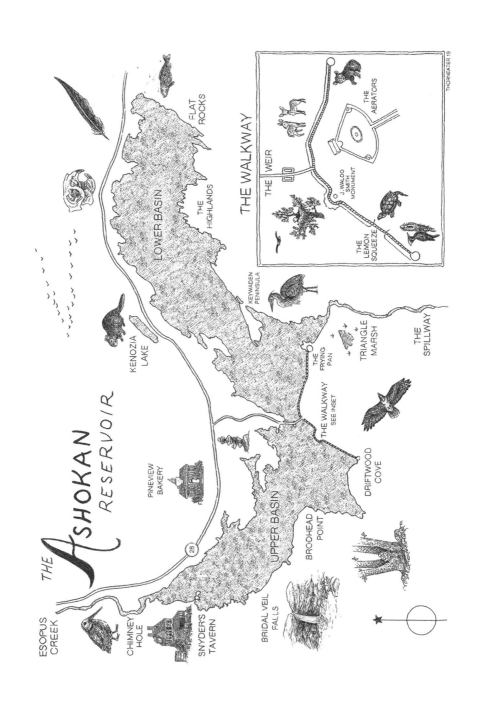

THE ASHOKAN RESERVOIR

ESOPUS CREEK

CHIMNEY HOLE

SNYDER'S TAVERN

PINEVIEW BAKERY

28

KENOZIA LAKE

LOWER BASIN

THE HIGHLANDS

FLAT ROCKS

BRIDAL VEIL FALLS

UPPER BASIN

BRODHEAD POINT

THE WALKWAY SEE INSET

DRIFTWOOD COVE

THE FRYING PAN

KEYWADEN PENINSULA

TRIANGLE MARSH

THE SPILLWAY

THE WALKWAY

THE WEIR

THE AERATORS

J. WALDO SMITH MONUMENT

THE LEMON SQUEEZE

THORNEATER '19

RESERVOIR YEAR

Fall

Day 1. **September 15, 2015, 7 PM**

Sunset walk along the Ashokan Reservoir under whisper-pastel sky. Two deer graze on the steep embankment below the walkway over the Olive-bridge Dam. I stand still, holding my breath as they work their way toward me. The doe stays a few yards downhill, but the fawn comes so close I can see white fur lining its ears and hear its teeth munching vetch.

A bicyclist passes. They spook and charge down the hill, white tails flashing. I turn to see western clouds streaked flamingo, with a sliver of new moon hovering over the cleft of Slide Mountain.

Day 2. **September 16, 6:20 PM**

Jazzed by yesterday's sunset, I come back for seconds. This time I set out from the opposite end of the walkway, the parking circle locally known as the Frying Pan, heading due west with the setting sun right in my eyes. The slanting rays gild the high grasses, backlighting every seedhead.

There's much more sensation of bowl and big sky from this side, an undulant skyline of Catskill High Peaks. A weir bridge carves the reservoir into two basins, Upper and Lower. Sometimes the shorelines are wildly different, one drought-low and studded with islands, one lapping the edge of the forest with no beach at all. These levels change often, as water's released into the Upper Basin from the Schoharie Reservoir, higher up in the Catskills, and into the Catskill Aqueduct, which ferries fresh mountain water to Manhattan taps. Right now both basins are low. I reach the weir just as the sun slips, slowly then suddenly, behind the ridge.

There's an instant gold halo. The peach-peel tints of sunset reflect on still water.

A lone grebe dives again and again. Each time a sudden swoop down, disappearing for minutes on end. We parallel each other for most of the last half mile, and never, not once, can I guess how far ahead of me it will resurface.

Day 3. **September 17, 4:50 PM**

The sun bakes my shoulders and leaches the late-summer green from the leaves so the flanks of the mountains look tawny.

Boneyard of driftwood. Dragonflies kiting.

I've walked here three days in a row, and each has been beautiful in its own way. What if I just kept on going? The thought streaks through my brain: *Take this walk every day for a year. Take notes.*

Just as quickly, the chorus of doubts. *Every day?* I'm a freelance writer. I don't do *anything* every day. I'm a serial breaker of vows to myself. I do get things done, in my shambling, eventual way, but I'm a compulsive rule breaker, even when I'm the one who made the rules. Could that change? Could I actually stick to a goal?

I don't have to make a decision about this tonight. Just come back tomorrow. Let's see how that works.

Day 4. **September 18, 5:20 PM**

Tide stripes from woods down to water: driftwood, bluestone, grass, dirt, mud. The Upper Basin's shoreline is way down, as if it's been drained overnight. A lagoon's formed since yesterday, out by the sentinel rock, which is now on dry land.

The cement poles flanking the Lemon Squeeze—the high, narrow stretch where this walkway crosses the thousand-foot dam—are made of a product called StressCrete. Why?

I look down from a dizzying height. Below, the remains of the Esopus Creek trickle under the dam. This narrow spill pond is flanked on one side by natural cliffs dripping with mossy seep. On the other, stone terraces march down the steep, curving hillside like rice paddies.

Toddler wearing magenta beret. Mother talking on cell phone, not *looking.*

Day 5. September 19, 6:40 PM

It's a sunny fall Saturday and the walkway is popping with life. A small Asian boy pedals a training wheel bike with his mother and aunt walking alongside. He's talking excitedly about bikes—thirteen inches, fifteen inches! As I pass, I hear him say, "Power walk! Insane power walk woman!"

Who, me? I slow down.

The next person I pass is a willowy woman in white, strolling barefoot with sandals dangling from one hand as if she's on a beach. She turns to me, beaming. "Isn't this *beautiful*? The clouds, the water, the way it reflects. You could come here *every day* and it would be beautiful *every time*!" She's singing my song.

Couple walking ahead. He has a water bottle in one hand; she's clutching a purse. As they start up the only small hill on the walkway, a rise leading into the thicket of oaks and tall pines where a pair of bald eagles has nested for years, he says, "Push through the burn. No pain, no gain," which I assume is ironic—the rise isn't steep—until she mumbles something whiny and I notice she's lagging. The man sounds annoyed. "Push through! You got a mile and a half to go. Push! Come on, *push*!" And I think, *I cannot walk behind you two.*

I sit on one of the weathered wooden benches set out at half-mile intervals. The sun's sinking behind a bank of gunmetal clouds and the sky's streaked with textures: cotton batting, burnout velvet, tie-dye striations, spun sugar. The colors change minute by minute, deep blues and purples licked amber, then rose.

Midstream snippets from cell phone talkers:

• "You're not listening. No. No, that is *not* what I said. If you need to be such a quote unquote *expert*..."

• "On a work level, it's kind of a wait and see kind of a thing. It's fine, the money is fine. I just need it in writing."

• "Don't be weird. Okay, you're attracted. Just don't, don't be weird."

The one human image I love: Walking in low-slanting light, I gaze down the long terraced slope of the embankment toward the edge of the woods, where the maples are starting to hint at the colors they'll turn. The shadow of the guardrail bisects the foliage midway up each tree, and my own moving shadow seems to balance on top of that line, like a tiny Philippe Petit.

Day 6. **September 20, 5:55 PM**

I don't feel like walking today, not one bit. I arrive with a suitcase of autumnal gloom, and the reservoir doesn't unpack it. Stiff wind, so the water is choppy, with whitecaps. The colors are supercharged, as if there's a gold filter over the sun. Grass seedheads shimmer fox red, and the last of the Queen Anne's lace has gone Havisham, white blossoms shriveled to dry brittle purses the color of tea. I hear, but do not see, a large flock of Canada geese.

Two strident-voiced women keep pace with me for a good half a mile, just far enough behind that I can't hear what they're saying, just the glass-cutting pitch of their voices and once, in a clear patch of silence, the lone word "AnNOYing!"

I sit on a bench until they pass, my new reservoir trick. Maybe I should stop coming at sunset. But the light is seductive.

The sun slinks behind the ridge, disappearing without much glow. The air cools down instantly.

I head back in blessed silence. Lone blue jay skrawking. Then I spot a Mexican family crossing the Lemon Squeeze. First across are two tiny girls, running as fast as they can and yelling in Spanish. Then everyone else in the family starts racing each other, laughing and hooting. Dad pretends to lose to a toddler son, teenage girls giggle and fist-bump. Six children, ranging from toddlers to teens, and the parents appear to still be in their thirties.

All of them look so happy being together outdoors that they part the clouds of my surliness. We trade smiles as we pass. Then I think, *These are the people Trump wants to deport.* And get surly again.

Day 7. **September 21, 5:50 PM**

Cotton-wool sky, not a hint of blue in it. The temperature dropped into the fifties overnight, and even without the sun I can see maple trees edging

toward yellow and red, a few outlier branches already turned. The water is waveless but rippled like '50s shower glass. Air thick and still. No movement of leaves, no birdsong. If I had to pick out an adjective, it would be *ominous*.

I drive home from Woodstock a few hours later, taking my usual shortcut on Reservoir Road, which crosses the weir bridge that bisects the reservoir. Right before I reach the bridge, a barred owl swoops over the hood of my car directly in front of the windshield, so close I can see the striped feathers and talons outstretched as it slams down toward some prey on the shoulder. I'm still gasping and whooping when I round the next curve and a young red fox streaks across the road. Animal portents.

Day 8. September 22, 5:58 PM

Reservoir mysteries:

Who were the elegant Sikh couple—white-bearded man in silvery turban, woman in flowing green silk and sandals—walking along the road shoulder toward Olivebridge?

What were the two men in the off-limits area looking for under the driftwood?

Why is that delicate stippling of cloud called a mackerel sky?

Day 9. September 23, 6:50 PM

Sun already behind the ridge, air cool and breeze up. I notice the curves of the mountains, even the distant ones, are sawtoothed with individual treetops. But the star attraction tonight is the eastern sky, in soft rainbow stripes—indigo, lavender, pink, amber, gold—and floating above all that color, a startlingly bright moon, already past half.

Slate-blue bird perched on a driftwood spar, a ratcheting indignant cry as it swoops away to land on a taller spar, doubling back after I pass. White throat, large bill, punk tattered crest, clunky flight: a kingfisher.

No walkers in sight by the time I turn back. Sacred silence, gathering dusk. Then I notice a reflection moving in the water at the shoreline. There's a man in a flannel shirt walking down at the water's edge, coming back from the point. He's way farther out than the rowboats, and he has no fishing gear. Hour of the scofflaw.

It looks like our paths will converge at the parking lot, but he melts into the woods. In the movie, I'd marry him.

Day 10. **September 24, 11:40 AM**

On impulse I go to the reservoir at lunchtime instead of waiting for sunset. It's like having a crush on somebody I can't wait to see. As soon as I set foot on the walkway, a flock of Canada geese starts bickering, takes flight, and resettles next to the water. A few steps later, a pileated woodpecker flies right in front of me, so close I not only gasp but clutch my heart like a character in a cartoon. Black and white with a brilliant red cap, it's the largest woodpecker in North America.

It lands on a leafless dead tree at the edge of the woods where it's joined by its mate, who lands higher on the same tree. They ignore each other for a while, each hopping upward and pecking fitfully at bark flecked with silver-green patches of lichen. Without warning the newcomer swoops away into the woods. The first bird pays no attention, continuing to peck for a few moments longer, then suddenly follows. It has the air of flirtation and sudden tryst.

Baking sun, and many more flowers out: knapweed, chickory, butter and eggs. Cabbage-white butterflies fluttering.

First signal flares of bright color. The sky overhead is a cloudless blue. Low cumulus over the western peaks, shadows dappling in Holstein-cow patterns. I think about phrases and images, boiling things down to essentials. Am I leaning toward poetry? The thought makes me snort. I've gone broke writing plays, screenplays, novels, nonfiction. Why not poems?

Crows strut on the guardrail. I spot two, then a third on the road, then a fourth in the grass, then a fifth flying overhead, sixth in a tree. It's like a child's counting rhyme. When I get close enough to notice the inky black sheen of their feathers, the two on the guardrail take wing and the rest follow suit, swooping down to the water's edge.

That moment before they land, meeting their shadows.

I walk back sweating in high noon sunlight, reminding myself to add a water bottle to my car stash of hiking shoes, windbreaker, notebook and pen. I don't know why I'm so determined to do this every day for a year, but I am.

I don't have to know why. I just have to keep paying attention.

I started to write every day when I started working outdoors in my twenties, living in the backwoods of Washington State and southeast Alaska. I saw new things everywhere; I wrote them all down. Like a facepalm it hits me what I have been missing: *outdoors*. Why I moved to the Catskills nearly three decades ago. This.

On the way home I stop and buy tomatoes from a guy with a table and sign in his front yard. Three for a dollar, apples and Seckel pears four for a dollar.

Day 11. **September 25, 7:25 PM**

I drive to the res straight from teaching. Two roller-derby girls in full combat gear—sleek black catsuits, sculpted helmets, red knee pads—sail off the path and circle the empty parking lot, using the wide space to practice. They skate backward, drop into low crouches, do lunges and tango-like dance steps. Both of them laughing, enjoying their badass moves. Then they step out of their skates and remove their protective gear, loading it into the backseat one piece at a time as they chat about haircuts, blow dryers, and Rite Aid reward cards. They get smaller and blander as each piece of armor comes off. Come back, roller ninjas!

They drive off and I'm the only one left. I walk out to the Lemon Squeeze bridge under darkening sky. Cliff swallows loop and skim, skittering over the wavetips.

Day 12. **September 26, 1:40 PM**

A long walk today, and the lesson is patience. I hear a bald eagle call out as I'm passing the stand of tall pines on the rise, a surprisingly high and thin *skree* that prickles the back of my neck. I stand peering up at the treetops, but can't find the source. I round the next curve and spot the usual eagle photographer, sitting on the bench with his long telephoto lens. "He's been up there all morning," he says, pointing up at a branch near the huge, pine-screened nest where an eagle sits, still as a post. "He's wearing me out." I wish him well and keep walking.

On the way back, same bench, same photographer. Eagle still on his branch.

Day 13. **September 27, 9:05 PM**

Tonight there's a lunar eclipse, and I drive to the reservoir with three of my oldest friends. I met Shelley Wyant when she was cast in my first produced play at Albany's Capital Rep, thirty years ago. She was the first person I knew with a house in the Hudson Valley, and her husband Bill Brinnier grew up right down the road. Alan Amtzis, a teacher and ardent traveler with "Ph.D." tattooed on one arm and a tarot sun on the other, has driven from Trenton to join us. He used to live nearby, and I remember him telling my very young daughter, "Always remember to look at the sky." Maya's now in her twenties, a student at Bennington College. I hope she'll go outside to watch the eclipse.

There are clouds scudding over the full moon, but we're optimistic. It's cold, and we're all wearing parkas, hats, scarves. I'm lugging two sleeping bags, one to sit on and one to wrap over our shoulders. Bill's brought a flashlight, but it's more exciting to walk out in the dark under a cloud-blurred scatter of stars. From time to time we hear voices of other moon watchers who've staked out spots along the guardrail. We can't see them at all. At one point, we stop walking and stand trading stories and jokes, and I suddenly realize there's someone sitting still on the first wooden bench, maybe ten feet away. "Oh, sorry," I say, and a female voice answers calmly from the darkness, "It's not *my* moon."

We walk out a bit farther and sit on the stone bench in a tight row, wedging our knees between it and the guardrail, using an unzipped sleeping bag as a group shawl. Alan's brought Moon Pies, an homage to a long-ago summer night when a group of friends lay on a blanket in my backyard to watch an eclipse, got high, and ate so many Moon Pies we all felt sick.

This time there's just one apiece; we're not kids anymore. A dark shadow is starting to creep across the moon's surface. It looks like a bite taken out of a Moon Pie.

It takes a long time. We get restless. At long last, the last strip of white disappears into shadow and the moon's whole disk glows an unearthly cinnamon red.

Total eclipse. Heart of darkness. We sit dead still, mesmerized by its primordial strangeness. No one says a word.

Within minutes, the clouds close back over the blood moon. But we know it's there.

Day 14. **September 28, 6:20 PM**

I don't have many ground rules for this, but I don't carry paper and pad when I'm walking. I notice whatever I notice, and memorize a few key-words to help me remember. Here are today's: *heron cloak veil stillness alchemy*

Which is either a very short poem or dialogue you might hear from a tarot reader at a Woodstock bar.

I came to the res in an awful mood, two weeks into this practice and already resentful and bored with the notion of doing it over and over again for a year. What's the point? Can this really make one bit of difference?

My house is too empty to stay in alone.

I walk out to the stone bench and sit, watching the sunset glow turn the cloud wisps from Turner pastels to a brief sudden flooding of neon-bright coral, then lavender gray. As the water gets calm, so do I. When I finally stand to walk back, a great blue heron angles over the water, its heavy big body in silent glide, to land at the water's edge.

Day 15. **September 29, 6:25 PM**

I fell asleep reading, and when I wake up, it's drizzling lightly. By the time I get downstairs, it's pouring. I put on my red raincoat, go anyway. A hard rain turns harder, high wipers sluicing with no visibility. I park next to three other cars. There's no one in sight, so I figure a few unfortunate walkers must have been caught in the downpour.

But I didn't get caught. I've *chosen* to set out in this slop. I sit in the driver's seat, changing from shoes to boots, listening to rain drum the roof of the car. If I had any doubts about getting obsessed, this should pelt them away.

Okay, let's go do this.

I grab my folding umbrella from under the passenger seat, and the pounding redoubles. Rain pummels the windshield as if I'm in a carwash, bouncing white off the pavement. I wait. Patience, patience.

I can't see the Lemon Squeeze bridge. The fog's socked it in, so both guardrails disappear into whiteness. And here comes a walker, materializing out of the swirling fog like a Kurosawa samurai. Her gait is unhurried. Why bother? She's already soaked. She wears a black raincoat, zipped to her chin with the hood up.

The rain is relentless. I wait for a break and there isn't one. But if I wait much longer, it'll be pouring *and* dark. Another lone figure looms out of the fog. As he gets closer, I notice he has an umbrella. So he didn't get caught out; he chose this too.

The third car's driver glides in on a bicycle, wrapped in blue raingear. Hardcore. When all three of their cars leave, I get out of mine.

Rain drums my umbrella. The moist air feels good in my nostrils. Low clouds comb through pines, a palette of dark blues and gunmetal grays. The haunch of the far shore is scrimmed over, shadowed. Beyond the point, where the bowl of the High Peaks should be, is a blank white horizon. The reservoir looks like an inland sea, endless.

I'm most of the way to the Lemon Squeeze when I think, *I'm the only living creature in sight.* As soon as that thought forms, I sense something over my left shoulder: the heron, gliding low and silent, disappearing into the dusk.

Day 16. **September 30, 10:15 AM**

Last night's biblical rainfall flooded my basement, raised the Vly Swamp to a lake, and turned runoff streams whitewater, so I drive down to the Spillway expecting a manmade Niagara. But the reservoir's been so low all summer that the spillway's wide cement tiers are still empty. The only thing feeding the falls below is a swollen stream east of the channel. The mountains look glum, a few stray plumes of cloud wisping upward.

I drive back to the Frying Pan, the only car parked on the circle. A chestnut-furred squirrel hops across the approach road, tail rippling.

Gray water, low chop. By the time I reach the first bench, it's raining again. Just past the quarter-mile mark, I see a large flock of Canada geese squatting on the path up ahead and wonder how close they'll let me come. The pavement is littered with olive-green poop curls; they've been here awhile. I count heads: seventeen.

They notice me coming, a flock awareness, necks tense and alert, a few restive spreadings of wings. When I get within a few yards, they start honking and—rather than take flight as I expect—waddle under the guardrail. Five birds take too long to cross and rush ahead of my feet in an anxious herd. One of them panics and lifts off, and in an instant the whole flock takes flight all around me. Whirr and clatter of wings grabbing air, indignant honks as they wheel in untidy formation, flying first toward the trees and then toward the reservoir, where they angle down onto the water, seventeen perfect landings, white wakes.

Day 17. **October 1, 5:10 PM**

Fall fell. Not much leaf color yet, but the green looks exhausted. The air's chill and grim. Short quick walk on my way to teach; my usual stroll is a quickstep march. I pause for a moment and a small, chunky bird plummets out of the sky and slams onto the top of a pole, long feet first. I gasp, "Are you a peregrine?" (Sam Gribley's Frightful!).

But no, it's a sharp-shinned hawk, a.k.a. "sharpie": gray back, reddish tail and chest, short sharp beak. She tips her head back and eyes me, then takes off, flapping hard and fast. Then she catches an updraft and soars.

Day 18. **October 2, 4:40 PM**

I go a little off grid. Gray and raining again, the premonitory "Cone of Uncertainty" for Hurricane Joaquin, and rather than walking out on the exposed walkway, I decide to follow the nearby fisherman's path to the rowboats so I can stay under the cover of trees. The trailhead's a short walk down Route 28A.

As soon as I step onto the road, I sense something above and look up. A turkey vulture floats nearly still in the air, framed between two lines of treetops. Vultures are carrion feeders, with heavy dark wings and raw-looking featherless heads adapted for digging in carcasses. The sight of it gives me a shudder. I walk fast down the shoulder, staying close to the guardrail, but even so, a speeding pickup truck almost clips me.

Sign on the gate: RECREATIONAL ACCESS ONLY, LICENSE REQUIRED.

Yeah, yeah, yeah. Sue me. I slip past the chain.

As soon as I step into wood, the air feels different. Lots of downed ash trees with mud-clotted roots, autumn-red poison ivy vines, white curls of paper birch bark. Wind rattling dead leaves. The burrow of something too big to be a chipmunk, its opening fist-wide, tunnel heading straight down.

Feeling vulnerable, I stay close to the tree line, picking my way between overturned rowboats, each chained to a tree. The familiar vista feels different with trees in the foreground instead of a guardrail. The angle is lower; rocks crunch underfoot. It's wilder, unpaved, with a sound of waves breaking.

I walk down to the edge of the water and stand on a flat rock, smelling a riverine funk. I find it as soon as I turn: the bleached spine and ribs of a very large, long-dead trout. Tailfin like ivory.

Day 19. **October 3, 9:55 AM**

Ghost mountains, gray on gray. Cold, wet, and blustery.

Day 20. **October 4, 11 AM**

Quick walk with my friend Teresa Giordano, a TV writer and documentary producer who's joining me at the Woodstock Film Festival. We're

crossing the Lemon Squeeze under an arching blue sky, the exact shade of the book jacket for Paul Russell's novel *Immaculate Blue*. There's a cluster of hikers listening as a guide narrates the history of the dam's construction, the Drowned Towns that were razed to stanch New York City's "water famine." Residents were paid a pittance for land their families had farmed for generations; some earned an additional eighteen dollars apiece to exhume their own ancestors' graves. The dam we're standing on now was erected below Bishop's Falls, site of a gristmill and popular inn. I'd love to stay and listen, but we've got movie tickets.

Apparently it's Reservoir Cleanup Day. Back at the Olivebridge parking lot, volunteers erect a pop-up canopy and line folding tables with clipboards and reservoir maps. I ask for one, saying, "We're on our way to a screening, but I'd love to stop at one of the cleanup sites later." As I walk away, prize in hand, Teresa says, "You didn't fool me one bit."

Back home, I pore over the map. Names! My usual walkway traverses the Olivebridge Dam, looking over the water at Brodhead Point, Van Steenburgh Cove, Ice House Cove. After the rise, with its double S curve through oak and pine forest, the walkway becomes the West Dike; the Reservoir Road bridge, where cars wait at a single-construction-lane light, is officially called the Dividing Weir. Beyond it are Shovel Cut, Burns Cove, Keywaden Peninsula. The map gives me new language.

It also shows dozens of "access points" for recreational use. Do you need to have a fishing license? I google the NYC Environmental Protection website. No, you do not! Coming soon to my life: an Ashokan Reservoir Access Permit from the NYC Department of Environmental Protection office in Kingston.

It's free! There's a windshield sticker! Whee!

Day 21. **October 5, 5:05 PM**

Water level much higher, so the round lagoon that formed near the end of the Driftwood Cove point has turned into a half-circle bay.

A solo grebe skids in for a water landing and almost immediately tips its neck and dives straight down. Again I guess where it will surface. Again I am wildly wrong. It pops back up near Driftwood Cove, shaking its head with a glint of red eye, then dives again. Gone.

A pair of wild turkeys struts along a mowed path below the embankment, grazing on grass seeds. Their bobblehead gait suggests Eric Idle and Michael Palin playing housewives. They look as if they should have purses.

I hear chirps and rustling sounds in the trees. Nuthatch, blue jay, song sparrow: the usual suspects. Then something large, dark: A crow? White wing patches and a bright slash of red as it flashes between tree trunks, lands on deadwood, and starts to drill: a pileated woodpecker, followed by its mate. They circle the trunk, pecking and hopping, then fly off in a double helix, flight paths crossing in midair.

The double S curve on the rise is the Mammal Zone. Two does and a teenage fawn, grazing in ferns, look at me and shift skittishly, raising white tails. Gray squirrels rustle through fallen leaves. A petite red squirrel sits on the end of a fallen log, tufted ears on the alert as its teeth scrape an acorn as big as its head.

Coming down the rise onto the West Dike, I see the same six crows, my little murder. It's like going to visit the neighbors. I sit on the eagle-watch bench, though the nest is bare, listening to waves lap the shore. There's a shimmering wedge of lit rainbow, a sundog. They always make me think of southeast Alaska, where I started writing like this. Taking notes on the things I observed, sometimes at the wheel of the sky-blue salmon troller where I was a summertime deckhand; its name was the Eagle.

The sun is so low it shoots spotlight beams over the mountains, turning the west-facing hillsides a neon green gold with deep purple shadows. Lone fisherman standing on Driftwood Cove, casting. Jerky movement of spinner through water as he reels it back in, again and again and again.

Day 22. **October 6, 5:45 PM**

Noisy parking lot tonight. Three tween girls in matching pink fleece unload bikes from the back of a pickup. Shrieking and laughing, they pedal away from the mother who drove them. She calls after their backs, "Be safe."

Yeah, right, Mom. They're off on a freedom jaunt.

The Virginia creeper on the cracked cement wall of the Lemon Squeeze bridge has turned red overnight. Not much bright red in the woods yet, just some muddy maroons and golds in a mostly green palette. The dignified colors come first, with a few gleeful streaks of exuberant orange. Drag queen sugar maples.

Today's walk is all about sky. The cloud cover is high and still, twisted into mottled shapes that suggest marbled paper, or marble. Then it clicks into place: it reminds me of bowling balls. Once you see this, it cannot be unseen. No matter how splendid the sky becomes, some part of your brain hears the clatter of pins and the clunk of resetting machines. You can almost smell warmer-scorched pizza.

A headlight comes down the hill. It's one of those goofy recumbent bikes, powered by a man in full spandex, sunglasses, and helmet. He looks like a happy fool.

When I get back to the parking lot, the last lipstick bruise has departed the bowling ball sky, and the tense mom is pacing with cell phone in hand, while a kid brother dribbles a soccer ball. It's been over an hour and mom's *pissed*.

Day 23. **October 7, 7:40 PM**

A Technicolor fall day, and I drive down to Nyack and back to see my aunt Joan in her anodyne nursing home. I chase a spectacular sunset all the way north, but get to the reservoir after it's faded to dusk.

I look up the difference between dusk and twilight. Apparently dusk is the darkest stage of twilight, just before nightfall. And twilight is subdivided into three phases: civil twilight, nautical twilight, and astronomical twilight, each of which has its own dusk.

So this, I suppose, is civil dusk. Mountain silhouettes above water that still has a bluish metallic shimmer, like mercury. I set off in darkness. All I can see ahead is the red antenna light on top of Overlook, the shoulder-shaped mountain embracing the village of Woodstock. The sky's clear but starless. Or is it? As I walk, I notice a few pinpoint shimmers, then more. I spot a whole constellation: Cassiopeia, her angled W first faint, then distinct. I stand listening as waves lap the shore to the wheezing of katydids. Two bats circle overhead as more and more stars come into focus. It looks as if someone were clicking on light switches, but no, they're all there all the time; what changes is light in the sky.

By the time I walk back to my car, it's gotten so dark (astronomical twilight) that I can see the Milky Way. The Big Dipper hangs over the narrows.

Footnote: dusk is sacred in the Hindu faith, and the Hindi phrase for it—*godhuli vela*—means "cow dust time."

Day 24. **October 8, 1:40 PM**

Today's breaking news: COLOR! Miss Ashokan has started to model for calendar shots. Flaming trees dot the hillsides, persimmon rose hips on the lone dog rose over the guardrail. Bouffant cumulus in morning-glory-blue sky.

A couple climbs over the fence, right next to the yellow NO ENTRY FOR ANY PURPOSE sign, to eat lunch by the water. I drive past a blonde Harley rider in chartreuse leathers, then wait beside orange-and-white-striped safety barrels for the red light to turn green.

Day 25. **October 9, 5:50 PM**

Light rain left a low-lying mist brigadooning the draws, with a twist of fog creeping over the Lemon Squeeze like something alive. One part floats out over the water and a second lies down over the treetops and creek far below. I lean on the cement wall for a long time, watching it swirl. When I look up, a doe has stepped onto the path and stands staring at me.

I hold her gaze for a long time, watching the fog shift around her. Suddenly she vaults the guardrail and dashes back down the embankment, passing a two-point buck and a second doe grazing. They both raise their heads.

The mist muffles sound. At the crest of the rise I turn and look back down the mile-long straightaway. No one in sight. Then I see something gliding behind the trees. Huge wingspan, white head. A bald eagle!

I move to the edge of the woods, craning my neck to get a clear view. The wind comes up, riffling my hair as the eagle soars over the water, hang gliding updrafts, then loops out of sight. When it reappears, bursting out of the pines on giant wings, my chest expands. A second eagle glides over the trees on the opposite side of the walkway. One disappears low on one side and the other appears from a much higher angle a split second later, an elegant dance in the darkening sky. It feels like a blessing. The air thrums with power. Feathers and mist.

The next person I see is a grim-looking exercise walker with headphones clamped over his ears. I don't say a thing. But when I pass a young couple a few minutes later, their eyes look alive, so I tell them, "I just saw two eagles!" The man gives a smug smile and says, "Yes, I know. They're the local bald eagles."

No, you don't know, I think. *Something holy just happened.*

I stand in the swirl of fog, feeling it dampen my cheeks, and look back at the trees just as one of the eagles lifts up from the treetops and loops back out over the water again. The couple is walking. They don't look up.

Day 26. **October 10, 6:10 PM**

Mob scene at the res today: perfect weather, fall foliage, Saturday night. I pass at least twenty people and four dogs, owners cheerfully flouting the posted NO DOGS rule. One of them looks a little like Chris, and I'm stricken with wagging-tail envy. Through the trees I can hear a large rally of bikers on 28A, motorcycles roaring past one at a time with a curve-hugging rev. Not much holy silence tonight, but infectious joy: every walker I pass has a beauty-fed grin.

The sun is already behind the ridge, and the air is so still that vapor trails crisscross white stripes across stray wisps of cloud. Someone's hung a strap from a crag on the Lemon Squeeze wall with a dangle of car keys. A story awaiting an ending.

On the far side it's quieter—most of the walkers stay close to the parking lot, taking snapshots of the sunset or helping kids onto their bikes—but the only wildlife I see is a chipmunk streaking across the walkway, flat out. I have the sense that my friends are lurking inside the forest, waiting for these interlopers to leave.

Then I remember *I* am an interloper.

The sky on the way back is a mix of pale turquoise and powder pink. Fifties nursery colors, the exact palette of *Pat the Bunny*. Can you say bye-bye?

At the parking lot, one of the dog-walker couples heads back toward the path with an odd, jangled urgency. The man is a Nordic-looking carpenter I used to see in the lobby of Marbletown Elementary School as we waited to pick up our kids. The woman he's with asks, "Did you happen to see any keys?" and I get to tell her I did.

The End.

Day 27. **October 11, 2 PM**

As I drive to the reservoir I can feel my senses sharpening, opening up like a camera aperture, ready to take more in. Passing the hardscrabble farm on Krumville Road with its random tumble of pens and outbuildings, I spot the massive black stallion who's always across the road from the rest of the herd, leaning over his fence with a yearning expression. A flock of pigeons wheels over the pasture in a tight formation, settling onto the ridge of the barn. Something higher up grabs my eye, and through tree-tops I catch a red glint. An exotic bird? Finally I get a clear view: a trio of mylar balloons, red, blue, and silver, high up in the thermals. At a leisurely distance below them a vulture glides, giving no fucks.

The goats in the pen by the Olivebridge Post Office are out in the sun, chomping hay.

Cars spill out of the parking lot and down both shoulders of 28A. The maple on the corner is a gasp-inducing red orange, the color of hot sauce.

Dozens of people are out on the walkway today. It's an upbeat, carnival atmosphere, more like a sunny fall Sunday in Central Park than a nature walk. Worshipping the god Recreation today: families, tourists, hipsters, rollerbladers, bikers, picnickers, leaf peepers, lovers, men wearing cameras with foot-long lenses, little kids on scooters and princess bikes, one guy reading on a bench with his bag and jacket spread out so nobody will join him (the Trailways commuter trick). A beaming white-haired woman in a motorized wheelchair, surrounded by three generations of family. Over-heard: Southern and British accents, tourists speaking Japanese, German, and Quebecois French.

And yet there are still things to notice. The milkiness of the sky just above the horizon. The airborne courtship of cabbage-white butterflies. The way a breeze riffles just one strip of water, like tinsel against the dark teal.

Day 28. **October 12, 8:40 AM**

Morning sun slants in from opposite side, so the mountains look more orange than green. Nineteen Canada geese bedded down on Driftwood Cove.

This time I'm the one who asks unbidden questions. Two women with binoculars are looking at two dark birds silhouetted on the sentinel rock, now nearly submerged. I ask what they are.

"Cormorants."

"Oh. I thought they were grebes," I say, and the second woman says, "I'm rethinking this. Cormorants are air divers, not water divers. I just saw that one go under while swimming. They might be grebes."

Air divers and water divers? So much I don't know about birds.

Then I spot a tall woman in exercise clothes reading a paperback book while she walks. As a writer, I'm thrilled by her intent concentration. As a walker, I'm appalled. Look where you *are*!

A big bird hits the water and skids along the surface in a series of splashy pings, taking off awkwardly and flying low over the water in a straight line, all the way across. Could it be an osprey?

Rounding the curve, a Waldorf mom pushes a baby in the stroller, holding the hand of a sullen blonde preschooler. We're having a family conference. "Sometimes we don't get to do what we want right away. Sometimes we have to wait for your brother."

After they pass, I look up at the eagles' nest. Sensing movement inside, I stand very still, wondering if I'm imagining things. With a sudden flash of sunlit white feathers, an eagle hops up to stand guard on the branch, posing like Fabio. Then a second eagle angles low through the trees toward the nest. It's thrilling and quick, but I see something silver glinting in the sun. So that was the big bird I saw in the water before—she was fishing!

This is so cool that when I see Waldorf Mom again, talking with a beaming Eagle Guy at the foot of the rise, I blurt, "Did you see that?"

"Yeah," says Eagle Guy, clutching his camera close like he just won the lottery. "She was down on the shore before. Brought a trout back to the nest."

"I just spotted her mate on his perch," I say.

Eagle Guy nods and says dryly, "He doesn't work."

Later, I spot the *other* Eagle Guy—call him Eagle Guy the Younger—for the first time since last year, sunburned and straw blond with a Howdy Doody grin, toting his camera back to his car. Eagle Guy the Elder is more stolid and seems to put in more hours. I wonder how they get along.

Day 29. **October 13, 5:20 PM**

Hudson River School sky, with towering banks of clouds and an Eye of God radiant sunburst.

Unexpected things turning yellow and brown: grapevines, banks of ferns, young white pines at the edge of the woods. How close together their trunks grow, like prison bars. Their dry fallen needles are the exact color of deerskin.

An acorn hits the pavement. Another. I crane my neck and see a squirrel harvesting. I notice the whole crown is shaking and spot at least five more squirrels, hopping from branch to branch, systematically shaking down nuts. Acorn factory, working the late shift.

Day 30. **October 14, 5:15 PM**

Abruptly colder. I walk with hands stuffed in the pockets of my fall jacket, starting to think about ice, snow, and wind. This is going to get harder, and soon.

The clouds are piled high, so dramatically lit I expect a Monty Python God to appear in that circle of gold and tell me not to grovel.

This is my thirtieth day on the res, and I have a proud sense of becoming a regular: I pass five people in two miles and recognize four of them. Even odder, they all seem to recognize *me*. The friendly slump-shouldered fellow I've passed a few times seems not only glad but relieved to see me, as if I'd gone missing, and the asymmetrical older gent with the Walkman gives me a courtly silent nod. The couple I've nicknamed The Cheerfuls calls out a synchronous "Hi!" from their bikes. I've thought of myself as anonymous, but it's like going to the same café every day; sooner or later the waitress knows your order. I've become a character in other people's reservoir walks as they have in mine.

I walk back to a thorough scolding from a lone crow, fan-flipping his tailfeathers on a branch and trading disdainful slow caws with a distant companion. Two more lofting high in the clouds. How the news is spread.

Day 31. **October 15, 3:20 PM**

Reservoir Mysteries II:

Why, on a sunny and windless day, are some spans of water entirely flat and some riffled?

Why does the sun's reflection pool at one end of the basin, sparkling so brightly it hurts your eyes, then skip over a dark stretch of water and reappear in scattered twinkles like fireflies?

Why would the otherwise handsome young man leaning over the Lemon Squeeze wall cut most of his hair short and leave a high ponytail sticking straight out from the back of his head like a tempera paintbrush?

Why racewalking?

Day 32. **October 16, 5:00 PM**

A clamor of avian squawks: Crows versus Blue Jays, Bronx-accented razzing. It sounds like a girlfight in the school cafeteria. *Did not! Did too!* Then the Canadian hockey team honks off the water. A small black-and-white downy woodpecker flies overhead, escaping the fracas. After a while the spat settles down, except for the world's most obnoxious songbird, the one that filibusters a monotone *ca ca ca ca ca* for hours at a time. The cacabird. Tufted Tourette's.

A bright-eyed student stops me to ask about hiking trails. It's his first time in the Catskills. He looks euphoric, and so am I. I get to be somebody's expert.

The sun slides behind Ashokan High Point, and the clouds turn Maxfield Parrish, golden on top and deep purple below. One seems to be spilling white rain. Crescent moon levitating.

Lone Nalgene bottle stands sentry in the parking lot, saluting the port-o-sans.

Day 33. **October 17, 4:50 PM**

In today's mail: NYC DEP Access Permit 127297, the size of a credit card, plus a kelly-green Vehicle Tag to hang from my rearview mirror. I exist!

Emboldened, I drive past the very full Olivebridge parking lot and pull up in front of the first fishing entry gate. Taking the access path through the woods, past rowboats chained to trees, I step onto the muddy strand. I walk past the trident point and head around the bend to the next cove, which I've never seen. A stiff wind churns up whitecaps, and the footing along tumbled rocks is unsteady. I watch the ground, wary of twisting an ankle now that I'm out of view. It's shady and cold where I'm walking, but when I pause to look over the water, the weir bridge is sunlit, its arches bright white, and the western slopes of the mountains are violet and orange. I'm all by myself. My lungs fill with air. There are forty more miles of beach to explore.

Walking back to my car with the wind at my back, it seems instantly calmer and quieter. I hear waves lapping stone.

Mudprints: large and small deer, recent fisherfolk, me.

Day 34. **October 18, noon**

Well, *that* was sudden! White veil over High Peaks, stiff wind blowing snow flurries. Water a roil of opaque gray chop. Dried grasses and Queen Anne's lace seedheads tattered by gusts that sting tears from my eyes.

Nevertheless, Asian tourists with selfie sticks.

Day 35. **October 19, 3:20 PM**

Introducing the Secret Cove, a spot so private and lovely I don't dare disclose its location, a short, golden walk from one of the fishing gates. When I park on the shoulder, two guys in tan vests stand talking in front of their trucks—gray Chevy, black Ford. They look surprised to see me get out, but I see (or imagine) one of them glance at my DEP mirror tag, and they answer my that's-right-I-belong-here nod with a half-swallowed "Hey," very butch. Secret handshakes of the off-roaders.

I walk past the gate (ENTRY BY PERMIT ONLY; I *got* this) and set off down a dirt road cushioned with layers of new yellow leaves and pine needles. Within minutes I can see water through trees on both sides: the road traces the ridge of a narrow point, with footpaths down to the water on either side. There are dozens of overturned rowboats huddled under the trees, gray, silver, and olive drab, many striped with long rainbows of fading and new permit stickers.

A sudden loud bang makes me jump: hunting season? Not yet! I spin around as an acorn bounces off a boat. The upturned metal keel makes a great echo chamber: it sounds like a cannon. A fusillade of acorns goes off as I walk down the point, like a drumroll. Which path to try first?

I set off toward the reservoir, marveling at the reverse-angle view of the dikes and stand of tall pines where the eagles nest. I walk down the rocky beach for a while, hunching my shoulders against a brisk wind, then recross the dirt road and thread my way down the far side—banks of mountain laurel, must come back in spring!—to a hidden cove with a pristine view of the western High Peaks, mottled orange in the sunlight.

And yes, I do gasp. So would anyone.

The Secret Cove's water has two distinct personalities. Turbid waves roll from the left like a fast-moving river; the right side is still as a pond, with a few rocky islets.

The slope from the road makes a perfect windbreak: the air around me is silent and warm. A few yellow oak leaves blow over my head, angling downward to land on the water. And then a bald eagle lifts up from the pines, slow and lazy, circling the Secret Cove's shoreline and flying right over my head.

Is it Fabio's wife? Is this where she comes to escape?

It's where I'll come. I'd stay on that rock all day long with a book. Or a lover.

Heart full as I make my way back to my car. This is just the beginning.

As I walk, I feel something scratching my shins and look down to see dozens of some kind of opportunistic seeds—small, brown, and flat, with twin prongs—porcupining my pantleg. The things that grab hold of us when we're not paying attention. The things that we carry back, things that might grow.

Day 36. **October 20, 5:40 PM**

The hard frost two nights back drop-kicked fall foliage into the end zone. There's still color, but it's more subdued, rusts and mustards in place of bright orange. Some of the leaves have dried right on the trees, hanging like brown paper bags. There are bare trunks and branches. Incongruously it's much warmer today.

The sun is already below the horizon, and the mountains look somber. Even the clouds are a dignified Presbyterian lilac, except for a small puffy clutch over High Point's left shoulder, doing the rumba in orange.

Someone's left a bouquet of dried grass and Queen Anne's lace on the window ledge of the DEC's never-manned guard booth. An offering.

Day 37. **October 21, 3:50 PM**

Bizarrely warm, with milky cloud cover and haze like a cataract. I decide to walk out on a long rocky spit near the bridge, where I've sometimes seen a lone fisherman casting.

As soon as I start down the path, I pass two fishermen in khaki and olive-drab camo. (Why do they dress this way? Can fish see through water enough to avoid, say, red stripes? Or is it just Outdoor Sportsman tradition?) They're carrying rods and buckets that look disappointingly light, but we trade friendly nods, and one offers, "Beautiful day!"

The dirt path is wide, with trails forking off on both sides. There's a surprising abundance of Day-Glo-orange blazes dangling from branches. A chipmunk scoots right past my feet, diving into a hole.

A fisherman stands on the cement jetty, casting into the fast-moving whorls and eddies in front of the weir, where the water pours through. I walk down to the shoreline, where every rock fragment and striated boulder is caked with dried mud. It looks like the surface of Mars.

It takes me a while to pick my way out to the spit. There's a great hue and clamor of seagulls, a klatch of them shifting position on a near-buried flat rock farther out on the water. There's a larger bird hunched on a lone rock twenty feet past the spit, and though its feathers are brownish, its posture says eagle. It lets me get all the way out to the end of the spit before it lifts off with what looks like disdain, and I see the ghost of white tailfeathers under the grunge. A juvenile, flight low and heavy winged, practically skimming the water.

Which completely surrounds me. I make a slow turn, taking in 360 degrees: mountains, water, dike, weir bridge with a line of cars crossing, more mountains. It's the same view the teen eagle had, moments ago.

I walk back through the woods on one of the side paths, past clusters of overturned rowboats. There seem to be more of them here, scattered along the woods' edge. I'm looking down—red winterberry, pale tuffets of moss—when I sense something moving through trees. I freeze, expecting a deer. But it's a fisherman, wearing brown Carhartts, Duck Dynasty beard, landing net in one hand, fishing pole in the other. He glides behind trees, soundless, leaving an uneasy charge in the air.

Day 38. **October 22, 5 PM**

Brooding sky. Three plein air painters with easels set up by the guardrail. I recognize two of them.

Nora's palette just got flipped by a gust and fell onto the path paint side down; she's scrubbing a vivid orange splotch off the asphalt. "I'm *such* a messy painter!" she grins, splashing more water and scrubbing again.

Dan Green, a legendary comic-book artist whose credits include *X-Men* and *Doctor Strange*, has rendered peak-foliage hillsides in black, gray, and white, an unclichéd autumn vista if ever there was one.

The guy I don't know has already folded his easel and stands taking reference photos. I wish I could see what he painted.

Day 39. **October 23, 4:40 PM**

Neighborhood coffee klatch at the res today. I spot my friend Deborah walking down our road. On impulse I ask if she wants to join me at the res.

When we park at the Olivebridge lot, our neighbors Andy and Frank pull in right behind us. We greet each other effusively. Then Andy says they'd like to take their walk à deux, since they haven't seen each other all week. This strikes Deborah and me as adorable—they've been together for what, forty years?—especially when they set off ahead of us, sliding their arms around each other's waists.

The water's deep aqua, with high chop and whitecaps. Stiff wind, brilliant colors. We notice the way color morphs on certain maples, so some of the branches are green, some tipped with pale orange, others scarlet. It's the tree equivalent of a golf tan.

Just past the eagles' nest, a brown-feathered juvenile flaps over our heads; could be the same one I saw out on the spit. We watch as it soars toward the nest, circling around as if wondering whether to drop by for dinner, then angles off into the trees.

We meet Andy and Frank coming back, and I ask them if they saw the eagle. They didn't, but Andy asks, "Did it fly with the dove?"

Frank wonders what I know about "the Eaglemaniacs"—their nickname for my Eagle Guys. They're especially curious about Eagle Guy the Younger ("who's *very* tan right now," Andy notes). How can he afford to be here all the time? Does he sell his photos? "From this he's making a living?" Andy asks in Yiddish.

He describes a few walkers he and Frank often spot: the aloof greyhound couple, the Estonian woman. Deborah's amazed that we've noticed the same people. I explain, "There are regulars."

Andy says, "Believe me, I could write a book."

I tell him, "I am, and you're in it." Hi, Andy!

Many years ago, Frank and Andy and I split the cost of a secondhand rowboat. It turned out to be much heavier and more unwieldy than we expected, and none of us rowed enough to keep on renewing our annual boat stickers and fishing licenses. (We never fished, but we stashed secondhand rods and a cooler in the stern so we'd look official, my first DEP deception.)

"What happened to the rowboat?" asks Deborah, and Frank answers, beaming, "We sold it to lesbians!"

More birds on the way back, including a turkey vulture that struggles against the strong wind, stiff wings lurching through turns. The sun's dropped behind High Point, and a ray of light slants out sideways. Deborah stops at the rail and exhales, gazing at the water. "About halfway through the walk, I felt as if I could see more," she says. "Like everything else—all the stresses and running around—just *slowed down*."

I know what she means. It's a physical sense of unburdening, growing alert, like doing tai chi and dropping down into your body.

Two crows, swelling moon.

Day 40. **October 24, 1:30 PM**

Gate W-27 is a parking pullout, not even a footpath. It's a short bushwhack, though—I can see water through trees, many bare, the rest yellow.

A small clutch of overturned rowboats, some covered with moss, abandoned. This must be where the antisocial fishermen go.

Sky wintry and gray. I walk down to the water, but nothing is grabbing my eye. So I sit on a rock, waiting for something to happen.

And that is what happens. I sit.

I see trees. Lots of trees. I hear distant cars passing on Route 28A and the halfhearted drill of a woodpecker. I think about the wilderness beaches

I sat on in southeast Alaska, with acres of popweed and long whips of kelp. I smoked Drum tobacco back then—rarely, but I carried a pouch that was given to me by a guy I'd fallen in love with when we were treeplanting in sleet, and drawing warm smoke deep into our lungs felt delicious.

When my back gets stiff and my butt gets cold, I head back through the woods, tracing a tumbledown stone wall that reminds me there used to be farms and quarries here, before the Drowned Towns. These woods are a ghost town. And that's when I see it.

Next to the wall is a massive oak tree that splits into not two but *four* separate trunks. Four tall, thick-barked golden oaks, joined at the base. How did that happen? I see a flat stone in the saddle, at least a foot wide and I can't tell how long, because living wood has grown right up around it, obscuring its base like the Sword in the Stone. It must have been decades ago: the stone doesn't wobble. It's surrounded by wood, by the flesh of the oak tree it's cleft into four mighty trunks.

The history's there for the taking, forest forensics. Decades ago, that flat stone crushed the apical bud so that four side shoots prospered. Then I realize that the stone must once have been part of the boundary wall, that some long-dead squirrel stashed an acorn beneath it that took root and grew, toppling the stone off the wall, where a sturdy colonial farmwife had placed it as her husband plowed. Could have been two hundred years

ago, many millennia after a glacier had lifted that stone from the bed of a dried inland sea.

Perspective.

It should be a druid throne.

Day 41. **October 25, 12:20 PM**

Today was about fast and slow. I stopped at the Secret Cove on my way to Woodstock, running late for my class. Strode down the path fast, chipmunks running in every direction, the cacabird sounding its anxious, arrhythmic monotone. Even the eagle I saw seemed to be in a rush, winging a beeline toward Boiceville.

And then I just stood on the shore.

I walked back much slower, and that was enough.

Day 42. **October 26, 6:28 AM**

First reservoir sunrise. Bitch-slapped by beauty.

I wake around six, see the Venus/Jupiter/Mars conjunction outside my window, and make an impulsive decision to drive to the Ashokan. I throw on warm clothes, reheat yesterday's coffee, and get there while it's still dark, only car in the lot.

The first thing I see is Orion's belt. The sky is a deep cadet blue, with just enough light that I can make out darker mountains silhouetted against the horizon. I know the water is rough by the sound of the waves and the cold wind stinging my face, but I can't see it at all.

As I reach the Lemon Squeeze, the sky turns pale blue at the edges. I lean on the cement wall and stare down at the creek far below. Reflections of stars on a glassy, mercurial surface, with two clumps of dots: sleeping ducks.

The sun takes its time. The horizon starts lightening, slowly. A distant jet draws a long vapor trail, like chalk on a blackboard.

It's cold.

I'm cold. I stamp my feet, windmill my arms. I'm impatient. I feel like a fan waiting outside the stage door.

I look over my shoulder. The western mountains are visible now, shot with shadowed fall color. When is the sun going to show?

It's all part of the process. Or is it? If you seek out transcendent experience, can it be authentic? Isn't the point of a miracle that it finds *you*, unexpected?

I pull my hood close, hunch my shoulders, jam both hands into pockets. I hear footsteps. A small woman in a white parka approaches, carrying something. Large flashlight? A thermos?

No, it's a camera with a long lens. Is there an Eagle Gal?

She nods as she passes me, probably wondering why I'm standing still when it's so cold and windy. Though the fact that I'm facing due east, toward that glow in the trees, might be a bit of a hint.

I'm finding this dawn kind of boring. No sunset theatrics, just a strip of bleached blonde getting brighter beneath the sky blue. Mars winked out a long time ago, followed by Venus and Jupiter.

I try to pick out the spot where the sun's going to make its debut. Come on, diva. Show your damn face.

Below me, a heavy bird wings off the creek and curves into forest. The heron!

The sun's upper edge burns through tree silhouettes. It comes up much faster than I would expect, and when it's high enough to see its flaming curve, I turn back toward the mountains.

I practically scream. The trees are hallucinogenic, magenta; it looks like the cover of Zappa's *Hot Rats*. It's a color that I've never seen, or imagined, in nature. And as I stand gasping, an eagle flies over my head. The magnificent colors, the great silent bird—the beauty slams into my body so hard that tears pour from my eyes. I'm thrown off balance, literally reeling, as I lurch after the eagle. I'm dead drunk on dawn.

I come to a little as I start to walk toward the rise. It feels good to move. Songbirds and jays call through trees. A squirrel runs across the path, its tail a semaphore. A short V of Canada geese flies high overhead, sunlight catching their wingbeats so they seem to flicker.

The mountains are back to their orange and gold autumn plumage. A few cars cross the weir, windshields winking in sunlight.

Seagulls wheel over blue water, bright white in low slanting sunlight. Ducks stir on the creek, sunlight catching their wakes. Three grazing deer stop and stand frozen, staring. A lone low cloud sits like a snood over Wittenberg Mountain.

A couple of walkers hunch into the wind, looking grim. His doctor is making him do it.

Blue water. Cold coffee. This.

Day 43. **October 27, 5:40 PM**

Cloud calligraphy, twilight. Nine deer grazing. A two-point buck stands apart, stomping one hoof like a petulant teenager. Cliff swallows loop, skimming wavetips.

A word I love: crepuscular. Of or pertaining to twilight, or animals active at dusk and dawn.

A twentyish couple emerges from the woods on the rise, looking giddy and guilty. A contact high. I follow the path they came off, which ends at a paved circle. Up seven stone steps, a hulking cement monument, streaked with lichen and Soviet in its ungracefulness, to the reservoir's chief engineer, J. Waldo Smith. All four doors are sealed shut, and spindly trees sprout from its roof like a Tim Burton set.

The guardrail lets out a shuddering metallic ping. I look back to see if someone behind me hit the far end with a stick, but there's no one in sight. Must have been cooling metal. Or J. Waldo Smith.

Day 44. **October 28, noon**

I set off in a drizzle, come back in a downpour. The tops of the close peaks are lopped off by clouds; they look like wet mesas. The High Peaks have disappeared, swallowed by fog.

The water is gray, opaque, striped with stretch marks. Pocks of rain stipple waves. It's a churning, uneasy mix. Makes me think of southeast Alaska, of steering a fishing boat for hours on end, trolling tide rips. My skipper picked up a drowned eagle once with the gaff hook. He slid the end claw off one of its talons and gave it to me. Then he dropped its body back into the sea.

The rain stings my face. I used to work outdoors in weather like this, I think as I open my folding umbrella. (I was younger back then, and I had better raingear.)

There's nobody flying, no bird calls. I spot one crow perched on the guardrail. It flies into the woods. Moments later, a loud series of caws, which I translate as "Check it out. Fool walking by with a fucking *umbrella.*"

Day 45. **October 29, 2:00 PM**

Lashing tail of the hurricane, beating the wind to a frenzy. So many leaves down! The mountains are brown, no more reds or bright yellows at all. In the wind shelter of the embankment, a lone row of backlit gold maples. Leaves blow off, swirling like butterflies. The grass on the hillside is littered with bright bits of yellow.

The water is turbid. Waves crash against stone, foaming at the mouth. A long line of fallen leaves bobs in single file.

Lone crow chased across the path by two pileated woodpeckers. Just past the rise, I spot my little murder, perched up and down a white pine. One or two ruffle feathers at me as I pass. Moments later, they're jeering. I turn, but it isn't at me: there's a lone crow overhead, flying so high it's blown sideways by gusts. The gang in the tree keeps on scolding till it's out of sight. Mean girls.

Walking back is much harder. I'm pitched back by headwinds, so every step is deliberate, effortful. Wind roars past my ears and stings tears from my eyes. Oddly, it's warm, and the sky is bright blue.

One biker, a woman in a red windbreaker, passes me four times; she's riding laps. A white-haired man in highwater pants and white socks sits up straight and determined, pedaling into the wind like Miss Gulch.

Day 46. **October 30, 3:50 PM**

Armored truck in the parking lot, next to the port-o-sans. Driver taking a leak, or a leaf-peeper heist?

Perp walk:

• White male with sternum-length beard cinched by rubber band, possibly going to Halloween party as Young Dumbledore.

• Racing biker, black shorts with suspicion of spandex, hunched over getaway vehicle.

• Older male bicyclist, butter-yellow golf sweater and chinos, two counts of White Shoes after Labor Day.

• Female flaneur in red beret, dingy parka, and fingerless gloves. I'm innocent, Officer Bluejay!

Day 47. **October 31, 4:30 PM**

My life of crime escalates. Busted by the DEC at the Secret Cove!

It's Saturday, Halloween, the last weekend of leaf-peeping season, so I skip the walkway and drive east on 28A, checking out entry gates. The first few are high above the water. When I see pickup trucks parked on the shoulder, I realize: hunters. Opening day is still three weeks away, but bow hunting starts in October. Include me out.

The sign on Gate E-17 has a fishing icon, and I can see water through trees. Beyond them, a flat stony beach with a shallow creek winding its way through the center.

I pick my way across it, tightrope walking from stone to flat stone. There's a pine-covered point on the far side, and I want to see what's beyond it. There's an inlet between me and it, so I circle its shore and clamber up a short cliff, grabbing exposed roots to steady myself. On top, I pass through a thick grove of cedars and pine trunks—soft needles, sweet smell—and come out at the edge of a truly secluded, deep-green stream-fed cove with a fabulous view of the northern Catskills. There's no sign of anything human. The forest primeval.

Worth every step, there and back.

I drive over the West Hurley Dike to loop back on Route 28, and because the clouds have gone very dramatic—think El Greco—I stop at the Secret Cove for the view. I sit on a rock gazing up at the sky, which now looks like cotton batting, muffled sun shining through like a flashlight under the covers. Not five minutes later, I hear footsteps approach from behind. Oh, I think, it's a fisherman.

Wrong.

The DEP cop is Central Casting, dark glasses, shaved head. I pull out my Access Permit. And that's when I find out my Access Permit does *not* grant me access to fishing areas unless I *also* have a valid New York fishing license and am "actively in the act of fishing."

"The sign on the gate says Recreational Activity By Permit Only," I tell Officer Bald. "I have a permit, and one of the listed Recreational Activities is hiking."

Well yes, he admits, you can hike in designated Hiking areas. Where are those? I ask. He thinks there might be one up by Brodhead, but "not on the water." In designated Fishing and Hunting Areas, you have to be fishing or hunting. You can't just tromp around looking at things.

I'm being interrogated on suspicion of not attempting murder.

I don't tell him that less than an hour ago I bushwhacked across a stream, climbed up a cliff, and crossed a cedar-and-pine-covered point to a hidden beach, with no fishing gear.

I don't tell him I'd do it again in a heartbeat.

I walk back past his cruiser—really, you *drove* down this quarter-mile spur?—giving its tire a discreet mini-kick as I pass. I'm not repentant at all, no more than I was when a childhood friend and I trespassed on the golf course behind her house and climbed into empty construction sites, but I'm mad at myself for stopping so close to the bridge on a weekend. The DEP cops must be scooping up tourists and iPhone photographers. And Officer Bald probably took down my license plate, so I can't get away with "Gee, Officer, I didn't know," at least not for a while.

But I will play ball. I will (a) get a fishing license, and (b) buy or borrow some gear, so if they track me down again, I can appear to be *in flagrante pescado*, caught in the act of fishing.

Yo, DEP: I'll be back.

Day 48. **November 1, noon**

Shades of gray. November is the new November.

Day 49. **November 2, 4:40 PM**

Post–daylight savings. Sundown before five just feels wrong. Deer, heron, squirrels, a few exercise walkers: the usual suspects. And me, Public Enemy #1.

Today I bought a New York State Sporting License ($25 at Marbletown Town Hall) and some used hip-boot waders ($9.99 at Goodwill). I went there to pick up some "weird '80s hunting videos" Maya spotted last time she came home and wants to use as found footage for an experimental film project. So I'm standing on line with a secondhand thermal undershirt, five deer-hunting videos, and olive-drab waders. I feel like I've changed local teams.

Or not. I run into the rule-bending neighbor who's offered to lend me one of his old collapsible fishing rods as a decoy and tell him I just bought used waders. He says, "Oh, now you're just embarrassing yourself. That'll just *prove* you don't know what you're doing. You wear waders for stream fishing, not for shore fishing."

Gee, Officer, I didn't know.

Day 50. **November 3, 1:20 PM**

Bare trees and midsummer sunshine, midseventies. A sleek gray snake, sunning on asphalt, stirs lazily as I approach and speeds up as I step closer, bombing down the embankment faster than I've ever seen a snake move, grass rippling above. About fifty feet down it stops, cranes its neck up and freezes, like a miniature Loch Ness Monster. At least two feet long, slender, shiny, no stripes. Young black racer.

Yellow butterfly on purple aster, last flecks of bright color.

Day 51. **November 4, 7:20 AM**

Nobody here but a school bus parked outside the porta potty (actual business name Call-a-Head, slogan inside the door: "We're #1 at Picking Up #2").

Mountains bare, foothills rusty. Riffled blue water and cloudless pale sky.

Seven deer at the edge of the woods, looking bleary, like club kids who've been up all night.

Songbirds warming up in the trees. Juncos perched on the Lemon Squeeze wall, letting out little trills. A small downy woodpecker, dalmatian-spotted with tiny red blaze, worries the top of a limb, then the bottom, then lets out a single sharp *cheep* as he flies to the trunk and starts drilling.

An eagle soars over my head, lands on a branch, sits still for a moment, and flies back again. She's checking me out. The nest's more exposed with the leaves gone, visible from closer range, but with the scrim of bare branches and pine boughs it's still hard to get a clear view. She flies over the path one more time in a near-silent glide, then disappears into the woods, somewhere down by the shore. I hear two shrill warrior shrieks, followed by a musical call that sounds almost exactly like *bibbity-bobbity-boo*. Eagle whimsy?

First walkers approach: older couple talking. She gestures, he shrinks.

Big man with a limp, coughing into his hand.

A *third* Eagle Guy, grizzled and slump shouldered, with a white telephoto tucked into his arm. Eagle Guy the Gray.

Rollerblader *texting*. Dude!

All before breakfast.

Day 52. **November 5, 4:50 PM**

Eerily warm. Bare twigs scraping gray sky. Heavy clouds floating on black mirror water.

Day 53. **November 6, 4:40 PM**

Pretty sure Thoreau never wrote up his field notes in the waiting room of a Jiffy Lube. And yet.

Fourth day in a row of bizarrely warm weather: seventy-seven degrees, a new record. Ignoring the omen of climate disaster, TV weathergirls in tight dresses joke about "No-Coat November." What's next, "No-Ozone December?"

The air is dead still. Layered gray clouds and no blue to reflect, so the reservoir looks like a bowl full of mercury.

A dad helps his toddler daughter balance on the guardrail while mom and proud grandpa look on. When he takes her down, her legs bounce in a tantrum while her arms exult: she wants MORE. Her unbridled energy reminds me of Maya, how she and her best friend Zane spent hours doing the Ministry of Silly Walks and riding their training wheel bikes on this walkway. It seems like a lifetime ago. I think of the phrase "empty nest" and wonder if birds ever miss dropping worms into gaping pink maws. I sometimes miss making school lunches, the daily surprise.

Everybody in Olivebridge needs a new muffler today. Car noises rattle through trees, with no lapping waves or wind sounds to cover and no leaves to baffle. A single dog barks somewhere across the water, plaintive, insistent.

I miss my dog. And my daughter. Is that why I'm doing this? Learning to spend time alone, to connect to a world that feels fuller than home. I may not be able to climb Machu Picchu or hike through Tibet, but I can get out my own door every day. It's a start.

Day 54. **November 7, 3:12 PM**

What a difference a day makes! Stiff headwind and whitecaps. Looks like fall, feels like fall. Is fall.

Mesmerized by the bobbing of dry grass seedheads and dead Queen Anne's lace. A flock of dark-eyed juncos flits from hillside to trees as I pass, crisscrossing flight paths like an elaborate shell game. Charcoal gray on top, white on the bottom, their plumage reminds me of nuns.

Fitness family of four: Toddler pedaling training wheel bike with a striped scarf swathing his face like a desert turban. Taut mom pushing jog stroller with baby's face almost entirely covered by a knit hat and blanket, only a strip of cheeks and pacifier exposed. Dad running behind in high-zipped black fleece and tights. None of this looks even faintly like fun.

Day 55. **November 8, 1:15 PM**

An unhappy milestone: first day I left home in a bad mood and came back in same. I have my reasons: I'm fighting a nasty cold, I missed my dear friend Karen's birthday party, my furnace went out, and I don't have the money to fix it. So walking is more of a chore than a pleasure, and finding the Olivebridge parking lot full doesn't help. I drive down to the Frying Pan, hoping the change of perspective will help.

More sense of human presence on this side. The fifteen arches under the weir bridge are a treat for the eye, like the Japanese bridge at Giverny. The same can't be said for the view-hog McMansions that dot the hills, much more visible now that the fall leaves are down. It's scenic but doesn't feel wild.

Many walkers, including a punkish blonde in black top, skirt, and tights who'd be right at home in the East Village and six SUNY New Paltz students of such perfectly assorted genders and races they look like a college brochure. Three bike racers in Team Overlook spandex. Dad teaching daughter to skate. The only wildlife in sight is a squabbling cluster of gulls.

Remind me again why I'm doing this. Three hundred ten days to go. There's no way.

And if I stop doing it, then what? I'll feel even worse. It's no win.

There will be days like this.

Day 56. **November 9, 3:10 PM**

Brightest color today is the water, a vibrant electric blue. It's close to full sun, but a deer stumbles out of the forest and starts eating grass. Within seconds a second doe joins it, and one after another a herd of seven melts out of the trees. I hear hoofs crunch dry leaves before I spot each one emerging from shadows.

A splash from the beach. Is Fabio's mate (she deserves her own name; it'll come) catching his dinner?

Nope. Ducks. Three of them, paddling and diving in shifting formation. One dives and the other two follow.

The patchy-barked sycamore's lost all its leaves, and its long-stemmed brown fruits dangle down from bare branches like spiked Christmas ornaments.

Pastel sundog amid scrim of clouds. As I drive home, I see it again, transformed into a vertical pillar of red, orange, yellow, the rest of the spectrum too faint to make out. It looks like a column of fire.

Day 57. **November 10, 2:20 PM**

Because every day means *every day,* I head out in a grizzling rain.

Treeplanting weather, what my long-ago crew boss called "Seattling." Not a downpour, just hovering damp, cold enough to soak into your bones.

The mountains are draped in white raincoats. High Point is pointless. I can't tell the peaks' silhouettes from the ridges of cloud, but I can see rain falling, milky, like special effects rain. Foothills recede into mist combed by high pines. It looks so much like southeast Alaska that I scan the horizon for trawlers.

The great blue heron lifts off from the creek far below, drawing in his long neck and legs to get airborne. His wingspan is vast. It's amazing to look *down* at a heron, the twin curve of blue and gray wings slowly fanning the air. Winging across the embankment, he lets loose a string of white poop.

Day 58. **November 11, 1 PM**

Indecisive sky. Every kind of cloud cover there is, with a few sky-blue eyes and a radiant patch of bright sunlight over the Secret Cove. Overnight rain left muddy runoff streams snaking through the woods.

Some parts of the reservoir basin are riffled, some flat. A meandering curve of flat water traces a path toward the Lemon Squeeze, like a river on top of a lake. It looks like the ghost of the Esopus, the creek that was dammed to fill up this valley with water. There was a waterfall right in that spot, Bishop's Falls, that powered a gristmill. Nearby was a wooden covered bridge spanning the creek, with boarding houses and shops on both sides. I think of the families who lived here and had to leave everything, hand-built homes burned to the ground. I think of the men paid a pittance to burn them, the immigrant workers who died laying stone for the dam. When we walk on the reservoir path, we are treading on ghosts.

Day 59. **November 12, 4:50 PM**

Dark, dank, damp. Damn.

Rainclouds bisect hillsides, decapitate mountains. Gray sky and gray water, like walking between two plates of a griddle. Lone runner, stiff shouldered, passes me coming and going.

Day 60. **November 13, 2:45 PM**

Colder, windier, grayer. November is boredom's bitch.

Boots on the ground. Natty man with white mustache *salutes* me. Eagle Guy the Younger just setting out, camera in hand, humming cheerfully under his breath.

Day 61. **November 14, 10:10 AM**

It begins. New snow on the High Peaks. Heavy clouds and fierce wind. A few stabs of sunlight bleach leafless tree trunks bone white.

Nanooked biker.

The reservoir roils. Not just chop, but whitecaps that curl high and crash over the stones of the dam, like Great Lakes near-surf.

I draw my hood tight. Red hat pulled down to my eyebrows, scarf up to my nose, fake-fur blinders on sides. I look like that kid from *South Park*.

A small slice of scenery, moving. Wind whips through my pants. I need long johns. This shit's getting real.

Here's the layout for winter walks: Olivebridge straightaway, windy as hell. Cement walls of the Lemon Squeeze offer some wind shelter. Second straightaway, windy as hell again. Rise, a bit calmer. Windy as hell to the weir bridge. Reverse and repeat.

Walking *most* days in agreeable weather is not a commitment. This is. Get out the long johns.

The last bright thing blooming: thistle-pink knapweed, bobbing low to the ground. Just in one spot, a scatter of new Queen Anne's lace that bloomed when the weather got warm and now tosses, wind-buffeted, dancing with the dead. My mind leaps to yesterday's terrorist bombings in Paris, including the Bataclan theatre, where my nephew Jeff often goes to hear music. He's safe, but more than a hundred are dead, and for what?

A line from Chekhov's *Three Sisters* jumps into my head, from lovesick Baron Tusenbach marching off to be killed in a duel: "You see that dead tree? It sways in the wind with the rest. So it seems that if I were to die, I would still have a share in life somehow." When I played Masha in college, I'd cry every time as I stood in the wings, preparing my own big emotional scene: a sobbing farewell to my lover Vershinin, played by an actor I secretly loved. I never acted so well in my life.

Not even the squirrels are moving today, no sound but the wind. And then the dark shadow: an eagle! Gliding high and fast, wings nearly motionless as she spirals up, fearless. Xena, the warrior princess.

Day 62. **November 15, 3:50 PM**

Big weekender crowd. I park next to a Zipcar. So many people on the path that I almost turn back to seek someplace quieter, but I don't want to get busted by Officer Bald. Besides, something's caught my eye: six people posing in front of a tripod, making playful leaps in midair. As I get closer, I see they're all young, Asian and Latinx. Four boys and two girls, dressed mostly in black, coordinating their gestures and leaps for the timer, then clustering around the camera to see what they got.

"Are you a band?" I ask, which makes them all laugh.

"A band?" echoes one boy.

"Looks like an album cover," I tell him.

They laugh even harder, and one of the girls pipes, "I wish!"

The air is so still that intact vapor trails stripe the sky. The sun's low and warm, painting dead grasses with magic-hour gold. One couple walks toward me, and all of a sudden an eagle lifts up *right* behind them, rising over the guardrail, so low and so close I can't speak but stand rooted, pointing up with both arms. They don't turn or look—*Why do they think I just did that, a small seizure?*—and I get the feeling the eagle is showing herself just to me. I swivel to watch her sun-gilded flight, reflected on still water. She lands on a distant tree, and I see the bough sway with her weight.

Sun slides behind High Point. The air cools in seconds.

Lining the shore by the rise, clumps of rusty dead leaves, like a funeral garland on water. I think about sweet Jeffrey Nelson, an old friend who died yesterday after living heroically with a long illness, and tears sting my eyes. This is why I wanted to be by myself on the walkway tonight. Above me the postsundown sky turns pastel, ripples of grapefruit pink, streaks of bright lemon. Jeffrey gave me my first theatre job, running the box office of a summer stock theatre in North Conway, New Hampshire, where I fell in love with mountains and sky, and with writing.

Also with most of the men in the company, including him.

Gone. It's fitting I started this project in fall. It's the season my life is in now, turning sixty this year, facing winter, the days growing shorter and so many flavors of loss all around and ahead, this beauty that changes so swiftly it aches.

A pale new moon levitates, rising through indigo. This one's for you, Jeffrey.

Day 63. **November 16, 1 PM**

A DEP cop is parked facing the footpath, window cracked open and engine idling, and I think, *Oh no.*

Was there more terrorism in Paris? Manhattan? What good could it possibly do to place one patrol car in this one spot when there are so many devious ways to access New York City's water supply? The Ashokan has forty-four miles of shoreline, most of it near public roads. What is this but an authoritarian dumb show, polluting the air and goading us to feel unsafe, even here?

This walkway was a working road when I moved up here in the late '80s. In the panicked weeks after 9/11, the state police erected a guard booth. As winter set in, the guards in the booth went from stern and commanding to listless and bored. When spring came, they grilled hot dogs on a hibachi, drew a face on a Wilson volleyball, and stuffed him an outfit. The return of humor felt like relief. Then they shut the road to car traffic, adding a row of retractable columns across it so DEP cars could get through for their pointless patrols.

I walk right past the cop. Not his fault, but I don't want him here. I'm aware of his eyes on my back as I pass. If my skin were brown, would he ask me questions?

It's another warm day, and the milky pale sky makes the hillsides look faded, like old Polaroids. I'm looking for something that I've never noticed before, but my mind is too jangled to focus.

Is it the way sunlight glints on the shore's edge like chaser lights? The odd beauty of dead goldenrod, glowing ivory in sunlight?

The cop car is gone by the time I turn back. Maybe he just ate a sandwich.

Day 64. **November 17, 2 PM**

Off-road adventure at the fishing gate by Brodhead Road. I've seen two more DEP cars on the prowl, so I can't relax, even though I have my fishing license tucked in my pocket. Don't want to be stopped and told no.

A makeshift gravel road through the woods comes out on the wide beach directly across from Driftwood Cove, at the long row of rowboats I see from the start of my usual walk. It's a dizzying shift of perspective.

There's art on the beach. Someone's left balanced stone cairns here and there, and there's a makeshift driftwood lean-to wedged between tree

trunks. The top of a broken, hollowed-out tree looks just like a mask, two round eyes, knotty nose, wide screaming mouth.

On the path back, a tiny black feather with white polka dots on both edges. Downy woodpecker?

A red-tailed hawk glides silently over tall pines, sun striking the bright fox-fur wedge of its tail.

Day 65. **November 18, 4:20 PM**

It's barely past four and I'm already driving with headlights. The walkway looks dark and mysterious. A child's pink mitten dangles from a metal NO DOGS sign, attached with the clip meant to fasten it onto some little parka. Lost and Not Found.

I don't see a soul for two miles, except for one biker in top-to-toe black who passes me silently coming and going. Black Rider.

The quiet is palpable. No birdsong, no waves. Distant traffic through trees. Then a sudden eruption of yipping and howling. Coyotes! A *lot* of coyotes; I hear individual voices, sharp, whooping, percussive. They've killed something and there's triumph and glee in the pack, bacchanalian.

Then silence. Just me and the dusk.

Day 66. **November 19, 10 AM**

Kurosawa fog swallows the mountains and sits in the low draws like cobwebs. A thick white mist rolls up the hillside like steam from a cauldron. The crowns of dark pines levitate over clouds.

A clatter of unseen crows, then long silence. A single duck honks on the water. I spot it swimming alone, off the beach near the rise. One small dot moving in all that still gray. Same as me.

I stand still and watch it meander, wondering why it's alone. And why I am. This self-sufficiency thing is important and valid, but sometimes you just want a hug.

When I turn back, two heavy dark bodies in still silhouette. Wild turkeys. They spot me, crouch into their dinosaur hunch, and scuttle under the guardrail, gobbling a warning returned from below. I cross and look down. Seven more turkeys, straggling into the woods single file. Big tom with a bobbling red flap on his neck, like a tie made of meat.

Silver mirror. There is no far shore.

Day 67. **November 20, 4:30 PM**

Sundown by four thirty, stars out by five. Darkness too soon, late fall's waning light.

The Driftwood Cove shoreline is higher than I've ever seen it. The beach is half-gone and the sentinel rock is an island. The creek tumbles under loose driftwood, making gurgling sounds like a bamboo marimba. Could this all be from yesterday's rain, or was there a water release from the Schoharie Reservoir upstream?

Some yahoo in West Shokan is target practicing for tomorrow, opening day of deer-hunting season. His gunshots ring over the water. I pass three groups of deer grazing on the embankment. The first group raises heads, wary.

The second is going through some hierarchical struggle. One keeps chasing others away from the cluster, running at them with head down. Finally two break and gallop off into the woods, white tails flagging. The challenger follows.

The third group stops eating and runs off as soon as they spot me. All typical whitetail behavior, but reservoir deer are so mellow. They know something's up. I hope they stay far from those gunshots.

I spot two eagles flying together, so far off and high that the only way I can identify them is their straight-shouldered wingspan. They look penciled against the sky, like faintly drawn eyebrows.

Moon just past half, tilted on a diagonal.

I'm bone-deep gloomy, and the cold walk at twilight does nothing to shake it. Sign on the DEP booth: IF YOU SEE SOMETHING, SAY SOMETHING. Dammit, I'm trying.

Day 68. **November 21, 3 PM**

Shoreline even higher today. Driftwood clots in loose rafts, some breaking free. A scatter of brilliant red barberries.

Just past the rise, a threesome brandishing cameras: Eagle Guys Younger and Elder chat up a middle-aged blonde in a pink tam-o'-shanter. Her telephoto is bigger than theirs. I ask, "Are you staking them out?" and the newbie says, "Yeah, we're the eagle paparazzi."

I walk across Reservoir Road where it crosses the weir bridge. The walkway continues on the Lower Basin, where the first thing I spot is a scruffy teen eagle, winging away from the press corps. A few seagulls flap up from the water, white wings catching light.

Fewer walkers on the Lower Basin, or maybe it's just that the sun's dropping low. I hear distant gunshots. Inept hunter, firing off shot after shot: one, two, then threefourfivesix, like e. e. cummings's Buffalo Bill. I hope he missed.

The sun slants bright yellow, then drops behind High Point. The eagle paparazzi are still hanging out, talking lenses and bagels. It's Bread Alone versus "Bodacious Bagels in Stone Ridge—the best!"

I nod up at the empty nest. "They're making you wait."

Eagle Guy the Younger looks at me, reproachful. "So what? It's a nice place to wait."

He's right.

Day 69. **November 22, 9:20 AM**

Why do runners wear such bizarre colors? Woman in silver parka, fuchsia leggings, and neon-spattered shoes checking stats on her app. Two guys, first in cobalt-blue beanie and fleece with tie-dyed spandex leggings, second in dignified black but with sneakers the color of Gatorade. Just as I'm thinking, "You look ridiculous," they greet me with a cheery, near-simultaneous "Morning!" in lovely British accents.

Male cardinal flying low, splash of bright red.

Crossing the weir bridge, I spot Eagle Guys Younger and Elder at the rail, by the NO PEDESTRIANS sign. Their lenses are trained on a spar tree next to the bridge, where Fabio sits posing in sunlight. It looks like an eagle fashion shoot.

Day 70. **November 23, 4:40 PM**

First subfreezing res walk. Thirty-one degrees with serious windchill.

Red beret and wrapped scarf under Velcroed hood, stiff as a crash helmet. Wind blowing so hard that a yellow metal NO ENTRANCE sign is flapping off the guardrail.

Two groups of deer acting frisky, charging after each other or galloping in solo circles like horses kicking up their heels. Are they doing it just to keep warm? It's mating season and hunting season; film noir for ruminants.

Day 71. **November 24, 3:50 PM**

No wind. Water so still that the cornflower sky and cotton-ball clouds don't seem to be reflected on its surface, but visible far beneath it, a world under glass.

As I'm walking back, a blonde iPhone photographer effuses about the late-afternoon sunlight on my pumpkin-colored parka. "You look so beautiful walking along! Like a golden apparition!"

Well, no one's called me *that* before.

The benches are gone for the season. Winter is coming.

A huge white almost-full moon rises right over the road, filling the vanishing point between two rows of trees like a light at the end of the tunnel. My heart rises with it. This is how joy feels.

Day 72. **November 25, 2:30 PM**

Leaf music: Single dry leaf skittering over the path makes a ratchety scratch. Small oak still covered with dry maroon leaves that blow like maracas, portentous. I half expect the sycamore to start crooning "Oye Como Va."

I hear wings flash open like a fan. I wheel around, hoping to see an eagle at close range. But it's a pileated woodpecker, swooping through trees. Its mate follows. They bob and weave, landing and hopping up pine trunks, then taking off again in their peculiar flight pattern: wingbeat wingbeat dip, wingbeat wingbeat dip, as if they can't quite stay aloft.

Delicate etching of backlit grass seedheads. First crust of ice on the creek spill below.

Day 73. **November 26, 4:05 PM**

Happy sight on the eve of Thanksgiving: seventeen wild turkeys crossing the road single file and fanning out into the woods.

Rust hills, purple mountains, and painterly sky, all reflected in not-quite-still water.

Just after sundown, three alto-flute hoots from an owl.

Maya's on her way home for the holiday!

Day 74. **November 27, 2:20 PM**

Dozens of people atoning for Thanksgiving dinner with reservoir walks. There's not even overflow parking in Olivebridge, so my brother David and I drive to the Frying Pan, where he nabs the very last parking spot on the circle. I hoped Maya would join us, but she's staying with her grandparents.

It's a mob scene. A lone fisherman in boots and overalls, portaging tackle box, two rods, landing net, cooler, and flotation cushion, plus two oars slung over his shoulder, heads down a dirt path to his rowboat. Everyone else funnels onto the walkway.

Only wildlife in sight is a shifting flotilla of seagulls. David's gait is shambling, bearish; I can hear him mouth breathing. We walk out a short way, then head back.

"What are you going to write about?" David asks me, and I tell him, "You!"

He stops at the Call-a-Head stall and calls from inside, "Did you notice their slogan?" But of course. We are brother and sister.

Bumper sticker: "got squirrels?"

Day 75. **November 28, 12:40 PM**

No Catskills, no foothills. Sheared off at the tree line by clouds so low that the crowns of the tallest pines poke into mist.

Steady drizzle. I'm inside the belly of cloud.

Still silence.

The monotone sky brings out autumn colors: dead grasses lion's-mane gold, silver-green lichen on tree trunks. The tips of bare branches are maroon: dormant buds. It's not even winter yet, and there's a promise of spring.

Day 76. **November 29, 5:20 PM**

Stacking two cords of firewood, belatedly prepping for winter like some lazy creature in an Aesop's fable. I don't stop till it's practically dark. Then shocking news: our dear friend Sandi Zinaman has died of a heart attack, two days after posting a Thanksgiving selfie on Facebook. Unable to take it in, I click open and stare at the photo. Sandi is beaming, her lovely face framed by a nimbus of red curls, a Pre-Raphaelite kitchen goddess surrounded by loved ones and food she just cooked.

First Jeffrey, now Sandi: my own generation. Aunt Joan in the ICU, Papa frail and shaky this morning, asking "What am I supposed to be doing?" again and again. November is brutal.

I drive to the res with a heavy heart. It's past sundown, so I'm surprised to see two other cars. Somewhere in the distance a large group exclaims, laughter floating though darkness. Damn. I am not in the mood for a party.

The voices come closer. They're speaking Spanish, mingled with gleeful shrieks of small children. This softens my irritation: those kids will remember this evening for years to come, that time we went for that really long walk after dark.

I pass them crossing the Lemon Squeeze. Six adults and three kids, looming out of the shadows. The first thing I see is a little girl's white puffer jacket. "Hello!" she calls, scurrying back to her dad as I echo, "Hello!"

They must wonder why I'm walking into the dark by myself.

But it isn't *that* dark. The mountains are midnight blue, silhouetted on blackberry sky. Venus shines overhead. As I walk, pinpoints of other stars

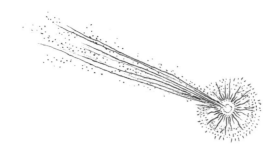

appear, a few blinking planes, constellations. The Big Dipper rests on Tonshi Mountain as if it's a shelf. I can't see the path up ahead, but I can make out bristles of pine silhouettes on the rise. It's darker in there, and though I'd planned a short walk, turning back at the rise, I'm drawn to keep going. My cheeks are cold. My breath sends out steam.

Walking through woods I can't see sparks a little frisson of fear. I stop several times, thinking I heard something move in the trees. I'm about to turn back when the brightest shooting star I've ever seen streaks across the whole sky, left to right, leaving a trail of white light like a comet. My fear is erased in an instant, flushed out by gratitude.

Day 77. **November 30, 2:55 PM**

First time back at the Secret Cove since the bust, and the scene of the crime is now underwater. So is my mood.

Broken tree trunks and stumps. Curled white birch bark, dead leaves. Simple grief.

I don't want to stay here; I don't feel at ease. I park at a fishing gate next to the West Hurley Dike and tromp over the windswept beach called Flat Rocks, its huge slabs of bluestone like a raked stage. A stone jetty juts into the water, and I clamber out for the view: shafts of amber light over the tops of the mountains. The rocks at the end are streaked white. I've discovered the gulls' Call-a-Head.

Day 78. **December 1, 5:10 PM**

Best thing I can say about today's walk is that I did it. Fog and cold rain after dark. Am I really going to do this all winter? I doubt it. It's going to get hard, and I'm going to start balking, and there'll come a day when I don't go at all, and the whole thing will end in a flurry of guilt and recrimination. Because that's what I do.

Do we ever stop blaming ourselves? I think of a poem Papa read me when I was too young, Randall Jarrell's "The Woman at the Washington Zoo," with its bleak final lines: "You know what I was, / You see what I am: change me, change me!"

Day 79. **December 2, 1:30 PM**

Driftwood Cove in fog and unrelenting rain. Fallen trunks and leaners, crisscrossed like a battlefield. Woodpecker-drilled pine trunk oozing white pitch.

No beach at all. Steel-drum rainfall on overturned rowboats.

Gulls flying over the weir bridge against whiteout fog.

Day 80. **December 3, 1:35 PM**

Squeezing in a short walk between writing deadlines, a shiva call for Sandi, and my Word Café class. Tumultuous sky: snowfall on western High Peaks, rain slanting down from the north, pale blue sky to the east, shifting Eye of God sunray piercing clouds in the south. All weathers at once.

Agitated gray chop at crosscurrents, no pattern of waves.

Something spirals up into the clouds over Brodhead Point. An eagle, far and high, searching for fish.

This is life. Too much of everything in all directions at once, the clash of storms and the beauty that rises, stirring our soul as it disappears.

Day 81. **December 4, 3:45 PM**

The Olivebridge parking lot's down to one Call-a-Head. Winter austerity.

Towering clouds look as if they belong on a rococo ceiling.

Shiny teal waves in obedient rhythm.

Seven deer grazing in a close knot. They spot me and freeze. Six stay still as posts, staring at me. The seventh, a yearling, dashes back and forth at top speed, darting around the adults like a skier racing slalom, then gets the memo and freezes. One doe stamps her foot at me, doing her best to look menacing. The doe next to her chews slowly, jaw moving sideways.

Day 82. **December 5, 10:30 AM**

It's Papa's ninetieth birthday today, which astonishes me. My dear cousin Elaine and her husband Fran have driven from Syracuse to surprise him and stayed at my house overnight. After breakfast we head for the res in their zippy red car.

The sky is a summery blue and the water is still. There are plenty of walkers and bikers today, and Fran greets each one with a hearty "Good morning!" Some answer, some don't. He seems miffed by the Garbos who vant to be alone.

I've noticed an inverse ratio of speed and equipment to friendliness. Contemplative walkers tend to nod, smile, or mumble hello; so do people on upright bikes. Exercise walkers with sunglasses, headphones, and/or cell phones ignore you. Runners ignore you with attitude. Rollerbladers look at you as if you're an obstacle. Bike racers look at you as if you're a cockroach.

There's an eagle paparazzi summit conference: Eagle Guy the Older, Eagle Guy the Younger, Eagle Guy the Gray, *and* Eagle Gal are all hanging out at the sweet spot past the rise, jawing with each other, cameras hung loosely around their necks.

We cross the weir bridge to the Lower Basin, then walk back and head back up the rise, where a couple stands staring up into a pine. Fran spots Fabio first, still as a block, two-thirds of the way up the trunk. After a long, disdainful pause, Fabio swivels his head, lets loose a stream of white poop, and resumes posing, motionless.

The eagle paparazzi converge, snapping photos, and we walk on.

Ever the expert, I point out three distant deer that turn out to be sun-haloed fenceposts. Fran thinks it's a riot.

Day 83. **December 6, 2:30 PM**

Hard frost in the morning. Rime glitters from each blade of grass: white-edged swords.

By midday the shadows are already long, which seems perfectly apt for Sandi's memorial service: dark too soon. The auditorium's full to bursting, a community stunned and heartbroken. The words of love, Abby Newton's cello, and the ethereal kaddish sung by Sandi's cousin wring us out. We weep buckets and cling to each other afterward, shaken.

Still in mourning clothes, Shelley and I drive to the reservoir. My dear friend borrows the spare pair of sneakers I keep in the car, which I love: she's walking a mile in my shoes. But as soon as we hit the path, it's discordant. I crave silent reverie; she needs to download. One of her cats has just died, and she's gotten a raft of bad medical news, which she recounts in a loud, angry voice. We're walking a few feet from two other people. I suggest we sit on a bench for a moment and let them go past. I sit; Shelley doesn't. She stands there, impatient.

The sky's milky over the mountains, an August haze with a winter bite.

When the strangers have passed out of earshot, I stand and we set out again. Shelley's talking about life's fragility, how none of us knows how much time we have left. "It's all a gift," she says, spreading her arms.

And an eagle appears. Flying right toward us, strong wingbeats. She comes closer and closer, then glides right past us with huge wings outstretched. We swivel and gasp as she flies to the opposite shore, disappearing into sunlit white radiance.

I turn to Shelley. "You just said, 'It's all a gift.' *That* was a gift."

We fall into each other's arms, hugging long and hard. We finally let go and walk on arm in arm, Sandi's big wings around us. My memory echoes the call and response we just spoke at the service with so many others: *We will remember her.*

We walk back in silence, squinting into the radiance. The waves look like crinkled gray silk.

Day 84. **December 7, 4:23 PM**

Early sundown, the western sky coral and turquoise. In postsunset half light I pick up two crumpled napkins to throw them away, then bend down for what looks like a third. It's a white mesh drawstring bag with something inside, an asymmetrical twist of metal with a mounted stone. Is it a crushed wedding ring? It's too dark to make out, but now there's an unfinished story, which gets a new twist when I pick up the object beside it, a potted-plant label.

By Subaru domelight I check out my booty. Jeepers Creepers White Periwinkle (*Vinca minor alba*), Part to Full Shade, USDA Zones 3–9.

Okay. But why was it lying on the reservoir walkway next to a jewelry bag?

It's about two by three inches, white organza with silver stars. Inside is a silver drop earring with a beveled red stone that might be a garnet. The silver is tarnished; it doesn't look new. It does look like part of a pair.

I remember passing two young women in boho layers: tiered skirts over long johns, long sweaters, fringed ponchos, embroidered Afghan hats. Did they exchange gifts? Let's say A gives B a pot of white vinca, and B reciprocates with new earrings. A takes off her old garnet earrings to try them on, stashing them in the gift bag, which she accidentally drops.

But where is the second red earring?

Day 85. **December 8, 4:20 PM**

After sundown. The sky is a whisper of nursery colors. It's mirrored in water so still the reflected mountains are photographically sharp in the shallows. A bit farther out a barely perceptible riffle lops peaks off their bases, a conjuring trick.

There's no hint of orange anywhere but the underside of a few cloud shreds snagging the crests of the Burroughs Range, like fiery steam rising from a volcanic chain. Within seconds the hot color fades.

Two walkers pass as I survey the reemerging shoreline of Driftwood Cove. Yesterday's scatter of rock tips is now a long narrow strip, like an alligator back.

The first walker, in orange puffer jacket, walks very fast with a comical swivel, swaying her whole upper torso. The next is a trim Asian woman in heels and a black tailored coat. She stops on the Lemon Squeeze, leaning over to look at the creek far below, then turning and arching her upper back against the angled stone wall to gaze up at the sky. As I approach she straightens up quickly, as if I've caught her in some intimate act.

The darkness and cold come down fast. When I return to the spot where Dan placed his easel, the landscape looks just like his black-and-white painting. He went home that night and Sandi cooked something amazing for dinner. I still can't imagine that I'll never see her again, her radiant smile at the Stone Ridge Library desk.

A DEP prowl car rolls into the lot. The cop in the passenger side gets out and goes into the guard booth, lowering three of the metal barrier columns. The driver rolls forward, and the columns rise back up. Floodlights snap off, cop locks up the booth and gets back in the passenger seat. Car begins its slow creep down the walkway.

Every night, around sundown. Just to remind us they're here.

Day 86. **December 9, 12:45 PM**

Water pale gray, mountains milky with haze, sky swathed in thick layers of dimpled cloud cover. It looks like a padded cell.

One blue jay shrieking.

White-bearded Santa Claus man in gray hoodie and watch cap, walking fast on the very small loop by the monument, circling around and around and around like a rat on a wheel. Santa Sisyphus.

Day 87. **December 10, 8:10 AM**

The sky is an unambiguous blue and the morning sun pinkens the haze on the mountains. They look like mountains in a dream.

Warm still air, springlike. Somewhere a woodpecker's drilling. A skitter of juncos, two rust-breasted bluebirds. Gray squirrel dashes the length of a fallen trunk. A flock of wrens drops from branch to branch of a sycamore, fluting a warning.

A tree falls in the forest. I hear it. It's actually only a limb, but the crack and fall draws my eye up to the spar tree where Fabio sits, preening.

I see Xena pass overhead, her straight-winged soar over the walkway, as if she's commuting to work. She flies back and forth twice, then comes in for a landing, right on the Lemon Squeeze wall. The sun catches the white of her head like a spotlight. Even from this distance, she's huge.

I walk in a steady straight line, no arm swing. How close will she let me come? It takes several minutes to reach the Lemon Squeeze. I see her head turn and her tailfeathers twitch, letting me know she's alert. Should I stop? But there's another walker heading out from the parking lot—if my approach doesn't startle her off the railing, his will.

I keep coming, eyes fixed and heart racing. When I'm about thirty feet from the great bird, she rises up slowly, glides over the wall, then circles back toward me, passing so close I can see downy gray tailfeathers under the brilliant white fan, her bright yellow feet and curved claws.

I watch till she disappears into the trees.

As I cross, I can't resist placing my hand on the spot on the rail where she sat. Then I realize the approaching walker is Eagle Guy the Gray. He looks surly. I spoiled his shot.

As I head home, a gray squirrel runs under my wheels with a sickening thunk, killed on impact. I drive away with a hollowness inside my ribcage. Why is death everywhere?

Day 88. **December 11, 2:50 PM**

First reservoir walk with a fever and stuffed head. It didn't occur to me to stay in bed. I guess I'm determined.

The trident point's back, breeze riffling the shallows. Ten or so ducks doing nothing. I trudge over the Lemon Squeeze bridge. I trudge back. Nothing but duty today, but I did it.

Fat yellow cat walks with disdainful slowness across Route 213 in the center of Olivebridge, stopping traffic in both directions, pausing on the center line to lick a paw. My new hero.

Day 89. **December 12, 1:25 PM**

Gray. Clouds. Mirror.

Talkative walkers. Kids on bikes.

> *same as it ever was*
> *same as it ever was*
> *same as it ever was*

Shaft of gold light on the crown of Mount Tremper.

Day 90. **December 13, 3 PM**

Ninety days. Do I get a red coin from Reservoir Walkers Anonymous?

The fall-to-winter transition is rendered bizarre by the warm spell. It's fifty-six, heading for sixty tomorrow. No snow predicted till after the new year.

I park at the first fishing gate, walking through a carnage of downed tree trunks in leafless woods. Some of the standing trees are blazed with orange spray paint. Textures of stripped bark and worm-eaten wood, hairy serpent of poison ivy vine climbing a trunk.

A fishy aroma hangs over the squelchy new beach, a rich mudflat stink. Old bones of bleached driftwood, with a newer high-water line of mud-darkened logs and stray bits of flotsam: a half-rotted tennis ball (thrown to a golden retriever?), a chunk of blue Styrofoam cooler, a twist of bright yellow twine.

I walk out past the rowboats. I can see people walking the walkway above the dike, hear shrieks of kids riding their bikes, but the strata of mudflat and ridge give me a new sense of perspective.

Ninety days in and I'm down by the water. There's something I need to get closer to, day by day, footstep by footstep.

Keep walking.

Winter

Day 91. **December 14, 11:30 AM**

Dense fog, no far shore. It's like being inside a wool sock.

Day 92. **December 15, 8:20 PM**

Fierce wind after dark, moonlight-edged clouds and a freckle of stars in the breaks. Maya's come home for the holidays and is dressed in Vermont winter layers except for her mesh running shoes; she gets literal cold feet. A hundred yards out, my adult daughter whines, "How much farther do we have to go?" And when I laugh at the echo of her toddler self, she zings back, "I hate how much you're enjoying how much I'm not enjoying this."

And then: helicopters! Two of them, loud and low, raking the water with spotlights. One pass overhead and they're gone. What the hell?

Day 93. **December 16, 2:10 PM**

Gray again, warm again. The usual clouds on the usual crests. A minyan of ducks on the creek spill, the sculptural twist of dried milkweed pods. The shore's even lower; that's different. But this phase is less about tracking changes than coming back to the same place, again and again and again. It's the dogged phase. The don't-give-up-*now* phase.

I still notice new things every time, but I'm actively searching for them. I'm not gobsmacked by firsts. That starry-eyed, blood-fizzing first-date sensation is mellowing into routine; it's not all exclamation points.

Oddly ominous greeting from a fellow walker: "Enjoy it while you can. And Merry Christmas."

Day 94. **December 17, 3 PM**

Umbrella walk, rain drilling the silk like a woodpecker. Low clouds blot out the bottoms of mountains. Peaks hover like Japanese ghosts.

Whiteout fog over the rise. The path is littered with drowning night crawlers.

Nothing moves in this landscape but me.

Day 95. **December 18, 9:09 AM**

Wall-to-wall carpet of clouds, gray for days. The wind is fierce, lashing up whitecaps. I South Park my hood, anticipating a monotonous slog.

To the west, a split seam in the clouds. Behind, turquoise sky. It's as if someone reached up and parted the curtains of this bleak day, revealing a bright one behind it.

Lone gull, sailboating in wind. Two wheeling crows, one scolding chickadee. A squirrel jitters across the path. An eagle lofts up from the woods in the distance, a thrilling brief glimpse. I stand stock still, holding my breath till I lose the white spot of her head over Brodhead Point.

Hairless black caterpillar with apricot stripes down the length of its body, inching along the Lemon Squeeze, in December. I carry it down to the end—it curls up in my palm, a tight spiral—and set it down in dry grass, where I hope it won't freeze or be eaten. What will it turn into if it survives?

Walking toward me, Eagle Guy the Gray, shoulders hunched, cradling his long white lens in the crook of his arm as if he were holding a baby.

There is no monotony.

Day 96. **December 19, 11:30 AM**

Blue sky, dappled sunshine with high airship cumulus casting irregular shadows. "Mom, you got some *calico-ass* mountains," says Maya. She and a friend are dropping me off; they'll be back in an hour.

It's windy as fuck. The water's whitecapped and opaque, streaked blue and olive by fast-moving clouds: you can see sun or shade racing toward you across breaking waves.

I walk fast to stay warm, watching two crows pick at seeds on the lee side. When I look up, there's an eagle flying right at me. As always, that inhale of thrill. I stop walking and whisper hello as she passes, flying across the path and over the woods. I swivel to watch as she joins her mate for a pas de deux in an updraft. They circle each other in rising spirals as if tracing a double helix, higher and higher. I watch till both dots disappear into clouds.

The eagle paparazzi march down off the rise, Younger and Older first, followed by Gray and *both* Eagle Gals, one pulling her gear on a scooter. They're moments too late; missed their calendar shot. But I didn't.

Day 97. **December 20, 3:30 PM**

My new favorite place to sit: a log by a runoff stream a short walk up the beach from Brodhead Point. The stream tumbles over a mossy bank onto driftwood hung with icicles, then trickles along the beach, where it waterfalls over stone steps. Water music in stereo: alto marimba behind, soprano gurgle ahead.

View to the left: western High Peaks with the tip of Slide Mountain photobombing its shorter neighbor Friday Mountain, a name I adore. To the right, the fifteen-arch span of the weir bridge, the eagle's-nest woods on the rise, the long jut of Keywaden Peninsula. Past-half moon starting to climb through presunset pastels.

There's a strange survivalist windbreak built out of driftwood boards leaning against a pine. Not a duck blind: no waterfowl hunting allowed on the reservoir, and it's too close to the water to legally take down a deer. Who built this? How long has it been here? A reservoir mystery.

The beach morphs from gravelly strand to large broken stones, crumbling bluestone steps, and smooth rock platforms crusted with frozen puddles.

I pick up a big piece of driftwood shaped like a kachina doll, and a dappled snaky root that fits like a staff in its hand. Toting this contraband under one arm, I hotfoot it back to my car. Drive home grinning.

Day 98. **December 21, 4:27 PM**

Earliest sundown of the year is a symphony of silver blues, the water like wrinkled satin.

Day 99. **December 22, 4:15 PM**

Weird warm spell continues. The light is December; the temperature is April. Daylong rain ended before early dusk, and the air is rinsed clean and fizzy with ozone. Fast-moving rainclouds break up overhead. Pastel rainbow shimmers ahead. Low shreds of white cloud sift through pine crowns, rising like ghosts.

A thick white mist rolls up the embankment, spilling over the path like dry ice in the footlights. Through the spectral scrim I make out a dark figure. Standing or moving? Human or deer? I strain to see, then hear a low, "Uh huh . . . When?"

Swirling mists reveal White Man with Cell Phone. When he passes a few moments later, he nods at me, phone still on ear, and says, "Hi." It's all I can do not to answer him, *"Really?"* But I nod back and let the mist swallow him whole.

The clouds roll apart, revealing a tooth-white moon. It casts a pink ring around itself, then disappears, lighting the cloud from within.

Three flat-backed black-and-white waterbirds glide on quicksilver water. Migrating loons, their shivery flute song the indelible call of the North. One tips back and spreads its wings, shaking off droplets. All three of them dive.

Day 100. **December 23, 11:50 AM**

Doing *anything* a hundred times in a row is cause for celebration. I'm astonished that I haven't missed a day yet. I'm not a person who sticks to things, but somehow I have. What's the glue?

Maybe it's the restlessness of this landscape, its constant changes. I set out to take the same walk every day, but I don't. I take a different walk in the same place, and the more I go back there, the more I see.

Today High Point is sporting a scarf of white clouds, like Mount Fuji. The water's glassine. One white duck swimming along the far shore. The *skree* of an eagle, unseen. *Come closer*, it beckons. *You're just getting started.*

Day 101. **December 24, 1:30 PM**

Christmas Eve, and it's sixty-seven degrees. Blessed, or bizarre?

Some magical soul has lined half a mile of Krumville Road with unlit luminarias inside gallon jugs. They're very evenly spaced, and I try to imagine how they were placed. Someone in the back of a pickup truck handing them down to a walker behind? When will they come back to light them?

Maya joins me on the res. She's reluctant at first, but she stops several times to gaze out at the view. She's especially struck by the textures of cracked cement walls on the Lemon Squeeze, and the random drip patterns of caulking used to repair them a long time ago. The rust-edged white streaks have a Lascaux Caves eloquence I've never noticed, though I've passed them a hundred times coming and going. Maya stops to take pictures, studying them with an artist's eye.

As we drive home, a hen dashes between two luminarias, speeding across to the opposite side. Maya bursts out laughing. "Look! It's a chicken crossing the road!"

Day 102. **December 25, 4:10 PM**

The sky's iridescent and silvery, like the inside of an oyster shell.

Summer Christmas frolic. A Korean family sets out with a small white dog, spots the NO DOGS sign, and carries her back to the car, where she yelps in soprano. Four men with booming Australian accents. Kids bombing around on new Christmas-gift bikes. A girl in a parka, boots, and tutu tightrope-walks down the center line while her relatives chat. Strangers greet me with "Merry Christmas!" as they pass, including an exuberant fat-tire biker with a headlamp strapped onto his Santa hat.

In the pines on the rise, three nuthatches swoop from tree to tree like drunks on a bar crawl. Fabio lets out two sharp *skree*s. You could cartoon-balloon it "Woman, Where's My Dinner??" He sits on his posing branch, regal and cranky.

Two deer on the hillside, a scatter of ducks on the creek spill. A swirl of white clouds like a galaxy, streaked with dark charcoal lines. God's calligraphy.

Day 103. **December 26, 4 PM**

My walking companion today: Margaret Wheeler Shengold, age ninety-one, in purple wool coat, rainbow-striped hat, lavender chenille scarf, and Easy Spirit sneakers, pushing her Rollator walker with Christmas-gift gloves.

The air is eerily still, and the reflection's so perfect you could photograph the scene and turn it upside down, and no one would see the difference. Mom says, "It's like a *painting*!" In her art-lover world, there is no higher praise.

Despite the eerie warmth, it's starting to drizzle, and we turn back before the Lemon Squeeze. Mom wants to keep going—"It's hardly raining at all!"—but I explain that if we're half a mile from the parking lot when it starts to pour, it'll be a long wet slog back, so best turn back now. She agrees, but just before we reach the car, she says plaintively, "I wanted to go the whole mile."

Day 104. **December 27, 12:40 PM**

One crow reels across the sky, wind-drunk. Drama overhead: scudding dark clouds, sun showers, shifting eyeholes of blue sky. To the east, a glowering tower of rainclouds. To the west, a scrim of dense white clouds obliterates the Burroughs Range; bright sun spotlights the foothills behind a theatrical scrim of white rain. It looks like Tír na nÓg.

A stocky bald guy greets me with a PC "Happy holidays," throwing both arms out and beaming, "Isn't this the *perfect* weather to be out here?" He's one of many people heading back to the parking lot; I'm the only one heading out, into a patch of bright sun with a light spritz of rain.

Rainbow weather. I scan the sky with Alaska-trained eyes. Seconds later a faint shimmer of rainbow shoots up from the shoulder of Ticetonyk Mountain, comes into bright focus, and fades away fast. I might be the only human who saw it.

Papa's been sick in bed all morning, filling the air with worry, so the private screening of rainbow hues feels like a gift.

A woman approaching jerks her eyes upward. I turn to see the straight-winged silhouette of an eagle, flying over the pathway like it's a train track. Coming closer and closer, Xena veers toward the Lemon Squeeze wall, passing so close I notice a missing pinfeather on her left wing. I swivel as she flies above me, then over a runner intent on adjusting her iPod.

Family of four on new scooters, parents on Razors and helmeted toddlers on pastel three-wheelers. Dad wears black Foster Grants and a girl's tiny parka draped over his head so it covers the back of his neck like a hot-pink keffiyeh.

Fast-blown clouds push shadows along the far shore, leaving the beach lit bone-white against violet hills.

Day 105. **December 28, 3 PM**

A blink of the eye, and it's *winter*. Twenty-nine degrees isn't cold for the end of December, but when it was seventy degrees two days ago you feel it right down to your marrow. The air tastes like snow.

The sky ranges from soft blue-white ombre to Percheron dapple. The water's opaque, an ambiguous shade of gray/blue/mud brown. Wind-riffled, no whitecaps.

A handful of walkers, all close to the lot: Hippie dad with toddler son on his shoulders. Group of five including three adults, a teen boy attempting parkour off the guardrail, and an underdressed sullen tween girl who wishes her brother would *stop*. One biker in a butter-yellow parka, turquoise gloves, and orange flap hat.

Not one bird, squirrel, or deer in sight. Not even a squawk from a blue jay. The locals are denning. They know what's ahead.

I pass two bundled-up middle-aged walkers, a serene-looking woman and a nervous man. Their body English doesn't say couple. (Coworkers? An internet date that's not going so well?) He, in a tenor voice that's pretending to joke: "I can't believe this is your *stroll*."

Day 106. **December 29, 10:10 AM**

First snow. Looks like snow.

But it's half an inch of slick ice, hard packed by sleet and freezing rain. The pathway's a nubbly skating rink. I toddle a few hundred yards like an emperor penguin, only to find my Manhattan-bound "waterproof" boots are not even close. Slush-soaked socks on the Trailways bus. Feh.

Day 107. **December 30, 12:20 PM**

Two miles in winter fog. White on white on white.

The pathway's a road to nowhere. I can't see the Lemon Squeeze, or the poles, or the trees on the rise. Not the opposite shore, not the Driftwood Cove point that I know is so close. On the thin wedge of visible beach, drift logs dusted with snow.

Two parked cars. Who's out there?

A three-tiered shape—half-melted snowman or cairn?—looms on one side of the path. The fog swallows everything quickly, even the red safety light at the start of the walkway. The whole world's soft-focus. The trees close enough to be seen are a blur of soft limbs. Cool mist moisturizes my cheeks.

Two round-shouldered women materialize out of the fog on the Lemon Squeeze. We speak briefly—Isn't this *cool?*—and keep going our separate directions. From midbridge, no markers at all. I can't see the end poles in either direction, just vanishing lines of white sky, gray wall, asphalt lined with white snow. When I lean on the wall and look down, the creek spill is gone, the geometry of mowed curves and retaining walls edged with snowfall and softened by mist.

There's something alive out there, I think. Moments later, a seagull wings out of the whiteness, using the path as a guideline. Later, one crow and a scatter of sparrows, swallowed by swirling mists. It's just me and the birds.

Then I spot a male silhouette emerging from fog, and my first thought is *Whoever you are, let's have sex* (one thing I haven't done yet on the reservoir!). The fantasy persists past uneven shoulders, slight limp—okay, he's not young; that makes two of us—but shatters on surly do-I-have-to-greet-you glare.

Nope.

I hear, then see, a common merganser, swimming alone on the vastness of gray with a few mournful honks. Then I spot a pigeon, strutting atop the wall of the bridge. As I come closer, it flies away, landing again a bit farther along. It does this three times, then flies over the water and disappears.

I hear, but don't see, several Canada geese flying high overhead, their individual voices distinct in the whiteout.

Day 108. **December 31, noon**

A jubilant day at the res. On the drive there, I see a woman lugging a life-size plastic Santa into the garage, her arms wrapped around his waist as if they're dancing. Matching neon-green spandexmen on matching red bikes.

The sky is improbably blue, heaped with cumulus. Maya's calico-ass mountains have a fresh grizzle of snow. The waves roll in audibly, a changeable-taffeta shimmer from gray blue to olive and back.

Even the parkas are colorful: red, orange, school bus yellow, lime green. Two grown women hurl snowballs into the water, cheering at every splash. A Tom of Finland–style leatherman (brimmed cap, aviator shades, shiny black jacket) greets me with, "You're smiling. You're *so right*. How amazing is this?" He spreads his arms wide to the sun.

Day 109. **January 1, 2016, midnight**

My old friend Karen Kessler has come from Connecticut to spend the holiday weekend, as she's done every year since her late-in-life soulmate Tate died of cancer. We fill two travel mugs with mulled cider spiked with Jack Daniels and drive to the reservoir just before midnight, layered in long johns and scarves and Karen's new fleece-lined Ugg boots. We're the only car there.

Soft clouds scrim the sky, which is lighter toward Kingston, a pale smear of gray on the near-black horizon. There's new snow on both sides of the pathway, some of it mounded up into a snowman that looms like a guardian.

We head into near dark, a just-in-case flashlight tucked into my pocket. When we hit the bridge, a realization strikes. "Karen? Have you got a watch?"

"No."

"A cell phone?"

"It's in the car."

"How will we know when it's midnight?" We look at each other and break into laughter. This is so us.

Karen chants, "Ten . . . nine . . . eight . . . ," and I join her on "Three! Two! One! HAPPY NEW YEAR!!!" We toast with our mugs, inhaling warm cinnamon, apple, and bourbon. The hot drink feels great in my throat. Karen says, "Okay, can we leave now?" We can, but I'd rather not. I've never been here on a cold winter night, at the start of a who-knows-what-this-will-bring year, with a friend and the glow of warm liquor. I don't want to give this up yet, but I am Karen's host, and there's champagne in the fridge and a fire in the woodstove.

As I take a deep breath, I hear a faint popping of fireworks from several directions at once. It really *is* midnight. We toast again, joining the rest of the world.

We can't see the fireworks go up, but their reflected light pulses and glows beneath the dense cloud cover, greenish and pink in the distance, like Northern Lights. It's lovely and kind of surreal. I think I see an owl flying over the bridge, a pale streak from darkness to darkness, but it's hard to tell.

When we reach the far side, the sound of the waves returns and we both fall silent, standing and staring at opposite shores. I know Karen is thinking of Tate, and I think of my parents and wonder how long we all have. There's a random scatter of lights across the near hillsides: cell tower, radio tower, McMansions. No moon and no stars. From a hillside somewhere in Olivebridge, actual fireworks, backyard edition, a volley of red and white spark patterns, *pop poppoppop*.

We turn on the flashlight exactly once as we walk back, to look at the snowman next to the path, which turns out to be a snow*woman* with pert snowball breasts and a tangle of long viny hair. She looks fabulous.

Day 110. **January 2, 7:40 AM**

I roll over in bed and see orange clouds. Winter sunrise. In less than ten minutes I've pulled on clothes, warmed up the car, scraped the windshield, made coffee, and left for the res.

Half moon fading, crow call. The rising sun hits the sentinel rock, turning it golden.

It also illuminates something white out on the Lemon Squeeze. There's a bald eagle perched on the cement wall. I keep walking, eyes glued to the spot. She lets me get very close before lifting off in an unhurried soar.

Later, another big bird, heavy bodied, with broad white wings and a white belly. Could it be a snowy owl? The regal predators sometimes spend the winter far south of the Arctic. Is that what I saw last night, in the first minutes of the new year?

New Year's resolution: keep going.

Day 111. **January 3, 8 PM**

I got back from New York after dark, so this is a boots-on-the-ground, okay-there-I-did-it effort. Cold, moon and stars clouded over, a few swirling snowflakes.

Flashing lights of a jet and a satellite, bright lights over Kingston: Dietz Stadium? Aliens? Weirdly, I'm spooked.

And very cold. Glad to get back to the car.

Day 112. **January 4, 10:40 AM**

First thing I see is the brown metal FORMER SITE OF OLIVE BRIDGE sign blowing in high wind. Clown time is over.

It's nineteen degrees and the wind chill is fearsome. The water is navy blue, striped with white combers. It sounds like the ocean. There's a dusting of snow on the Burroughs Range; the crest of Slide Mountain is white.

There's not a soul moving. Knife blade wind needles my face.

It would be so easy to give this up, right here and now. Who would care?

I would. Keep going.

Day 113. **January 5, 3 PM**

Winter digs in. Single digits last night. Pale blue sky, cloudless and mercifully windless. The cold is austere. The only bright color in sight is the leonine gold of dead grasses on snow. At the foot of the dike wall, a glaze of ice coats spikes of driftwood in sculptural forms.

Two ducks swim toward the ice-rimmed shore. Only one walker, a tall woman in a silver parka and earbuds.

I finish the walk alone. Praise to my long johns. Praise to my scarf, gloves, and hat. Everlasting praise to my wool socks and puffy down parka.

Day 114. **January 6, 6:10 PM**

Cold, after dark. Grumpy and utterly not in the mood, I pull into the empty parking lot muttering, "Of *course* it's empty. Why the hell would anyone do this?"

I slam out the door and see stars. A whole skyful.

Oh. That's why.

Short walk, but it's freezing and bracing and calms me right down. On the way back, I could swear I hear wolves somewhere high on the mountain. Not coyotes (high-pitched yips, very familiar) but a low, mournful, spine-piercing musical howl I haven't heard since I lived in Alaska. One lead animal and some answering barks, amplified by chill air.

Then an owl, asking (like me), *Who? Who? Who?*

Day 115. **January 7, 3:40 PM**

Temperature soars back into the thirties and everything comes alive! Pileated woodpecker swoops over the path, red blaze flashing in sunlight. Six deer frolic on the embankment.

Fast movers: a racing biker in yellow Team Overlook jersey, a sprinter in royal-blue shorts. A pair of reconnaissance crows squawks and circles above.

A slant of gold haze casts a mountainside shadow the shape of an angel. The creek spill is frozen in swirls. Stalactite icicles cling to the cliff, with a gurgle of water moving behind.

Santa Sisyphus walks his exercise circle in front of the monument, again and again and again and again.

A gull wings a beeline from west to east.

Early winter sundown, the bright white disc haloing pine silhouettes. The Burroughs Range High Peaks turn blue and the sky pulses lemon. A companion-animal old couple strolls in the afterglow, their bodies unconsciously leaning together.

Day 116. **January 8, 2:20 PM**

I stop by the Frying Pan on my way to interview the elusive artist/author of Thorneater Comics. A Catskills holy man with a chest-length beard like a beaver dam, he grew up near the reservoir and draws it obsessively. I can't wait to meet him.

White sky, sun veiled by dense clouds. As I walk, a flock of about thirty juncos flies up and down the embankment hillside, spreading their nuns'-habit wings as they bob and weave. Squadron of Canada geese takes off from an islet, flying low to the water and honking like furies.

Day 117. **January 9, 10:20 AM**

Quick stop on a day of grim errands—driving my antique Subaru up to Kingston, where I'll rent a more roadworthy car to move Aunt Joan to the "memory floor" of her assisted living. My brother is meeting me there.

The weather matches our task. It's overcast, drizzly, and moody, a Northwest funk. I arrive in a bleak mood and leave feeling human. Thanks, reservoir.

Day 118. **January 10, 3 PM**

I set out into patchy, fast-moving fog that bares and erases mountains so fast it feels like a conjuring trick. Other walkers loom out of cool mist: Six elderly Asians, one playing Chinese music on headphones. Two dads holding hands with young daughters. Old couple with cane and umbrella.

Veils of white isolate ridges of pines in the draws. On the Lemon Squeeze, an awestruck photographer in a red parka takes a few shots in each direction, then just stands still, gazing out at the changeable sky. He turns his head as I walk past, and his eyes are lit up. We nod without speaking, and I feel a magnetic kinship. He's not just seeing this too, he's *feeling* it too, this beauty no words or photo could capture because it's all movement and grandeur.

Above us the clouds curl and part like living things. A shaft of blue sky emerges from turbulent gray and closes back up in an instant. It goes to my heart like an arrow, some inchoate sense of peace overlying our sufferings and storms, and I'm suddenly weeping. Thinking of Sandi and Jeffrey and Tate, all the people I love who have died, and who will die, the grief and the beauty that we can't hold. This is why people invented gods, trying to build a container for something too vast to contain.

There's a storm swooping in from the west. Its veils lash down High Point and pummel the water. The photographer turns back reluctantly, heading back toward his car. I wait till the first drops start pounding. No drizzle—it goes from not raining to downpour in seconds, with high winds to match. I poke up my folding umbrella, which turns inside out in the wind. I decide to embrace getting wet. And then I hear thunder.

It's January, for Christ's sake. It shouldn't be forty degrees, and this should be a blizzard, not rain, and there certainly shouldn't be *thunder*.

And if there is thunder, there's lightning, and standing exposed on the top of a dam between two metal guardrails, right next to a body of water, is pretty damn stupid. So back to my car I go, thunder booming around the far hills like Rip Van Winkle's ninepins. Good choice, since the rain sluicing off the hem of my parka has soaked through my pants and my long johns. It's worth every shiver. I feel like a happy drowned rat.

Day 119. **January 11, 1 PM**

Cold wind and whitecaps, new snow on the Burroughs Range.
Two eagles fishing. Black-backed gull flying pirouettes.
Brilliant blue sky with David Bowie in it.

Day 120. **January 12, 2:10 PM**

There are rumors of "snow squalls," so as soon as the first flakes start swirl-ing outside I head for the res with the same heart-pumping glee I felt as a kid when I looked out my bedroom window and saw a day of no school.

Maya used to wake up the same way, yelling, "Snow day!" and charg-ing outside to scoop up a bowl of new snow to drizzle with warm maple syrup.

The snow's coming in from the west, so the mountains have vanished. The pines on the point are the soft silver gray of old tintypes. The flakes are fat and wet, not sticking to pavement, though there's a white tracery over the logs on the beach.

There are two other walkers, a man making tracks far ahead and a young woman in Uggs, ambling along taking selfies in falling snow. Far ahead, the unmistakable bulk and white head of an eagle, flying low over treetops.

By the time I reach the rise, the snow's falling thick and fast, sticking in patches. The fast walker's disappeared, leaving no footprints, and Selfie Girl has gone back to her car. I'm the only one left.

The woods are a painting, snow falling on cedars. The aerator buildings and bridge that usually seem like a slap in nature's face are transformed by the snowfall to fairy-tale castles. The weir's arches dissolve into white. It's astoundingly quiet. I feel like I'm inside a snow globe.

If you want to know what infinity means, stand in a heavy snowfall and look straight up. Endless dots drifting down. They look oddly dark against the sky's whiteness, from fat individual flakes falling into your face to swirling dots overhead and nearly invisible specks even higher, and they go on falling and falling and falling, world without end.

So I'm startled when a DEP car pulls up behind me, and a guy who looks vaguely like Louis CK gets out to unlock the chain across the dirt road by the monument circle. "Figured I'd get out here and do some work before it gets too sticky," he says.

Okay, I'll bite. "What kind of work?"

"I'm an engineer. Checking some data down by the dam, while I can still get there."

"Oh," I say. "I've seen you down there. What are you checking?"

"Water pressure. If you see me get stuck down there, holler. When the snow gets real deep, they give the cops snowmobiles; I get snowshoes. I oughta ride with them, right?" And he's off.

Later, I walk to the guardrail and see his car far below, parked next to one of the orange-capped pipes. He raises a wave.

A ponytailed blonde runner in black tights and white parka overtakes me, breathing hard. She looks like Amy Schumer. (Everyone looks like a comedian today. Is it me?) A flock of juncos scatters around her. By the time I've crossed the bridge, her footprints are covered by snow.

Dried Queen Anne's lace seedheads fill up with snowflakes, rewhitening. They look like cotton bolls.

I hear the loud rumble and scrape of a plow sanding Route 28A. Clark Strand observed in *Waking Up to the Dark* that we secretly crave the disturbance of storms, which interrupt our artificial routines, plunging us back to the basics of daylight and darkness. That may be, but we sure thrash against it, doing our best to preserve set patterns even when the weather tells us to stay home. Or go for a walk.

Louis CK drives past me, stops at the end of the walkway, and gets out to jigger the mechanism that lowers the columns so he can drive through. He turns and calls out, "I waited for you!" Then he looks at me closer and asks if I live in The Vly, and did I use to walk an old pooch on the road?

My god, this is a small town. I tell him my dog died; that's why I walk here now. He tells me where he lives, where his mother lives, moves on to fixing his roof, former dogs, having tea with his mother, leapfrogging from chitchat to monologue, and I'm starting to glaze. The snow's falling thicker and faster, and though I tell him I want to drive home before it gets too deep, he leans in like a bur.

But I shake him off and head back to my car.

What a difference an hour makes. My rented Hyundai is under an inch of new snow, and there are ice crystals crusting my eyelashes. My parka is heavy with snow.

The rental car doesn't have four-wheel drive. I white-knuckle it uphill and turn onto my road, which is literally trackless, lined on both sides by snow-covered pines. The snowfall is granular, turning everything pointillist. Judie's horses are bunched by the fence, blankets dappled with snow.

Day 121. **January 13, 7:20 AM**

The dawn is indeed rosy fingered, High Point glowing shell pink in single-digit windchill. No one out yet but me and the snowplows. One pulls into the parking lot just ahead of me, and when the driver sees me pull over to park on the shoulder—*not* in the lot he's about to plow—he backs up to block me, blinking his lights, so I'm forced to U-turn back onto the road.

I'm meeting somebody for breakfast, so there's not enough time to drive to the Frying Pan, where doubtless some other DEP plow is deeply engaged in scooping up less than two inches of snow. So right before I

drive across the bridge, I pull into the NO PARKING strip and trudge to the guardrail and back in a she-wolf wind. Technically, it *is* a walk on the res, but I feel like I'm cheating.

At least it's illegal.

Day 122. **January 14, 2:20 PM**

Fresh graffiti on the guardhouse, under the circle-slash dog-silhouette icon: NO DOGS, DIPSTICK! Some irate runner who stepped in Saint Bernard poop? Or is the DEP getting truculent?

Youthful blue sky going gray before my eyes. Looks like snowfall on the western High Peaks. There's a skim of ice edging the point, but it's still open water, except for the snowed-over creek spill.

It's cold. Not hurts-to-inhale cold, but raw. I turn back at the rise. There's a man on the Lemon Squeeze walking two dogs. Defiance!

I hear the insistent, irritant drone of the cacabird hitting its one note again and again, a Republican filibuster of a birdcall. Scanning the trees behind Driftwood Cove for the perp, I spot the red crest of a pileated wood-pecker, hanging nearly upside down from a branch picking dried wild grapes off a vine. He's not very dexterous, but he's persistent. For at least five minutes he pecks, nearly slips, clings, and rebalances over and over, filling his bill. Without warning he streaks off the tree, his drunken-lurch flight path dipping so close to my head I can hear the air swish through his feathers. He disappears into the woods.

Moments later, another big black-and-white bird swoops over the path in the same direction, and I notice the scolding has stopped.

Is Mrs. Pileated the cacabird? How can such a spectacular bird set up such a *geschrei*? Their domestic life suddenly seems like a '50s cartoon. Henpecked husband hits the bar while his wife nags and nags.

A few stray snowflakes float, indolent.

Day 123. **January 15, 4 PM**

Mattress clouds, mirror water.

Twin set of deer tracks across creek-spill snow.

Day 124. **January 16, 2:20 PM**

Warm sun, a convivial day at the res. A muscular runner in shorts, paced by a girl on a bike, passes me four times, coming and going. Also an inline skater with whopping thighs, two bikers in neon jerseys, and a family from some fundamentalist cult. Not Hutterian Brethren, not Amish, not Orthodox Jews, but the hierarchy is unmistakable. The dad walks ahead proudly with three little sons, trailed by mother and daughter in dowdy long skirts.

An artist sits on the stone bench, sketching with chalk pastels. Just as I reach him, he slips his pad inside a plastic bag: incoming drizzle.

Two flat-backed black birds swim side by side—loons or cormorants? One of them flaps wet wings bent at the elbows. Cormorants.

I hear a crow caw and turn to see three of them swoop in like Nazgûl.

Brand new signs on the rise:

RESTRICTED AREA

KEEP BACK!

EAGLE NESTING AREA—DO NOT APPROACH!!

The fine print says that coming within 350 feet of the nest may cause abandonment and that bald eagles are federally protected, with a fine of up to $100,000 or imprisonment for killing, harassing, or disturbing them.

The signs are much closer than 350 feet. So whoever stepped over the guardrail to nail them up oughta be behind bars.

Day 125. **January 17, 3:30 PM**

The Ashokan is back in her winter plumage. I walk down to Brodhead Point, ice-edged and lapped by gray waves. A hairy woodpecker takes a jazz drum solo, knocking loose fragments of lichen and bark. The wind stings my cheeks and I shiver.

As I walk back through the woods, a crow calls four times and I stop in my tracks, noticing a faint path that may be a deer trail. I head down it until it joins up with an old footpath leading through a break in a tumbled stone wall that must be a hundred years old; several thick oak trees grow through it.

The crow calls again and flaps off, indignant. I step over a downed trunk across the path but stop at the next, peering into a dense grove of pines. I don't know why, but I know I should turn back right now. A wash of fear runs down my neck like cold water. I walk back fast, trying to shake off the chill.

Day 126. **January 18, 1:30 PM**

Wind wolving out of the west. Snowfall on the High Peaks. Elemental.

Two crows fly high overhead, buffeted sideways. A red-tailed hawk flies up the embankment, hits the headwind, and changes its mind.

Everything's wrapped but my eyes and nose (numb). Navy water churns, tossing whitecaps against the stone dam, old waves slamming back against oncoming in plumes of white foam, oceanic.

I pass two solo walkers with grim faces leaning hard into the wind, then spot a pair of round women in bright colored layers, like rosy-cheeked rag dolls. I watch them stagger out into the wind, laughing hysterically, and hightail it back to their car.

But the Badass Prize goes to the petite older woman pedaling her bike in hot-pink parka and snow pants. Respect.

Day 127. **January 19, 4:50 PM**

Single-digit windchill cuts through every layer I've got. When it gusts it's hard to stand upright, let alone walk. Feral air burns my nostrils.

Three-quarter moon rising amid lambswool puffs of pink clouds, incongruous springtime pastels. I call bullshit.

Day 128. **January 20, 8:10 AM**

Yesterday's Great Lakes gusts threw a skim of ice about ten feet up the dam and sheared off a lot of dead grass, which clumps on the pavement like cut hair.

The creek spill is an ice rink. I'm the only live thing.

Meditations on endurance and persistence. I don't have much of either, but here I am. Because it is there. Because I'm obsessed with—what? Putting one foot in front of another, again and again and again and again.

Day 129. **January 21, 9:30 AM**

The Secret Cove is starting to freeze from the edges; the shallows are white.

On the side facing open water, the boulders are sheathed in ice as if they've been dipped in plexiglass. The crest of Slide Mountain looks like a snowshoe hare.

For some reason, or no reason at all, I'm deliriously happy to be outside in this austere beauty. Hello, ice! Hello, wind! Hello, birches!

And that is what's new today. Joy.

Day 130. **January 22, 3:20 PM**

Cold, gray, and raw. After stacking more firewood onto the porch in a grumpy, self-pitying snit, I set out for the res and a snarky voice in my head says, "And now for the voluntary phase of your masochism!"

I have no zest for this walk. My heart used to race as I drove down Vly hill, past the hardscrabble farm with the yearning stallion hanging his head on the fence, past the Olivebridge Post Office and the white church. I couldn't wait to arrive; I felt an electrical charge as soon as I set foot on the reservoir pathway. Yesterday I got a flutter of random joy, but too many days now feel dutiful, grudging. The thrill is gone.

Not gone, dormant. Like everything else in this season, it's hibernating.

The sky's hunkered down for the snowstorm to come. It's not windy, just grim. Ice platelets are starting to form along Driftwood Cove. What else is new?

Whatever it is, I can't find it. Is there anything I haven't noticed yet? Where's the surprise, the small revelation? *Give me my numinous*, I mutter, not quite aloud. *Give me an eagle-god, a bear-god, a deer-god. Red fox would be nice.*

I don't think it works like that, my better self answers. *You don't get to place orders.* And that's when I notice a ripple on the gray sheet of water, and up pops the flat-backed dark grebe I keep seeing. I watch it dive, stay under, and pop up again, a bit farther away each time, alone against all that vast gray.

What's the lesson? I ask half ironically, and the answer pops in: *Keep diving.*

Day 131. **January 23, 11:30 AM**

The blizzard that's pounding New York and points south hasn't hit yet, except for the nor'easter wind, which is mighty. I twist my scarf over my face, tie my hood over my hat, and pull on my '60s leather ski mitts (my family *keeps* things).

The sky's wrapped in flannel, the sun a white smear. And yet there are reservoir walkers. It's Saturday, dammit, and people are out.

Fellow travelers:

• Black dad with two teenage kids.

• Guy racewalking with cross-country ski poles.

• Eagle Guys Older and Younger, staying out of the wind on the lee side of the rise. They circle each other like raptors.

• Mother and daughter in layers of colorful shawls.

Twelve students with various accents cluster to watch a Nordic guy in a fox-fur hat and a Turkish guy in a puffy down parka step over the guardrail, daring each other to roll down the long steep embankment. Friends cheer them on or caution against it, pulling out iPhones as the two men lie down side by side. Fox hat guy clutches a GoPro minicam in one hand, holding it over his head for the roll action. Some "should we or shouldn't we" banter, then "one-two-three" and they push off, rolling at different angles in a fast, bumpy, uneven V.

Long pause. Verdict yelled up from the foot of the hill: "Not. Worth. It!"

We all greet each other with the apple-cheeked camaraderie of the demented. Mad dogs and eaglemen, out in the midday storm.

Day 132. **January 24, 1:30 PM**

We got exactly NO snow in the blizzard. Not one flake. It's the Winter That Wasn't. I had visions of coming down here in heavy snowfall, logging my walks on cross-country skis or my uncle Lou's snowshoes, but the storm front stopped right below Newburgh.

I crave winter white, so I go to the Frying Pan, searching for ice.

Frozen mud crunches under my boots. The shallow cove has frozen solid, with small slicks of ice between stones on the beach. Watching my step, I miss the moment the two eagles glide off a tree overhead, but there they are suddenly, one flying high and one low, winging away from me across the channel.

I walk to the edge of the water. The part that's not yet frozen solid looks like a Slurpee; the ice pebbles rattle in waves. I follow a sculpted ice ridge down the beach till I reach sheet ice. The surface is smooth, greenish gray, and translucent, and I have the urge to skim a stone on it and see if it cracks.

I do, and it doesn't. The stone bounces and slides like a hockey puck. Beyond it, the ice turns opaque. White as snow.

Waiting at the light to drive over the weir bridge, I spot something for the first time. Mounted right above the white metal traffic sign that says WEIGHT LIMIT 16 TONS is a smaller sign in safety yellow. It says NOTICE. I want one.

Day 133. **January 25, 2:50 PM**

Watercolor sky with a lemon-gray haze veiling the sun, like a Turner seascape. There's pack ice floating along Driftwood Cove and the dam wall, trying to get a grip.

Beatbox competition: A pileated woodpecker sets up a ruckus and swoops from the rise to the pine forest, shrieking a monotone note the whole way. Then a crow flies out from the pine forest, over the path, and onto the rise to land in the spot she just flew from, cawing at top volume. Hard to say which bird is more obnoxious, but I think the crow takes it. There's a playground jeer in its call, a *nyaah-nyaah-nyaah* rasp that sounds like it's mocking the woodpecker.

Skateboarder in a striped hoodie and rust-brown skinny jeans. He sails down the walkway, whistling.

Day 134. **January 26, 2:10 PM**

I'm greeted by a crow moaning above Driftwood Cove like Cassandra: *kuh kuh kaa, kuh kuh kaa, GAAAAAH!*

I walk out under one sky (milky cloud cover) and back to another (glowering rainclouds). Yes, *rain*. It's forty-four degrees. Yesterday's ice rafts are already melting. In a normal winter, this might be a welcome January thaw, but there's been no serious freeze yet.

I'm yearning for snow. It brings a fresh canvas, a promise of death and renewal. Without it the landscape is drab; it's looked like November since November. Not to mention the global implications of snowless northern winters and violent storms in the south.

The tinkling music of waves lapping over and under the dwindling ice sheets. Ice-water marimba, a dirge for the earth.

Crow circles the cove, ululating.

Day 135. **January 27, 7:20 AM**

Bliss before breakfast. I wake early, a little hungover, and though the lightening sky is dull gray, I'm compelled to go down to the res.

If you feel a mysterious pull to do something, listen.

I grumble through pulling on clothes and drive down Vly hill, convinced this is going to be anticlimactic. There's a cool wedge of clouds in the east, but so what? I could have rolled over and gone back to sleep.

Stiff wind, low sun swaddled in clouds. Lone crow, then a seagull, then more crows. A *lot* of crows, agitated, vociferous, flying back and forth as if something's up. *Take me to your leader*, I think. I turn my head, and of course—it really does feel like *of course*—there's an eagle flying right toward me, straight down the path.

She flies right over my head. It's my snaggle-winged Xena, her yellow feet bunched and her wingbeats an easy lope. I watch her fly all the way down to the tree line along Driftwood Cove. Then she cuts a diagonal across open water to fly back over my head. She veers off toward her fishing beach, circles around it, and flies back *again*, buzzing me twice more before disappearing into the trees on the rise. The last time I see her, she's high in the thermals. The sky's an extravagant tie-dye. The sun has turned apricot, bisected by a dark line of clouds so it looks like a blurred figure eight, almost like one sun on top of another.

Past the rise, I hear crows vocalizing again and look up. There's *another* big bird. For a moment I think it's an eagle, but the wings are too arched, the tail too long and straight. It's an osprey, the fish hawk, sleek brown-and-white grace.

I feel sated. That carbonation of spirit—that *something will happen*—recedes, and I walk back without craning my head up to scan the sky. I notice things nearer the ground: how a thick fallen limb has been caught in the palm of a spindly branch, how a trio of leaning dead trunks splay out like travois poles.

The ice rafts have disappeared, melted and swallowed. The wind's dying down, with a weird scent of premature spring in the air. The sun is still swathed in a tent-caterpillar cocoon of low clouds, but a few shafts peep over to land on the tops of Cornell and Panther Mountains, the only snowy places left. The mountains gleam white, then the rising sun shifts to illuminate first lower peaks, then the shoreline near Boiceville, then Brodhead Point, then the path where I'm walking. A glow.

Day 136. **January 28, 4:50 PM**

Reservoir tranquil today. A soft pastel sunset, no drama. There's a dense clump of cloud that looks just like a penis. (It really does. If you asked ten people, "What does that purple cloud look like?" nine would tell you "a penis" and the tenth would say something prim but be thinking BIG DICK.)

Bacchanal of coyotes, high in the hills.

Day 137. **January 29, 11:10 AM**

Today's sermon: disappointment. I look up from my desk to see swirling snow, pull on my reservoir clothes, and race out. My road is a wonderland. Fluffy white flakes on the windshield, etched beauty of new snow on pines.

By the foot of Vly hill it's no longer sticking—dashboard thermometer edging above thirty-two—and by the time I arrive at the reservoir, *four miles away*, there's no snow at all.

The sun's come out. Fuck.

I feel cheated. First the nonblizzard and now the nonflurry. A dusting of white on the High Peaks, nothing at all on the pathway or grass. Same old gray.

I have had it with gray.

I walk anyway, watching a mismatched pair of mergansers, salt and pepper ducks, bobbling over cold waves. Later, the slow-motion drum of a pileated, the telltale flash of red crest high up a trunk. Platoon of blue jays, oddly silent.

The sun slips behind clouds, and a walker just setting out fumbles to tighten her hood. She says in a Scots burr, "Bit nippy today!"

Yeah, well. Not nippy enough. The snow on my Subaru's melted, and I console myself that I'll get to drive back uphill to that Vly microclimate, the trees and road lined with fresh white. But it's gone, every bit of it melted.

And that's why we write. Because everything changes.

Day 138. **January 30, 4 PM**

I try a new path through the woods past the spillway. Great slabs of white ice heaped along the shore, solid but riddled with turtleback cracks in the center. I stand on the beach with my hood up and hands jammed deep into my pockets, trying to channel my inner Shackleton before it all melts.

I'm in a bleak mood and the walk doesn't help. Two private planes buzz the res, burning fossil fuel to give rich people a view. That doesn't help either.

Day 139. **January 31, 4:30 PM**

I'm meeting my playwright friend Mark St. Germain for a walk, and I arrive late with a delightful excuse: I got stuck driving behind two antique farm vehicles. Right ahead of my car was a rattletrap tractor with an Amish-bearded farmer in faded felt hat bouncing on the seat. I couldn't see what was ahead of the tractor until it turned onto an adjacent field: a team of spirited draft horses pulling a long wooden wagon. Entranced by their bouncing gait, I stayed behind the tractor, crawling at five miles an hour so I could keep watching. The horses' manes gleamed in the sun.

Mark is late too, so I walk out a little and perch on the guardrail, listening to two bikers talk to the ski-pole guy about how much they're missing the snow this winter. The air smells like plants, and the magic-hour sunlight glints gold.

Mark arrives; he got lost on the way. We set off side by side. Lot of movie extras today—proud dad holding the upraised hands of a new walker in a fleece onesie, the earphoned gent in the black leather jacket, small boy wearing sneakers that flash as he runs, even a Fabio sighting on his posing branch by the nest—but the main event is conversation, rich and abundant. We talk about writing projects and youthful ambitions, success, satisfaction, our parents and kids, being sixty. (Mark's sixty-one and I'm fifty-nine, but we average out, like Mark's Santa Claus beard and baseball cap.)

Squinting at the darkening sky, he says, "I just feel that ambition piece falling away. And it shouldn't—I still need the money—but it just doesn't matter as much as living my life."

And I realize for the first time that this plot-free description of brief daily walks is precisely the point, that at our age it isn't about the grand gesture, but the details and textures of day-to-day life, the magnificent usual. How we go on.

As we're saying goodbye at our cars, I hear Canada geese overhead. "Well," says Mark, "that was another walk."

Day 140. **February 1, 5:10 PM**

The sky's streaked with heavy blue clouds bottom-lit an intense yellow gold. I walk down toward Flat Rocks, moving through the woods fast as if I'm about to be late for a meeting, and I'm not surprised in the least when an eagle takes off from a tree and circles above my head once, twice, three times. I see the adjustments of feathers and feet to bank into the thermal, white tailfeathers lit up with gold as it soars out of sight.

I walk down the windswept beach to a sheltered spot and stand rooted, watching the sky turn from gold to flamingo. Waves crash like applause. This kind of sunset could start a religion.

Day 141. **February 2, 3:45 PM**

Cold with low-slanting sun. No one on the path but a young mom in a buffalo plaid shirt and black leggings with a round-faced toddler riding a Radio Flyer red car. She coaxes him to stay on the center line, but the kid keeps veering to one side (guardrail above steep embankment) or the other (guardrail above ice-edged water). The mom is amazingly chill, walking along with her hands in her pockets, letting him ride far enough ahead or behind that I can't help but picture the car and kid sliding under a guardrail to sudden disaster.

I don't miss that anxious hypervigilance, saving Maya's life every few hours, but I do miss the insular sweetness of the mom-toddler bond, the warm touch and constancy of our connection. A few days ago I saw a woman waiting at the end of her driveway for her daughter to get off the school bus, and the sheer joy of the exuberant, ponytailed kid flying into her arms brought tears to my eyes.

Sometimes I feel too alone.

Maya learned to ride a tricycle right on this path. Later she and her friends zoomed far ahead on two-wheelers. I remember calling, "Turn around BEFORE the bridge!" and feeling my heart in my throat as they rode out of sight.

The water is low. There's a sandbar I've never seen, ice lining its edges.

It's Groundhog Day. No shadow seen. Early spring, says the stupid tradition. Okay, but how about some *winter* first? Snow. Make it snow.

Day 142. **February 3, 2:30 PM**

It's been raining since dawn, and I have a bad attitude. *Okay, time for your self-indulgent white lady who-cares walk.* But I go.

I am studying stubborn.

The reservoir is a cloud sandwich. Dense bank of boiling white cloud over still water, then a clear slice of mountains, then more heavy clouds. There's mist rolling over the bridge, a thin crescent of free-floating ice. The sky's grizzling light rain, which feels cool on my cheeks. I'm the only one walking.

After a few minutes the rain stops and a giant black bird flies over the pathway, wings bent at the elbows, blunt tail. Could it be a raven? If not, it's the mother of all crows.

As I drive away, raindrops spatter the windshield, and I can't help grinning. I slipped it in, right between storms.

Day 143. **February 4, 5 PM**

Sunless sundown in unending gray. A cold, windy trudge under cloud cover pulled into furrows, which edge into pale cotton-candy pink blue, then catch fire. A 360-degree, eye-popping, tropical Catskill sunset. High Point silhouetted against bands of flame.

Out of drudgery, splendor.

Frustrated by trying to document sunsets; it can't be done. Even masterful photos capture only a sliver, since the experience is a constantly changing surround. Words catch even less. At their best, they can send off sparks that ignite someone else's imagination. But the sunset I witness is not the same one you envision. The heartbeat gets lost in translation, leaving only a glow of shared awe.

The sky's so amazing I long for someone to share it with, right here and now, though our feeble "Oh. My. GOD!" gasps couldn't touch this, no more than the bike racer who whizzes past with a yelled "What a night!"

But he saw what I saw. Nobody else did.

So these words: a small striking of tinder and flint. Can you conjure the bonfire, sky seething with beauty?

Day 144. **February 5, 1:30** PM

Temps in the thirties, windchill off the charts. Teal combers churn up whitecaps. Wind lashes my face as I walk on the edge of the water, near Bill and Shelley's chained rowboat.

Around the corner, wind-shadowed by land, it dials down from gale to stiff breeze. Driftwood sculpture park: split trunk like a temple gate, next to a cluster of bristling roots. Startled flock of ducks takes off, skidding on water.

Then an eagle, blown sideways like paper, flaps over the channel. A second joins it for a sky ballet.

Day 145. **February 6, 1:10** PM

The usual walk in the usual gray with the usual weekend crowd. Did I notice one thing worth writing today? Only this, as I'm leaving: old guy in Ray-Bans who zips his black jacket up to his chin, reads the sign on the guardrail, and declares in purest Bronx tones, "No Entrance for *Any* Purpose? What fools!"

Day 146. **February 7, 5** PM

Driving over Ohayo Mountain a bit before sunset, I turn onto the dead-end road tracing its ridge, lined with Wealth-Seeks-Altitude homes with spectacular views. I can see the whole reservoir laid out below, the intricate shoreline of coves and peninsulas. So much to explore!

But the sun's sinking low, so I opt for the usual pathway instead of new woods to traverse after dark. As I drive across the weir bridge I spot an eagle flying high up, heading from Upper Basin to Lower. I follow.

I park by the spillway and head for my Shackleton spot. The ice has receded since I was last here, chunks tossed up on top of each other like sheets of foam-core insulation. Their edges are straight, maybe two inches thick. I walk down the beach till it hits a short cliff I can't pass, and sit down on a perfect throne boulder. The yellow sun perches on High Point's left shoulder.

The stillness is perfect. The mourning dove's call echoes over the cove, and that's all I can hear. The mountains turn ultramarine, and the water's slight scintillation shifts their reflection in ripples of black, blue, and gold. I breathe in, I breathe out. I am part of the stillness.

The sun sinks. The air tightens, colder.

There's a sudden loud beating of wings on water, with honking so clamorous I laugh out loud when the V of geese rises: three birds.

I walk back through the woods under a sky tinged with sherbet pastels. The beaver pond glows with pink ice.

Day 147. **February 8, 3 pm**

Anticipation of snow! The cold has clamped down and the air is raw. There's new ice lining Driftwood Cove, and the sky is an India inkwash.

One crow flying in un-corvine silence. It's coming.

Day 148. **February 9, 11:20 am**

Woke to snow, snow, snow! Only a few inches, but enough to change the world. Snow in the trees, every bare branch and pine tree a black-and-white masterpiece.

I shovel my car off and follow the plow down the hill, seized with the get-down-there urgency I've learned to heed.

The High Peaks are white! For the first time all winter, a true winter landscape!

At the guardrail, a mother and daughter in matching blue parkas throw snowballs over, the child's trilling laughter a soundtrack for my own glee. The ice on Driftwood Cove has refrozen; it's covered with snow. The cove is a solid white canvas, until I walk far enough out on the pathway to see an incursion of meltwater. There's a sinuous black and gray shape in the snowpack that looks like a modern art mural.

I notice a loud engine sound coming closer. Is it a plane? Helicopter?

No. It's a DEP ice cutter. Red, with a giant fan on the back like a bayou airboat. It's cutting a channel through floating ice, heading straight for the dam by the Lemon Squeeze. Without even thinking, I'm yelling, "Fuck no!" The boat noise is deafening, grinding through ice. My euphoria bursts into shards like the ice pack.

All right, yes, this isn't an unspoiled wilderness—it's the New York City water supply—but what is this *for*? There's no way this half inch of ice is a threat to the aqueduct entrance, and even if it were, couldn't those grinning guys on the airboat just do what needs to be done and go back? But no, after plowing the edge of the dam, they veer out across open water and joyride around Brodhead Point, out toward Boiceville, and along the entire Upper Basin for no earthly reason, except that the weather is nice and they're men making noise with a combustion engine. Your Tax Dollars at Play.

I hear that damn boat every step of my walk.

I strain for distraction, try to make myself notice things. The angular gray-and-white patterns of newly chopped ice look like '50s Formica, but there shouldn't *be* newly chopped ice. I can't concentrate on anything but my rage. Is this why I felt so compelled to come down here this morning? *Why?*

And in asking the question I answer it: to bear witness.

I spot the EAGLE NESTING AREA—DO NOT DISTURB signs and fume: Which is more of a disturbance, my hiking boots or your damn airboat? Of course there are no eagles: if I had wings, I'd fly away too.

The airboat pulls up to the opposite shore, near the weir bridge. *Good*, I think. *Turn off your toy, boys.* It's silent a moment, then the engine revs loudly once, twice, three times, an amplified bellowing like a bull elephant.

After, the silence reverberates. Dozens of juncos—the largest flock I've ever seen—flee through the trees, swooping from cedar to cedar, not staying long on any perch. I could swear they look anxious. Years ago, when this stretch of road was first closed to traffic and the shoulders of 28A were clear-cut and bulldozed to widen the bypass, I drove home late and saw a herd of deer wandering through the wreckage, disoriented and stricken, like refugees crossing a battlefield. It's an image that haunts me: *We did this.*

But it's complicated. If humans had not interfered with nature, damming a creek to hijack mountain water for a city too big for its britches, I wouldn't be walking here now. The preservation of this irreplaceable watershed to filter tap water maintained a great swath of wildland, crucial habitat for many species, including endangered bald eagles. Without New York City's entitled impoundment, this land might be lined with strip malls and chain stores, Bed Bath & Beyond.

There are bones in this dam. There are workmen who died to fill up this valley with water, displacing twelve towns and unearthing their dead. Wounds leave scars. This peerlessly beautiful place is a welt on the earth, a tribute to Man the Despoiler.

The pine boughs release little siftings of snow. One falls on my face and I'm grateful. The sun's gotten high—a delirious, spring-skiing brightness—and as I walk back I unzip my parka and shed gloves, hat, and scarf. It's warming too fast: it'll all be over by this afternoon. The snow mural is already gone, melted into gray ice.

Lessons in evanescence. Like everything else in life, you had to be there when it happened.

Day 149. **February 10, 2 PM**

Heavy heart on another memorial walk. RIP Ed Littlehales, ninety-five, a.k.a. "The Old Forester," irrepressible landlord of the knotty pine summer cabin on Skaneateles Lake my family rented for decades. A retired Forest Service administrator, Ed's clarion by-golly voice and hearty laugh were the soundtrack to August. He routed brown and buff wooden signs for each cabin—LOCUSTWOOD, PINEWOOD—and bounced through the woods on a noisy four-wheeler well into his nineties. There's no finer place to remember him than walking near water, surrounded by pines.

This is the third time I've walked here in mourning, and the realization stabs like an icicle: I'm laying the ground for a grief I can't fathom.

This is where I will come when my parents die, the place I can cry and keep going, connected to something much bigger than me. These daily walks, steady as plowing, are breaking a trail for the losses to come.

It's colder and windier, churning gray chop. The Formica-patterned shards of ice are backed up by floating white sludge, with waves undulating beneath.

The mountains are grizzled, with few spots of sun. And then—at the same spot I saw Sandi's eagle—I see her again, the broad-winged T silhouette gliding right toward me.

The same spot. It gives me a shiver. And yes, it may just be coincidence—this is their usual flight path—but somehow I'm more comfortable with animal portents than with the idea of ghosts, gods, or miracles. That is an actual bird. I recognize Xena's snaggled left pinfeather.

I do a gasping 180-degree pivot as she flies overhead—my "Hills Are Alive" move—and watch as she wings down the rest of path. At the spot where she usually banks over the water and flies out to the point, she keeps going straight, and lands with a fluster of wings on a spar tree right next to the parking lot.

I follow, holding my breath as she lets me get closer and closer. I can see pinfeathers fluffing and twitching, the grasp of her talons, the way her head angles from side to side, wary. Then I hear the cry of a second eagle and spot his silhouette high in a pine down the point. Xena must hear it too, but she's playing it cool.

A woman gets out of her car, sees my still focus, and approaches quietly, craning her head toward the eagle. "I know you," she says quietly, and her gaze looks familiar even with most of her face covered by hat and hood. Her name's Laura; a friend of a friend. She tells me about a former job where she watched her colleagues band eight-week-old eagles. Once she held an eaglet in her hands while a coworker drew blood samples. "I felt such a spiritual connection to it, and the beating of its heart," she marvels.

Laura tells me it's mating season and that Xena looks "perky." I point out the potential mate in the pine. He calls again, three short notes. Xena leans forward, fanning as if about to take off, then resettles onto her perch without ever glancing his way. I feel like I've happened on some kind of slow-mo eagle singles bar.

Laura sets off on her walk—it's numbingly cold, and I'm tempted to head for my car, but I'd love to see an eagle take off from the tree at such close range. A guy pulls in, parks, and gets out, slamming his car door. Xena flinches but doesn't take flight. As he passes he flashes thumbs-up and says, "I saw one in that same tree two years ago. Just sat there for hours. Must've been fifty people here watching." He keeps walking.

I wait. I'm cold, shifting, restless. Should I stay or should I go?

Xena leans forward again and lifts into the air, spreading her white tailfeathers in a wide wedge. She makes a slow curve above Driftwood Cove—it wouldn't be far off to call it a runway strut—and lands a bit closer to the dude on the piney point barstool, who ignores her.

Of course he does. This could take hours.

Just before I get into the car, I turn back for a last look and spot two eagles wind-dancing over the rise. The Old Forester would have loved it.

Day 150. **February 11, 12:20 PM**

Two words: WIND. CHILL.

It's supposedly twenty degrees, but the Wicked Wind of the West is arctic. I'm layered in two sets of long johns (silks and waffles) plus sweater, wool scarf around neck and Curly Girl fleece pulled over my lower face, vintage ski mitts, Black Marshmallow parka, hood over hat, wool socks, Pac boots. I am in fact warm enough, which feels like a triumph.

A snow squall is rolling down off the High Peaks. It's obliterated the whole Burroughs Range, and as I walk it descends on High Point like a scrim, blowing a granular swirl sideways over the water.

Blue-gray chop. A lone female merganser, swimming between floating clots of white pack ice, fluffs out her wing feathers, then dives.

The metal NO ENTRANCE sign next to the Lemon Squeeze flaps like a yellow clown bow tie. This wind is *not kidding*.

And neither am I. One hundred fifty walks! Two hundred fifteen to go!

As I walk back I realize how I have noticed/named/mapped every foot of this route: there's Fabio's posing branch, the travois poles, the squirrels' acorn factory, the spot where the guys rolled downhill, Maya's Lascaux-textured bridge cracks, where we saw Sandi's eagle (and Ed's), the lunar eclipse bench, Nora's paint splat, the cacabird's grapevine. It's an intricate private geography.

Day 151. **February 12, 1:30 PM**

Judie's horses stand still in their blankets. They know.

The wind's blasting again, so I go to the Frying Pan to look at the Shackleton ice slabs behind the spillway. The whole channel is frozen solid, congealed around islands.

Pulling my hood drawstrings tight and my second scarf over my nose, I venture out onto the dike. The Lower Basin has gone opaque overnight. The ice stretches all the way out to the center, where there's a restive strip of gray water. The rest of the reservoir looks like a sheet of tin. Nothing moves but the wind.

Day 152. **February 13, 11:30 AM**

It's ten degrees, probably the hot spot on a day that will plunge below zero by nightfall. Even the chill Hudson Valley Weather dudes are throwing out phrases like "northwest winds will *howl*" and "dangerous." And, um, "Wind chills between −15° and −40° are possible. . . . Prolonged exposure of bare skin, to these conditions, could result in frostbite or hypothermia." *Damn.*

I suit up in full expedition gear—two layers of everything, plus an ancestral Russian *ushanka* hat with muskrat fur earflaps, too small for my head but SO WARM.

I drive down past father and daughter farmers in Carhartt jackets and padded coveralls. Even the Yearning Stallion looks subdued, possibly yearning more for his warm stall than the two muddy draft mares across the road.

Remarkably, I'm not the only car in the lot. There's even a school bus. I assume some driver is taking a very cold pee, then spot a gaggle of teenagers huddled against the wall of the Lemon Squeeze bridge.

It's a *field trip*? In this?

Apparently so. There's a shifting of bodies that clearly says group-selfie-okay-now-MY-phone. Some teacher is nuts.

He's not alone, though. I also spot three solo walkers in full Adirondack gear. We are badass, we Reservoir Folk.

Wind like cutlery. Making me stagger.

Harsh beauty. Stark bright sun on wintry palette. Snow squalls over the western and northern High Peaks, blinding white. Every kind of ice: white beach pileup, skating rink, crackled clear sheet, layered angular shards, smooth sculpted and glistening. In the center, a stretch of teal-blue open water, churning with combers. I see several seagulls.

I *don't* see the DEP flyboys out having fun on their airboat.

Back in my car, I unwrap several layers. My fleece scarf is wet from my steaming breath. In the rearview mirror, I see tears frozen under both eyes. As I pick up my coffee thermos and start scrawling notes, a black car pulls in and two guys in pea coats, sunglasses and hipster beanies get out. One has his coat open, displaying a chestful of ironic jewelry over a turtleneck. The other has fingerless gloves. I give them five minutes.

The first two teens dash in off the pathway and hug the bus, laughing. More follow in clusters.

The hipsters streak back to their Zipcar. I look at the dashboard clock, grinning. Five minutes exactly.

Day 153. **February 14, 2:30 PM**

Valentine's Day broke at nine below zero, wind chill minus twenty. If eagles are mating in this, they're insane.

I wait till the afternoon temperature soars to a balmy eleven degrees and park at the Frying Pan. The spillway channel is still glassine, the Lower Basin a striking divide between tumbled white ice and brilliant blue waves. It hurts to inhale, a dry burn in the nostrils.

One crow holding forth: *Fuck fuck* COLD, *fuck fuck* COLD.

I'm with him.

Day 154. **February 15, 11 AM**

Temps in the single digits again, granular flurries descending from milky sky. The reservoir is a buffet of ice textures. On the smoother parts, wind-blown snow gathers in cracks. Out past the striated path where the ice cutter went through and fragments refroze, the ice pack meets gray open water clotted with floating chunks.

Looks cold. Is cold.

Eight crows in a flying wedge.

A flock of at least thirty juncos lines the pathway on the wind-sheltered inside wall of the Lemon Squeeze. As I cross the bridge, they shift and reshift, never flying more than a few feet before they resettle, then take off again, chirping with indignation. It's like walking through a roomful of balloons that keep bouncing ahead of my feet.

Day 155. **February 16, 5 PM**

Temperature shot up by forty degrees, and the overnight snowfall morphed into sleet, and then biblical rain.

After the flood: rainbow, half moon, sunset pink, melting ice. A delirious beauty.

Day 156. **February 17, 3:30 PM**

Ice.

Sick of ice.

Sick of looking at ice.

Sick of writing about looking at ice.

Sick of doing it *every damn day.*

The ice sheet's let go of the shore. Its edge is submerged, an unhealthy whitish green like the edge of a scab. Can I go home now?

And as soon as that thought forms, an eagle wings up the embankment, white tail fanned, and glides toward the rise. Hard on the heels of my *wow* is *oh shit, now I have to keep walking.*

I don't *have* to, of course. But I do. I've chained myself to the wheel of this miracle du jour, and I can't turn my back on an eagle.

Face full of wind. Fingers cold. Heavy quilting of blue-bellied clouds. There's no sign of the eagle, and I'm about to turn tail when I hear a loud BOOM. I jump.

The ice sheet is cracking. I stand still and listen. Rough music of ice breaking up, bangs and belches and sharp sudden snaps, like a neck in a noose.

Then I hear three *skrees*. Then two, and three more. Then the bibbity song, liquid and musical. This eagle is courting.

I walk up the rise. *Skree, skree, skree.* There she is, sitting high in a pine about fifty yards from the nest. She shrugs her wings, sits. Sits some more.

A second eagle wings past with deliberate slowness, his tail pulled in tight. I'm not interested, I just happen to be gliding by, looking fine.

Skree, skree, skree. A staccato descent, neither squawk nor song.

I pause on the Lemon Squeeze, staring down at the iced-over creek spill. My fingers are numb, and I think of the time I drove back from St. Louis after Philip and I broke up for the last time, and ran out of money. I couldn't afford a motel, so I slept in my car at a rest stop somewhere in the Appalachians, wearing every garment I had, with my coat as a blanket. I woke up to ice crystals inside the windshield. Could not feel my fingers or toes. Hobbled into the restroom and thawed myself under the hand dryer. I can still feel that sensation of *I could have died.*

Day 157. **February 18, 3:30 PM**

Midwinter breakup. I'm down on the beach near the Frying Pan. The ice sheet has cracked into large jagged sections, their edges forced upward like jigsaw pieces jammed into wrong slots. There's an ice ridge a hundred yards long that looks like the vent on a peaked roof.

I have a sudden urge to stand *on* the reservoir, while I still can. I step onto the ice between two rock islands, no more than a yard from the shore; I'm no fool. I bend down to break a smooth knob of ice off one of the rocks, putting it in my mouth like a popsicle. It's cold and refreshing, a lingering savor of iron and earth.

Past-half moon rising through cloudless blue sky.

Small percussion of creaking and splits farther out, then a sudden great BOOM, belch, and heave. A big section of ice cracks off and drops, water gurgling around it, sending shock waves under the ice. I step back fast, grateful for earth.

Walking back through bare woods, I spot a dead cedar with dozens of woodpecker holes. I hear the drill of the architect, then spot him at work. He's a red-bellied: dove-sized, raspberry beret.

On the path, a small downy feather. His?

Day 158. **February 19, 4:10 PM**

Cloud cover a blue and gray Rothko with soft bleeding stripes. Very small child waving giant orange mittens.

Day 159. **February 20, 11:40 AM**

Sunny Saturday morning. The air smells like spring. Iced-over cove melting wholesale, with water on top. It looks like a mopped floor.

Exuberant crowd. Jog strollers, training wheels, bicycle bells.

Two middle-aged mooks:

"Whatta day, huh?"

"A Cadillac!"

Day 160. **February 21, 9:20 AM**

Bluebirds!

Day 161. **February 22, 5:40 PM**

Gray-pink-blue sky looks like scratched litmus paper. The basin's refrozen, ice striped with reflected pink streaks. The cold clamps down hard. Colors fade. Maya's gone back to Vermont after too short a visit and I'm shrouded in empty-nest gloom.

And then: Full moon rising, an electric streak of children's-aspirin orange. Bare trees backlit like Halloween.

I want an owl.

Day 162. **February 23, 3:40 PM**

Snow is general all over Olivebridge. Unexpected swirl out of the west.

Day began with a red-shouldered hawk winging over the road in front of my car, its cinnamon bulk angling into a swamp. An omen of . . . what?

Pay attention.

The mountains are a granular whiteout, Brodhead Point a soft blur, the iced-over water a sheet of flat white. There is no far shore.

Snowflakes sting my face, windblown. The woods are a pointillist shimmer of snow-edged bare branches, pines, and red buds. I sense something wild and stop walking. Five deer on the edge of the forest, so

perfectly camouflaged I would have passed them without even noticing. What made me stop? A musk, a stomp, an inhale?

I stand watching them for a long time. They see me but carry on grazing, nosing up moss. When I turn, there's an eagle gliding right toward me, no more than ten feet off the path. Its giant wings bank, curving over the beach.

In an instant, the walk has gone mystical. Life in italics.

Day 163. **February 24, 1:30 PM**

There's no worse weather than heavy rain, just above freezing. The air is dead raw. It's like getting slapped in the face with a fish. Hard to believe I used to plant trees in weather like this and go "home" to an unheated tent. I was a lot younger, and maybe a little bit tougher. The glue: I was madly in love with a fellow treeplanter who didn't reciprocate. He shared a canvas tipi on the far side of camp with a Dutch Boy–blond wannabe Indian and his malamute, while I tossed and turned on my canvas cot, wearing long johns and sweatpants inside an itchy wool blanket inside a lumpy down sleeping bag, a turducken of misery.

Things we do to ourselves.

Today, it's a walk in this grizzling slop. Now as then, the salvation is beauty. The fogged-over mountains look like the western Olympics, clouds combing through pines. Raindrops hang like crystals beneath every thorn of a dog rose.

Day 164. **February 25, 12:20 PM**

Second straight day of hard rain. The Driftwood Cove beach point is gone, the waterline practically up to the rowboats. The change is so sudden I blurt, "Oh my god," flushing two hooded mergansers, who take to the air side by side, their mismatched wings beating like weathervanes.

Quick stop at the res on my way to see my aunt Joan in the Nyack ER with a probable stroke. Life is weather.

Day 165. **February 26, 3 PM**

Joan is stable but frail. She can't speak. A grim cloud of fear.

My car's in the shop, so I settle for a microwalk with David and Papa on our way to Kingston. Papa gamely gets out of the Honda in his stocking cap and black leather jacket, striped scarf hanging out from the bottom like tzitzit, clutching his cane with one of the black gloves I lent him.

The knife blade wind almost knocks him down, but he takes my arm for a few short steps onto the pathway—just far enough to see ice on the cove—before I say, "Papa, let's turn back." He lets go of my arm and beelines back to the car, leaning into the wind.

David says later, "He looked so *determined*, as if he was battling monsters."

A few hours later I'm driving my own car back home as a past-full moon rises, the color of gouda. I don't care how cold it is (nineteen degrees, says the dashboard thermometer; less with the wind chill), I'm taking a walk.

Just as I open the car door, a star falls. Not a shooting star but an actual *falling* star. It drops with a fizzling shudder behind the dark trees, like the last down-drifting spark of a firework. "I see you," I whisper, heart racing.

And that would be more than enough, but now I really want to walk out on that path beneath this wild sky full of stars that leave glittering trails.

I look up at the few constellations I know and the millions I don't, and the mountains are black in blue moonlight that brightens as the gold moon comes over the hill. It is very amazing and I'm very cold. Wind whips through my pant legs. My cheeks burn and tingle.

I think of my ninety-year-old father, huddled under a fleece blanket on the Honda's front seat as we drive away. "Are you warming up yet?" I ask, feeling guilty for his three-minute exposure. He nods and then says, "It was kind of exciting."

Day 166. **February 27, 5:40 PM**

Just after sundown. Apricot afterglow on pewter ice. First three deer stepping out of the woods for the evening.

Day 167. **February 28, 3:20 PM**

Temperature shoots up to sixty degrees, like a bud bursting open. There's an Easter-egg-roll fragrance of mud mixed with chlorophyll. A redtail soars over a pasture, and craning to watch it, I notice a row of tapped maples, not the ubiquitous blue plastic tubing that looks like IV lines, but old-fashioned galvanized buckets. *Drip. Drip. Drip.* It's spring!

The Olivebridge lot's overflowing. I join half a dozen cars parked outside the lines. It's a Sunday carnival. Everyone's punch drunk on sunshine.

The whole ice sheet has floated away from the dam, a good hundred yards from the shore. Dozens of seagulls wheel, catcalling; more of them perch on the ice raft. As I walk east, it floats farther away, a half mile of ice bobbing over the waves like a bath toy. A band of crows circles overhead, letting off raucous caws, like avian bikers in black leather jackets.

Lots of actual bikes out, from blinged-out mountain bikes to Toys "R" Us training wheelers. An intense-looking girl, about seven years old, sings a serious song to herself as she rides way ahead of her family.

When I was her age, I pedaled all over my neighborhood in a lush New Jersey suburb, usually with my favorite bear, Mary Plain, in my handlebar basket. I used to narrate my rides; the secret to my phenomenal brilliance as a Famous Book Writer was going to be that I started practicing early. "She pumped her blue Schwinn down Magnolia Avenue, taking a left at the Fichters' driveway and coasting into the parking lot of the Presbyterian Church." Author! Author!

I also practiced narrating while running back and forth in the living room, bouncing both hands off the wall near the door and zigzagging back through the furniture. My parents called it Run and Tell, and I did it so often the white wall was covered with handprints.

If a kid tried that now, she'd be dosed up with Ritalin.

Day 168. **February 29, 9:20 AM**

Ice sheet GONE, presto. Sound of waves lapping.

Glowering clouds, a light drizzle. A few small chunks of ice bob on waves, and I remember one day in Alaska when my skipper gaff-hooked a stray chunk of glacier ice, vivid turquoise and startlingly dense. He broke it in chunks with a hatchet and mixed them with rock salt in the outer wooden barrel of an old-school ice-cream maker. We filled the inside tube with wild salmonberries (like giant raspberries the vivid bright orange of salmon roe) and sweetened condensed milk, and cranked till our arms ached. Best ice cream I ever ate.

That year I spent bumming around with an ill-fitting backpack—in some ways the most lost I've ever been, and certainly the wildest detour off the beaten track—gave me more than everything I did right. My first produced play is set in southeast Alaska, my first published story on Vancouver Island, my first novel on the Olympic Peninsula. Fiction postcards from the road less traveled.

The fact I'm a writer at all is a gift of that trip, my notebooks the one thing I could carry when I fled New York. The play I began on the train across Canada and the happenstance luck of a youth hostel on Port Townsend's gorgeous Fort Worden peninsula, also the home of a US Forest Service barracks where I found a day job and of the great Copper Canyon Press, where the great-hearted cantankerous poet Sam Hamill taught me to set letterpress type and made me want to write things that came from my heart, guts, and brain. I'd already been piling up tinder (high school newspaper, workshops at Wesleyan, the New Hampshire summer stock theatre where Jeffrey Nelson and Jean Passanante were producing new plays by John Sayles and Adam LeFevre), but the flint and steel that ignited it came from that walkabout year, from walking by water and scrawling down details of birds, trees, and weather in notebooks.

Full circle. Migration path.

A hundred or more northbound Canada geese clamor overhead, changing leaders in midflight so the deep V curves into a shifting parenthesis.

Day 169. March 1, 6:30 AM

Sunrise on the Ashokan. Joining me: one bald eagle, two hooded mergansers, four bluebirds, six vociferous crows, dozens of seagulls, nine white-tail deer, eight wild turkeys, and two shiny dark minks, loping along fallen logs like elongated housecats. The neighborhood.

Day 170. March 2, 4:30 PM

Snow squall over the western High Peaks. The wind is insane, whipping up whitecaps so high they bounce off the dam and smack into each other. The water's opaque and brown, turbid with silt. Nobody's flying, not even the gulls.

Day 171. March 3, 4 PM

Spring's being coy. Cold closes back over the day like a fist. There's fresh ice on the shore and along the dam. Driftwood bobs in the cove, rolling back and forth with every wave.

The sky's an elaborate quilting of chevron and herringbone patterns. White blaze of swathed sun.

Day 172. March 4, 8:40 AM

Silver water, still as glass. Light snow falling in sun, a mysterious scrim. A pair of dark waterbirds glides by, slow and elegant. Heavy bodies, curved necks. Could they be black swans? They notice me stopping and set up a cantankerous honking: two Canada geese, silhouetted on white.

Day 173. March 5, 6 PM

Token cowboy-boots-on-the-ground reservoir stop on my way to host Robert Burke Warren's book launch for his debut novel *Perfectly Broken*, but today's real walk was a spontaneous visit to John Burroughs's Slabsides, the hand-built "rustic cabin" where the great nineteenth-century naturalist went to write, sometimes hosting such guests as John Muir and Theodore Roosevelt.

Born in Roxbury, high in the Great Western Catskills, the young Burroughs taught in a one-room schoolhouse in the relocated village of Olivebridge, less than a mile from the Ashokan dam. He went on to write hundreds of essays on nature and literature, publishing twenty-three books between 1861 and his death in 1921. It occurs to me for the first time how he saw these valleys change, as one reservoir after another was built on the fast-moving streams he had paddled and fished.

Leaving poet Anne Gorrick's house after an interview, I spot a rusting historical marker along Route 9W. I make a quick U-turn, drive over a railroad track, and follow John Burroughs Road up a steep hill. A few cars are parked near a dirt road with a low chain across it, which I step right over. ("Oh, really, officer? I thought that meant no *cars*." If it comes up, which it doesn't.)

Rocky escarpment to the left, breathtaking steep gorge to the right. Glimpses through trees to an iced-over pond far below. Sounds of Canada geese honking back and forth, chatty. After a short walk the trail rounds a boulder, and there it is, rugged and scruffy, perched on the rocks like a sunbathing bear. There are steps leading up to Slabsides' cedar-pole porch, and off to one side a small cluster of stumps; must be where schoolchildren and tour groups assemble. I am all by myself, and that feels just right. I breathe in the cool mossy air, feeling my lungs and my spirits expand.

Wooden sign on a tree:

> If I were to name the three most precious resources of life, I should say books, friends, and nature; and the greatest of these, at least the most constant and always at hand, is nature.
>
> —John Burroughs

Day 174. **March 6, 5:40 PM**

Robins yanking up worms! Songbirds serenading!

Sundown sky is so still that vapor trails crosshatch the air, every white-pink scratch mirrored on water. First concentric pops of fish coming up to the surface.

Purple velvet mountain, coral crown of thorns.

Day 175. **March 7, 1:30 PM**

Two men take turns pushing a third in a wheelchair. As I approach, they veer toward the guardrail and stare down the hill for so long that I head over to see what caught their attention. Are the minks back? A fox? Flock of robins?

I don't see anything down there but dry winter grass. As we walk toward each other, the man in the chair lifts his hand with a mischievous grin. The friend pushing the chair and the one flanking it look amused, I assume by my veer to the railing. "I wondered what you were looking at," I explain, and one of the friends deadpans, "We were thinking of pushing him over."

All three of them laugh, especially the man in the wheelchair. That kind of affectionate, easy black humor that's only possible when there's deep love underlying it. Don't pity me, it says, grinning. I'm having much too much fun.

The sun seems especially bright on my skin as they pass.

Seagulls dive-bombing, twisting in air like white kites.

Day 176. **March 8, 5:20 PM**

Water so tranquil the whole reservoir looks enameled, reflections as solid as mountains and trees.

New hiking sneakers. They work.

Day 177. **March 9, 4:40 PM**

Bizarre, sudden summertime heat: seventy-nine degrees. Motorcycles parked in the lot, people walking in shorts and sundresses, flashing pale winter legs. Small girl in pink sunglasses and matching bow.

Pale blue sky with a scatter of stripe-edged lenticular clouds, including one that looks like the Guggenheim Museum.

Nostalgic *ping* of a bicycle bell.

Day 178. **March 10, 3:30 PM**

Towering clouds, dark and steely, casting an unearthly light. I'm hosting two novelists, my old friend Laurie Alberts and one of her friends, for a book tour event at Woodstock's Golden Notebook bookstore. They're thrilled by the reservoir views and the calm of the walk after dragging suitcases through the rush-hour chaos of midtown Manhattan this morning. It's drizzling a little. We pull up our hoods.

Laurie, who lives off the grid in eastern Vermont, has been painting a lot. She notices light and shapes, says the colors are "soft." The mowed grass on the side of the dike shows the first licks of green. When we cross from one side of the weir to the other, the water in the Upper Basin is mud brown and turbid, wind-riffled. The Lower is vivid teal blue. Yin and yang.

Canada geese honking northbound all day. Rites of spring.

Day 179. **March 11, 8 AM**

Laurie and I take a brisk, windy walk from the Frying Pan side. Whitecaps rolling in. Mountaintops still under wraps.

Before we leave, Laurie stops at the Call-a-Head, and I head down the fishermen's path to the water's edge. Just as I'm coming back out, a DEP squad car pulls up, and the first black DEP cop I've seen says in his most officially humorless voice, "See that sign over there? You're not allowed in the woods." And rather than drag out my fishing license or tell him I'm checking a rowboat, I just say "Okay."

As we walk to my car, Laurie says, "A few seconds later, he wouldn't have seen you."

Day 180. **March 12, 3:20 PM**

Squirrel chases another across the road, about six inches behind. They cavort like spring breakers. *That* time of year.

Dry-gold hillsides getting a green undercoat, swollen pink buds on the trees. Walkers in pairs holding hands. Two Chinese girls riding white bikes side by side.

Overhead, a striking formation of thin wispy clouds that hook upward at one or both ends, like attenuated commas and parentheses. I look them up when I get home: *cirrus uncinus*, a.k.a. mare's tails. The name conjures celestial hoofbeats and flying manes, sisters of Pegasus.

Day 181. **March 13, 3 PM**

Sunny Sunday, with a spring-ahead bonus of daylight. Parked next to my car, a BraunAbility van with a side ramp. A bearded young man sits on a pea-green hand-powered recumbent trike, looking proud of his stylin' machine. His girlfriend clumps around inside the van, resecuring the ramp. When they pass me a few minutes later, he's pumping hard and she's practically running to keep up, improbably dressed in an embroidered poncho, capris, and Birkenstocks.

"Next time you're feeling athletic I'm packing my sneakers," she pants, grinning.

"I *told you*," he teases, pouring on speed. She dances alongside, flapping her poncho like Stevie Nicks. They look so glad to be out here together that it hurts to imagine the probable reason he's using that trike: wounded veteran.

A couple pass by me on fat-tire bikes. The man's pulling a toddler trailer. Inside it, a moon-faced boy looks bored in his screen hut.

Three fireplug-shaped walkers approach in lockstep, like something out of *The Wanderers*.

But once I reach the far side of the Lemon Squeeze, I'm on my own. The beach by the rise is a lot more exposed. There are swirls of driftwood in four distinct parallel stripes, from silvery white at the top to damp brown at the waterline. There are also some objects stuck in the stone dam: a blue plastic flip-flop, a white Clorox bottle, a sun-bleached child's desk.

A *what*? How have I never seen that before? You'd have to be standing at this exact spot to make out what it was. I stare down at soil-browned water, imagining a one-room schoolhouse from one of the drowned towns beneath. Maybe it sat atop one of the ruined foundations that show through the shallows in drought years: tumbled stone walls, cellar steps.

Something makes me look up, and I turn toward an oncoming eagle. She passes so close I can see the reptilian texture of clawed yellow feet, hear feathers slice air.

Why do we hold our breath when something astounds us? It's not a decision; more reflex. My lungs fill with air, twin balloons.

Day 182. **March 14, 2:10 PM**

Cloud-lopped mountains, raw drizzle, crows being crows.

On the edge of the pathway, small kelly-green stitchings of crown vetch amid the dead grass.

Day 183. **March 15, 9:20 AM**

The Ides of March, midpoint. Halfway through my reservoir year. From the end of the road I can't see any mountains; they're socked in with fog. Welcome to the unknown.

Closer in, the tops of the mountains are shrouded, but glimpses peek through, like the Rider-Waite tarot deck's Seven of Cups: a figure with his back to the viewer stares at seven gold cups hovering out of a dense bank of clouds, each filled with a vaguely ominous treasure. What'll it be, miss?

As soon as my feet hit the path, there's a ruckus of Canada geese. A dozen or so are hanging around the rock jetty that juts into Driftwood Cove. They set up a racket, and the cry is echoed from behind the point by what sounds like hundreds of frat buddies. Then the crows get involved. Word is out: Red Hat Walking!

A pair of geese takes off from the water, skid-splashing into the air. They fly low, then touch down again like a small pair of seaplanes. As I keep coming closer, the male (larger and louder) flaps his wings back and forth, spraying droplets. As he honks, his long black neck stretches and dips like a cobra.

In the woods, songbirds trill. I hear mourning doves fluting, a cardinal's jaunty *cheer-cheer*. Juncos scatter ahead of me, hopping and swooping. I'm happy to see them. My peeps!

One hundred eighty-three consecutive walks. Miraculously I have not missed a day yet. What does it mean to do something 183 times in a row? I have no grand conclusions, but then again I am far from concluding; 183 walks still to go.

Only this: I have never not come back with something to write. There is life going on every day. We have only to notice.

Spring

Day 184. March 16, 6:40 PM

I leave the Poughkeepsie train station under a portentous sky: thunder-heads, lightning flashes, an eye-of-god opening so wide the sunlight seems to pour through from a giant bucket. Of course I drive straight to the res.

Quicksilver water wreathed in low mist. Air washed with ozone, storm-tingly. Fresh puddles on the wet pathway, rain slanting from peach-tinged gray clouds in the east. An alchemical feeling of SOMETHING WILL HAPPEN that I rarely get anymore. Not an eagle. Maybe a dragon.

I'm the only one out here. I take a meandering stop-and-start walk and that shivery sense never leaves me. What is it?

Rain starts to fall. I turn back, but the sky's so spectacular that I keep stopping and watching it change. When I reach the Lemon Squeeze, I see another walker approaching, wandering from guardrail to guardrail and stopping to look up, like me. It's a man with a camera. My first thought: Good luck catching *this*, buddy. Next thought: I recognize him.

Tall guy in a jean jacket and navy watch cap, nice squint lines around his eyes, always says hi. Which he does again. Then he says, "What's your name? I see you out here all the time, in all kinds of weather." And offers his hand for a shake.

I tell him my name and forget his at once. I'm so shocked that a not insane, kind of handsome man just introduced himself to me in a rain-storm on the res that my brain goes insta-sieve. But he's friendly and direct, and before you know it we're side by side, resting our arms on the Lascaux wall and talking as if we just met at a bar. He asks if I'm an artist (was it the beret?) and when I say "Writer," he says, "That's an artist," which is a good answer.

I ask if photography is his main work, and he tells me no, he just loves shooting sunsets. "You must live nearby," he prompts. Why yes I do. "Are you writing a book?" Why yes I am.

We both seem astounded to find ourselves conversing in post-thunder drizzle and really not minding. And just at the point where I'm starting to wonder, *Am I being pushy? Is he? Is this weird?* he says, "Well, I'm going to push on," lifting up his camera to make sure I know it's not me.

I tell him, "I'll see you again," and he nods.

His eyes are bright and he's looking right at me. "Enjoy."

The Sunset Man takes off to catch the tail end of the light, and I walk to my car with what can only be called a shit-eating grin. Even if I never see him again, this would still be a cool thing that happened. But I'm sure I will, and I feel oddly relaxed about not knowing when.

Is this Plot?

Day 185. March 17, 2:15 pm

Gusty winds rattling trees, a few big splatty raindrops. Drama-queen sky at war with itself: poufy cumulus jousting with gunmetal storm clouds. Rain showers bunched in the mountains, some stray shafts of sun.

Graffiti on the guardrail. *amandawong*, you are seen. *RoyRo77*, ditto.

Day 186. March 18, noon

White rain slants over the High Peaks. Over Ashokan High Point, four white vertical slashes, as if a wolf clawed the sky.

Day 187. March 19, 9:20 am

Mitten-cold. Very red buds against very blue sky. Mountain silhouettes crisp. Water a changeable taffeta: mud-sky, mud-sky, mud-sky.

The water level is rising again. Three crows land on a just-submerged jetty and strut like they're walking on water.

Beaver swimming near its lodge on Kenozia Lake, dark fur in wet spikes.

Day 188. **March 20, 9:30 AM**

First day of spring is ironically freezing. I'm walking into the wind in full winter gear and my eyes are tearing.

Three crows swagger on grass that's still struggling toward green. One defiant tall tree with pink catkins.

A white-haired woman in a forest green hoodie greets me with "It's much better on the way back." This turns out to be true; much less fierce with the wind at my back. Eagle Guy the Gray trudges out from the parking lot, shoulders hunched, camera cradled. He doesn't look happy.

It strikes me that I've just seen reservoir avatars of the parents I'm going to New York to visit: Mom making the best of things, Papa wind-bent, dutifully doing what he's always done.

On the train to the city. Sky's gray, Hudson's grayer. This wide, mighty river is fed by the freshwater streams of the Catskills and flows south to the sea, roiled by twice-daily tides as saltwater flows north from its mouth. Its Algonkian name, Mahicantuck ("waters in constant motion") is sometimes poetically rendered as "The River That Flows Both Ways."

The Ashokan was the first of an extensive system of Catskill reservoirs that now includes the Cannonsdale, Pepacton, Neversink, and Rondout to the west; the northern Schoharie empties into the Ashokan via the Esopus Creek. The water they gather flows down to New York in great underground aqueducts, tunneling under the turbulent river. The tap water I'll drink tonight on East Ninety-Third Street has taken the same southbound journey I'm taking right now, forest to city, mountains to sea.

Day 189. **March 21, 6:50 PM**

A light spritz of snow glitters lawns. At the res: snow squall, sunset, moon-rise, bald eagle, ALL AT ONCE.

To the west, whiteout mountains and snow blowing sideways. Turner stormscape, wind roaring across open water that's mustard, green, olive, brown—every color but blue.

To the east, gibbous moon calmly rising through clouds.

On the path, six ecstatic students dance and whoop like coyotes.

Day 190. **March 22, 4:15 PM**

Driftwood on the move. Sticks and rafts break loose from the winter-long clot in the cove, floating away on sudden high water. Stray branches sort themselves into an uneven line bobbing alongside the dike like a shuffling breadline.

A photographer with a tripod sets up near the rise. I feel my breath catch, but it isn't the Sunset Man.

Family of four, including a boy in a puffer jacket with sleeves the color of Gatorade. He holds his arms out to both sides as he runs in a serpentine pattern, weaving from guardrail to guardrail. "Hi baby deers! Hi grown-up deers! Hi cutie deers!" He's passed by a bike racer whose vest is the same rancid green.

One turkey vulture circles lazily, strolling on air. Copper half moons on the underside of its dark wings.

Several chestnut-capped tree sparrows bustle inside a thicket of brambles, constructing nests nothing will raid. I watch as they swoop in and out bearing twigs.

Just before dark, the pterodactyl glide of a great blue heron over the path.

Day 191. **March 23, 1 PM**

Fishwife gulls trash-talk on the Brodhead Point beach. Also actual trash, washed downstream by winter meltwater. I fill both arms with flotsam, a messy embrace. The things I carried:

four water bottles
one gallon jug
one rotting flip-flop
kid's Nike sneaker, full of wet leaves

Glad tupperware lid
plastic Oreo cup
Dr. Pepper can
staring doll, matted blonde hair
plastic straw
beef jerky wrapper
Cranberry LifeWater bottle
pink sippy cup
Builder Bar wrapper
Chinese takeout box
turquoise barrette
Bud Light bottle
long twist of fishing line snagged on a stick

All this near the one fishing path I've seen that actually has a trash barrel. I throw it all in. Doll staring skyward.

On the path back, some broken twigs topped with bright red maple flowers. Up close they look otherworldly, like tiny space lobsters.

Day 192. **March 24, 5:30 PM**

My friend Sarah Harden meets me for a walk in perfect spring weather. An actress and old-time bass player with stunning white hair, Sarah still has the straight back and turnout of the ballerina she was years ago. She walks at a clip.

Red buds, calm sky, mountains a soft milky blue.

Sarah admires the geometric stone terracing next to the creek spill ("That is *so* cool!") even though looking down from this height gives her vertigo.

A crow sees us coming and sets up a yammer, which I translate as, "Check *this* out. Red Hat's got a buddy!"

Second crow: "Yeah?"

First crow: "Gentrification."

As always when I walk with someone, the distance seems short. We cover the two and a half miles to the weir bridge and back in no time. The sun's sinking low and the wind comes up sharply. The water riffles like silk, and a couple of Canada geese veer over it, angling past High Point. "Beautiful," Sarah sighs.

She heads home to her husband, and I walk back solo to sit on the first bench and watch the sun set. The sky looks like masses of lilacs. One long incandescent contrail, etched onto the sky by a plane that glints silver and pink.

Where is my Sunset Man?

Day 193. **March 25, 3:30 PM**

Insane March wind. Car judders over the bridge, door nearly blown off when I open it. Peacock blue water with whitecaps tossing.

Four crows, two big and two smaller. The small ones flap like kites. Even the seagulls aren't flying today. They huddle in bunches on two rocky islets.

Two sure signs of spring: a fresh sandy anthill with tiny ants clambering up through the hole in its center, and wild onions spiking up higher than grass blades. I break off a juicy spike, hollow like a chive, and chew its sharp, garlicky green, stringy and pungent.

I circle the Frying Pan, studying bark variations. Fine-grained maple, camo-patterned sycamore, shingled white pine, horizontal scarifications of black birch, fibrous red cedar, gray ash with flayed-looking tan strips.

One tree has grown almost completely around a rusting metal sign— I can still make out the word FISHING, surrounded by bark. Someone's tied a lost maroon hoodie around a young maple, its arms in a permanent hug.

Day 194. **March 26, 2:30 PM**

Off-road trifecta! Fishing gate E-22 is a keeper. An old paved road, half grown over, leads to a dirt road with an ancient NO TRESPASSING sign. I go.

Long stone wall, with a high-angle view across railroad tracks down to a hidden lagoon with a scatter of waterbirds. I step over the tracks, which feels really forbidden. A steep narrow trail snakes down to the water. Another trail winds up the hillside and out of sight.

A frisson of fear tips my instinct: Come back here and explore, but not by yourself. Too steep, too far off the beaten track. Something doesn't feel right.

I drive down to Flat Rocks instead. In the grove of pines below the road, I find a sculptural balance of large stones like something you'd find in a Japanese garden. I walk past chained rowboats and wind-bonsai trees at the edge of the beach and onto the wide shelf of rock, where it's sunny and peaceful.

One crow on a spar tree, announcing my presence. Lulling music of water on stone, an irregular slap-gurgle-slap. In the mud I find stray tufts of down, and one three-toed bird print the size of my hand, no webbing, sharp claws digging deep. Could it be a bald-eagle footprint? Why is there just one?

I drive back over the West Hurley Dike and turn onto Basin Road, passing the Reservoir Inn and making an impulse stop at Gate E-15, where a grassy path traces the top of the Woodstock Dike. I walk out past several calm inlets and small rocky islands. It looks like Maine.

Two scaups skitter into the air. Then a thrilling sight: a northern flicker, tan winged and white chested with flashes of yellow. He's flying right toward me with stop-and-start dips, veering to land on a dead tree above a still pond. There's no other motion except for a pair of Canada geese idly swimming on one of the inlets.

Then the sound you least want to hear when you're alone in the woods, or think you are: a truck door slamming. I spot the driver ahead in the distance, on the Route 28 side. DEP cop, fisherman, duck hunter, creep? I don't wait to find out.

I walk away fast. I don't like having my back to him, wearing a pump-kin-tan parka with a white fake-fur ruff on the hood. *I'm not a deer,* I chant silently. And: *shit, shit, shit.* I don't want to get caught here. I have my fishing license in my pocket, but I'm clearly not fishing, just out for a walk.

It's no more than ten minutes back to my car. As I'm walking I spot a crow feather in the tall grass and bend quickly to scoop it up, sticking it into my pocket without breaking stride. Protection.

When I step back out through the gate and reach the car, I put a hand into my pocket for my magic feather and it's gone. Must have flown out on the path. Sacrifice to the reservoir gods.

Day 195. **March 27, 6:50 pm**

I took a long steep hike with a very fit friend and her dog, so I'm footsore and weary when I reach the reservoir just before sundown. The mountains are milky pale blue. Pigeons wheel over the bridge, and I say out loud, "Honey, I'm home."

Day 196. **March 28, 2:20 pm**

It rained all morning and it's still overcast and raw. So am I. Just got turned down for a bank loan I needed for Maya's tuition. I have no Plan B and I feel like an absolute failure.

I trudge down the path. By the time I get back, there are a few breaks of blue in the clouds. The metaphor lies like a lox on the counter but does not help my mood. Sometimes words are just words.

I'm back at the car before I realize I've observed nothing that I haven't seen before, which leads directly to *who cares, who wants to read this crap anyway, why are you even doing this?* Rabbit hole.

First green weeds growing though cracks in the asphalt. That's all I got.

Day 197. **March 29, 8 am**

Ocean-windy. Obstreperous crows.

Two stocky birders walk hand in gloved hand. He's got a rambling red beard, she's got a scarf over her face and wears her binox like a necklace. They lean forward, wind-buffeted.

Waning moon low in pale sky.

Day 198. **March 30, 4:40 PM**

The wooden benches are back for the season. I stop for a ritual sit on each one. It *is* spring. It is.

A small crow sets out, flapping its wings against minimal wind. Another crow sets up a shrill cry: nagging mom.

Beginning rollerbladers. Kid in front, mom working hard to keep up, dad lagging. "Noah! Wait for mama and papa at the pole!" CAW.

Two does emerge from the cedars. One has a round white patch of bald skin between her shoulder blades; must have been grazed by a bullet. She dips her head, munching new grass.

Day 199. **March 31, 3:30 PM**

Summer temperature (seventy!), chilly March wind, budding trees: all seasons at once. Storm clouds rolling in, so dark and heavy it feels like the soundtrack should be "Night on Bald Mountain." Every so often the white sun burns through, spilling liquid silver across the dull water. Just as quickly, it's gone.

One gull flying pirouettes, brilliant white against deep purple peaks.

I pick up a branch from the pathway and sidearm it over the guardrail. It lands with a pleasing splash.

Wind-tossed white pines, paler green at the tips. That flayed-looking hardwood I've noticed looks flayed because it is: there's a pileated woodpecker working it over, drilling for emerald ash borers, the invasive insects that are killing these elegant hardwoods all over the Northeast. I notice a pile of shaved bark at its base.

Beaming grandpa pushing a curly-haired toddler on one of those trikes with a pole. She asks him, "Who lives here?"

Oh honey. It's such a long list.

Day 200. **April 1, 9:50 AM**

My older brother Larry and his wife Laurie are visiting from France, and we're driving to Bennington to see Maya. Late start, but we grab a quick reservoir walk on our way. It's delta-warm, windless and humid. It wants to be raining.

Water and sky moody blues. Timeless silhouette of a man in a drifting rowboat, pole angled over the water.

All the way to Vermont we see men in waders and vests climbing out of their pickups or standing hip deep in trout streams. Opening day.

Day 201. **April 2, 5 PM**

Olivebridge is yellow. Bright yellow coltsfoot and banks of forsythia lining the road. A silver-blue heron takes off from a reed-edged pond, retracting its long neck and legs like landing gear.

Larry and Laurie have come back for more. We set out from the Frying Pan, layering on scarves and hats. The wind's come up, with clouds banking over the peaks. Laurie pauses to take a snapshot of the mountaintop where David Bowie's ashes were scattered.

Larry keeps noticing spray-painted GPS triangles and geodetic survey markers. Near the weir bridge, he spots the chain-link-fenced weather station and rain gauge. He recognizes a gray metal control box on a green pole by the guardrail and looks down the hillside for tilt meters hidden beneath safety-orange barrels. He regales us with tales of installing tilt meters and seismometers in the Caribbean and Aleutians, getting stranded in Zodiac rafts and mud-bottomed fishing boats. Great stories, but far from the first time I've heard them. Larry did fieldwork for Columbia's Lamont-Doherty Geological Observatory more than twenty years ago; like me, he's now mostly deskbound, staring at a computer screen and nostalgic for working outdoors.

Triple eagle sighting! First Fabio, silhouetted on his posing branch. Then we hear agitated *skree*s from the woods. Xena's head pokes up from the nest as a third eagle—not their brown-headed offspring but some uppity white-feathered rival—flies between pine boughs to buzz the nest. The interloper swoops past several times, very close. Lots of *skree*s back and forth. It's an aquiline telenovela.

When we emerge from the trees on the rise, the sky has gone melodramatic. There's a white veil of rain falling over the western High Peaks, with heavy dark clouds rolling toward us so quickly we're sure we'll get soaked. We turn back, walking fast, swiveling often to look at the mutable skyscape behind us. The rainclouds get stuck on the ridge, dumping their load, then shred and dissipate, leaving a sky full of God holes. A few shafts of sun spotlight the far shore.

A white-haired biker, barrel-chested in spandex, pulls up and asks if one of us can take a photo of him with his iPhone. Larry obliges, though he's not an iPhone user. The man is posing against that white sun, so his face is too dark in the shot. Larry wants to change angles and try again, but the man says it's fine, the photo doesn't have to be great. He just got a new artificial leg and wants to show his doctor where he took it out for a test drive.

"How's it working?" I ask.

"Great," he says, beaming. "A little bit stiff in the knee, but he can adjust that. It's great." He hops back onto his bike and sails off, pumping hard with both legs.

I would never have known.

Day 202. **April 3, 11:45 AM**

I wake up to three inches of SNOW, clinging to every branch. I want to drive straight to the res, but the power's gone out and my house is cold. I stoke up the woodstove, go out and sweep snow off my windshield, only to find orange safety cones blocking both ends of my road. Snow-heavy limbs must have fallen on power lines, causing the blackout.

A few hours later, the lights click back on and I drive to the res, past snow-clotted forsythia bushes and daffodils bowed to the ground.

New snow on the mountains, white all the way down.

The wind is immense. Flock of gulls scatters like paper scraps. An eagle *stops* in midair, then gets blown sideways. Ocean whitecaps smash into the dam wall so fiercely that spray blows up over the guardrail, twenty or thirty feet high. A driftwood log pounds like a battering ram. A merganser bobs on the waves like a bath toy.

On the lee side, pines lace-edged with snow. Kelly-green clover sprouts along the base of the Lemon Squeeze wall, where the snow's blown away.

Roar of wind, flapping the hood of my parka. Standing still makes me feel like a scarecrow. Lone male bluebird perched on the guardrail, feathers puffed out for warmth. The wind is so loud he can't hear me approach till I'm no more than six feet away. Startled, he swoops toward the woods, staying low to the ground so he won't blow away.

A few hardy souls venture out: Santa Sisyphus, a Goth exercise walker bare-calved in capris (is she nuts? training for the Iditarod?), Eagle Guy the Younger (bareheaded and smiling). A gay couple dressed Chelsea-style walks out about fifty feet. They gasp at the view and scurry back, leaning against each other and laughing hysterically. Country living, *too much!*

A flurry of new flakes blows into my face. I look up and an eagle is flying right toward me. She flies over my head—giant wingspan, those bright yellow feet!—banks over Driftwood Cove and circles back, fighting gusts. I watch as she rides the wind down the whole length of the pathway and back to the nest.

Day 203. **April 4, 11:50 AM**

Four *more* inches of snow overnight; April Fools'! I shovel my car out and head for the res in a fresh round of snowfall. The just-plowed road is lined with pissed-off robins. What happened to green grass and worms?

There's no wind and the snow falls straight down in a pointillist stipple. The mountains have vanished. The point at the far end of Driftwood Cove is a dark smudge, and beyond it the water and sky meld in seamless mourning-coat gray. There is no far shore.

There's also no color. The pink-budded hardwoods are obscured by falling snow, and the snow-lined pines look black and white. New grass and green clover are buried. Only the higher dead grasses and weeds poke up through snow cover, their dried blossoms hatted with white. It's a total erasure of spring. The whole world is gray on gray, pixeled by tiny white flakes.

I make out the faint silhouette of a walker returning. Is it my fellow bad-weather ecstatic, the Sunset Man?

Nope. It's another guy I've seen here before, hunching in wool cap and sunglasses. We pass on the Lemon Squeeze, greeting each other with weather talk. (Him: "Well, *this* is surprising." Me: "It's kind of magical." Him: "More snow in these past two days than we've gotten all winter.") We nod and keep going our separate ways.

Moments later I stop and stand still, looking out for a long time at nothing at all, the horizonless gray and the granular snowfall. The hush is profound. It's so quiet I hear snowflakes land on my shoulders. My hair and eyelashes gather wet crystals.

On the way back, a reddish-brown fox sparrow hops down the path right in front of me like a familiar. I think she's relieved to see something else moving.

Day 204. **April 5, 2:10 PM**

Spring-winter tug-of-war. Swedish blue sky versus raw winter wind. I think wind is winning.

The mountains are white, the water turquoise and mud colored, silvered by sun into crinkled blue foil. The east-facing slope is a bright golf-course green. At the foot of the hill it turns white again, shadowed by trees, snow crisscrossed by deer tracks. The buds reassert their pinkness, the pines their deep green.

Three tapered gray chimney swifts fly high-speed loops in triangle formation, chirping a high, constant *squee*. Juncos hopscotch the guardrail. A tiny brown creeper works its way up a tree trunk. There's a natty gray catbird, a rust-striped towhee, a jackhammering woodpecker. Woods coming back to life.

Eagle Guy the Younger sits on the guardrail, camera at his feet. He's got his eyes on the nest, though there's nothing to see. He hums to himself, keeping warm. As usual he wears no hat or gloves. "Beautiful day," he says.

Day 205. **April 6, 2:30 PM**

Killing frost late last night. The bright yellow forsythia lining the road has congealed to a limp, sullen mustard, and rust-colored magnolia buds hang like used tea bags. The three pregnant nanny goats next to the Olivebridge Post Office lie on the ground in a rump to rump triangle, keeping each other warm as they chew hay.

Four people in expedition gear come off the pathway, speaking Chinese. We trade nods as I pass, fellow travelers.

I see a male bluebird in the same spot as before, his back royal blue and breast hot-sauce orange. He looks like an avian Mets fan.

Other signs of spring trying to happen: green patches of clover, crown vetch, and dandelion defying the snow. I break off a leaf of clover to chew, releasing a sharp tang of chlorophyll.

The water's opaque olive gray, and the wind coming from the southeast sends it riffling *away* from the dam, so the waves look backward. Fish come up to the surface, leaving pockmarks and concentric ripples, like inverted raindrops.

The sky is a white velvet burnout. A few crows take roll call.

I head back to my car as a blonde woman strides away fast from her SUV. I see blue-jeaned legs bending over the tailgate, and as I approach I hear a man muttering under his breath. Did they fight?

As I pass, he looks up with a sheepish grin, and I see that he's changing his daughter's diaper. Just like that, my narrative shifts 180 degrees.

Never assume.

Driving home, I turn on the car radio: slow movement of Mozart's clarinet concerto. The lifting strings and warm-honey melody pull forth an instantaneous pang: it's the music I played as I lay on the living room rug for five minutes, waiting for a home pregnancy test result, the time that the answer was yes.

I think of that young dad with his diaper bag and have the insane urge to drive back and tell him, *Don't blink. It goes by in a flash.*

Mozart plays.

Day 206. **April 7, 3:40 PM**

Daylong drizzle turns into a violent windstorm and lashing rain. When it lets up a little, with sun slanting through, I head straight for the res, seeking rainbows.

None to be seen, but the air's rich and sweet. There's still snow at the high elevations, but the hillsides and woods are washed clean.

Far below in the creek spill, I see something move: great blue heron, stalking toward something near shore. It's a second heron. Herons are loners—I've never seen two in the same place—so my interest is piqued. An outstretched neck, a quick back and forth, and the first heron wings off, landing a few yards away. Courtship or turf war? I watch for a long time, but they aren't telling.

Outside the Olivebridge Post Office, I spot an elderly man in British country-gentleman garb, khaki trousers tucked into his wellies. He stands ankle deep in a puddle, stomp-splashing like a kid. "Just the right depth," he says, gloating.

Inside, talk of rainbows. "I saw five in one day," says the postmistress.

"All at once?" asks her customer, startled.

The postmistress shakes her head. "There was a double rainbow right out here, then I drove to Shandaken and saw a *different* double rainbow, and on the way home I saw one right over the res."

"Oh, I *love* them. They're so beautiful. You can't believe how bright the colors are."

"Nothing like that in the crayon box."

"That's because the colors are made out of light," says the gent in the wellies, who's just walked in. "Those other colors are not."

Mansplaining the rainbow. Thanks, fella.

Day 207. **April 8, 8:30 AM**

Cold clear air, flippy little whitecaps.

Lone heron reflected on sparkling water.

Day 208. **April 9, 8:10 AM**

Driving home from the thruway last night, I braked for three animals in less than ten minutes: a streaking red fox, a zigzagging bunny, and a stolid beaver trudging from swamp to swamp, leaving wet footprints across the road. I stepped out of the car to a sky full of stars and a barred owl calling.

So when I wake before the alarm clock with sun pouring in through the windows, I'm positive there's something I need to see right away. I pull on my clothes, reheat yesterday's coffee, scrape ice off the windshield, and get to the res minutes later.

The whole sky clouds over while I walk, as if I'm being stalked by a shadow. My feet hurt. I'm cranky. A preening runner stands at the rail doing showoffy stretches in spandex. If I were an old-country witch, I would hex her to gain fifty pounds overnight.

A speedskater dressed like Darth Vader passes me four times, hands clasped behind his back and wheels whirring on pavement. The loud noise makes me wince.

I spot a big bird in hunched silhouette on a tree far below. Eagle or vulture? It doesn't stir. I move on.

The eagle nest's empty. A loud diesel engine revs over the weir bridge: truck pulling a giant RV. Everything is an abrasion today.

As I turn back, I spot a pine cracked several feet from its base, leaning onto a neighbor, its trunk smeared with waxy sap. *Everything breaks*, I think. I'm feeling worse as I walk, a first.

Pay attention.

Gray squirrel, rustling through windfall branches. Blue jays shrilling. Pileated woodpecker in slow-motion drill, like a rap on the door.

Three small crows fly out of the woods, trading nasal caws. Teenage drivers.

I stop on the Lemon Squeeze. The big bird is still in the same tree. No point waiting for it to move after what must be a half-hour sit, but a glum, clomping walker is dogging my heels and I want him to pass me already. Just after he does, the bird spreads its wings: great blue heron. It glides out of sight in three wingflaps, but I got that intake of breath, that transcendent gasp. And, I suppose, a lesson in patience, though I wouldn't have seen it take off if I hadn't been impatient with the glum clomper.

At the parking lot, a woman with a Nikon case greets me with "Anything out there today?"

I tell her I just saw a heron take wing, and she's thrilled. She *loves* great blue herons. She tells me, "I'm not even walking today. I have to bring my dog to the vet, I just stopped on my way for the view." I nod and say, "I've done that too," and head for my car, spirits lifted at last.

Parked beside me: a rusty white pickup with emergency flasher on roof, American flag and slat hiking basket in back. Dreamcatcher on windshield, several decals for American Mountain Men. Bumper sticker: May the Forest Be With You.

Day 209. **April 10, 1 PM**

First dandelions in bloom. It's a beautiful day in the neighborhood.

Sunshine + Saturday = a crowd.

Six sullen teens hunch by a van while an earnest woman holds forth, lecturing them about something or other. One smokes, four stare at their phones, one pretends to be listening.

Bright yellow Corvette with vanity plate USNSEALS.

Overheard on the pathway:

• Man talking to woman with arms folded over her chest: "Well, it happens. I don't wanna dwell."

• Daughter: "You're *so mean.*" Mom, grinning: "I know!"

• Family group. Littlest kid, chasing sibs: "Wait for MEEE!"

Even so, there are moments of peace. The water's glassine. When I stand in the sweet spot between the Lemon Squeeze and the rise, there's no sound at all. Ears full of stillness.

A row of daffodils blooms at the foot of the hill. How did they get there? Some DEP maintenance man with a poetic streak, or did a rogue walker roll bulbs down the hillside to see if they'd take?

The creek spill's developed some kind of algae bloom, so it's streaked with unearthly blue green. The heron glides from one side to the other, takes a couple of steps, then flies back. That's three days in a row now. I hope he's a fixture.

Shrub that looks like witch hazel, budding in acid-green tiny curled fists.

Day 210. **April 11, 4:20 PM**

The day's drab and gray as a pigeon. Light drizzle turns to a hard rain as soon as I park, so I switch to the first fishing path for a tree-covered walk to the edge of the water, so high now it's practically licking the rowboats.

More blowdowns than last time I was here, including a large white birch. I notice a long hardwood trunk with a mud-packed root ball. As I circle around it, I flush out a flicker at very close range, red at the nape, white back patch, a flurry of yellow-tan wings.

Then I spot a water-smoothed board with partial orange lettering, part of a hand-lettered boat stern. It's split so that only the bottom third of each letter is visible, and some of the paint's chipped away. It looks like this:

I can't puzzle it out, and I'm getting soaked, so I pick it up. I speed walk back to my car, planning to toss the contraband into the woods if I spot a DEP cop. Path clear, road clear. My heart's beating fast as I reach the car, drop the board on the floor, and drive off. *I got away with it,* I gloat. Then two headlights appear in my rearview. I look up. A cop car.

Oh shit. I'm going to get busted for poaching driftwood?

I turn right onto Route 213. He follows. He hasn't flashed lights at me yet, so I keep on driving. By the time I pass the firehouse, I've almost convinced myself that the road was clear when I pulled out, so the cop couldn't have seen me toting the board and just happened to be driving the same way. *Right? Right??*

I reach the barn on the corner and signal right, holding my breath for the moment of truth.

I turn right.

Cop goes straight.

I breathe. I grin. *Thank you!*

Back home, I set my treasure on the table and sketch out partial letters, invoking my inner crossword nerd.

That first straight line could be almost anything, but the next, with its pedestal foot, must be an I. Then a vertical line–V combination that must be an N, a vertical-diagonal that must be an R, a right angle (L or E?), another R, a vertical-curve (D?), then L or E again, then a could-be-anything nub.

I puzzle it out: _ I N R (E/L) R D (E/L) _

It's a boat name, I think, and all of a sudden I see it:

TINKERBELL

Day 211. **April 12, 4 PM**

Big birds on the move. Two herons on Vly Pond, a wild turkey with wings pumping hard in midair, and *hundreds* of crows flying over the Hurley Flats corn stubble. The flocks come in clumps, heading southward, as if there's some gathering they're all attending. Mass murder of crows?

I grab a quick walk near the West Hurley dike, sure-footing bluestone. The Flat Rocks are covered, and wind whips the high water higher. I don't spot any birds, but I pick up a beautiful snow-white gull feather.

Day 212. **April 13, 1 PM**

After several postponements, I'm meeting Sandi's husband Dan Green in the parking lot. He's wearing a brimmed hat, a hoodie, and round opaque sunglasses. He gives me a toneless hello and halfhearted hug and I say idiotically, "How are you?"—a really wrong question for someone whose wife died four months ago. Dan just shrugs. No need for words.

But we have a good walk. The sky is clear blue, with a few puffs of cloud. There are walkers in parkas and walkers in sundresses. They're both sort of right.

I show Dan the residual splat from Nora's overturned palette, which makes him smile. He says that was the first and only time they met there to paint *en plein air*, and I ask about his black-and-white painting. "Just something to try," he says, shrugging. We talk art and art school. Dan tells me he hitchhiked cross country to attend the School of Visual Art in New York. He met Sandi there. They were nineteen and twenty years old.

Dan tells me he's only seen an eagle here once, sitting still in a tree. We talk about Sandi and her love of birds, his not-yet-gelled plans to move west. He has the feeling that people are getting impatient with him and his grieving. He's late with some comic-book artwork and can't get it done. "I think I'm more emotional than most people," he says. I tell him I'd worry more if he *weren't* emotional. It's the people who bottle it up who can't heal, and things take as long as they take. Dan's in tears, and I brim. I don't know what to tell him.

We've reached the rise. He takes a deep breath, filling his nostrils with pine scent. "I love that smell."

I show him the nesting site just as an eagle takes off, flapping soundlessly through the pines. "I'm glad I saw that," Dan says. So am I.

There's a lone Canada goose in the long grasses just over the guardrail, its head glossy black. I take a step closer, and it takes off with a clatter of wings, webbed feet paddling air. It sails onto the water and lands like a seaplane, bobbing on its own wake. Dan says, "Nicely done."

Day 213. **April 14, 4:40 PM**

Short walk en route to a Word Café reading I'm hosting. The sun's out and spring's on Take Two. New daffodils blooming. Two goldfinches perch on a flowering crabapple. Spring peepers earning their name. These dime-size tan frogs inflate their throat pouches like miniature bagpipes, greeting spring nights with a jubilant chorus of treble-clef shrills.

Blue water, green grass. A man with a shaved head does yoga stretches, perching the sole of one foot on the opposite knee.

As I drive away, a tubby, bristling raccoon steps into the road, reconsiders, and trundles back into the underbrush.

Day 214. **April 15, 5:10 PM**

First thing I see is two broad-winged birds riding high on an updraft, a slow, lazy spiral in front of a rising half moon. Eagles or vultures?

I raise a hand over my eyes to watch as they circle. Even squinting into the sun, I can make out a white wedge-shaped tail and head. But the second bird is all dark. An immature?

No. When it angles away from the sun, I see copper half circles under both wings. One eagle, one vulture, sharing an updraft like bros.

Day 215. **April 16, 10:30 AM**

Busted again, this time by a genial black DEP cop on an olive-green ATV.

It's a splendid spring morning. Approaching the weir bridge, I impulse-park on the road shoulder next to the gate by the Shovel Cut. Seven pickups and me.

I've been eyeing this gate for a while, and I want to walk down there and see who's out fishing. There's seven or more of them; safety in numbers.

The sun bakes a waft of dry pine from the trail, a wide dirt road parallel to the shoreline. It goes much farther back than I thought, with rowboats chained to trees on both sides and smaller spur trails to the edge of the water. At the first turnoff, two old-timers shoot the shit in shaggy-fish story tones I remember from the café where I waitressed in southeast Alaska. The fishermen ate at the counter, rolling a dice cup to see who'd get stuck buying everyone's Hungry Man Special. Colorful, yes, but the sore loser always undertipped the breakfast waitress who plied them with Bunn-o-Matic black coffee.

Until I climbed onto a salmon troller with one of them. The day before we left port, my new skipper bought me breakfast. I sat on a stool at the fisherman's counter with a mile-wide grin and left my coworker a ginormous tip.

I keep walking. There are six rowboats scattered at intervals on the flat water. Each has two fishermen, one in the stern and one in the bow. It's silent as church. I hear chipmunks scurry, the dip-splash of somebody's oars.

Lots of ash trunks flayed bald by emerald ash borers. The road gets uneven, dredged into deep ruts of dried mud. I remember driving to Chaco Canyon in Laurie Alberts and Tom O'Neill's vintage Travelall (off white, with a doll's head glued onto its roof). When our foursome drove in at dawn, after huevos rancheros at a roadside diner in Cuba, New Mexico, the entry road was frozen solid, with red-dirt ruts so broad Laurie photographed Tom and our friend David lying inside them. After we hiked through the unearthly stone ruins, the afternoon sun turned the road to mud soup. We got stuck several times, and as we pushed and shoved the

Travelall out of the slosh, a reservation school bus tore past us, angling up onto the shoulder and spraying the gringos with mud.

There are signs nailed to some of the trees. One says CEDAR COVE. A songbird trills from one of the cedars, and I follow its call.

The view is serene, and as soon as I settle onto a log by the water, I hear an engine on the dirt road. *Fuck. DEP.*

The cop drives his ATV over and climbs out, leaving it idling. I show him my fishing license and explain that I'm thinking of buying a rowboat.

"Gotcha, but you can't be down here without fishing equipment," he says. "Look, it's a beautiful day. If I could just sit on a log and chill out enjoying the view, I would. Got a rod in your car?"

I don't. "Not today."

"Bring it with you next time," he says. "Even if it's just a little folding rod, you hear what I'm saying? You just gotta be down here to *fish*, okay?"

He tells me the DEP runs an auction on unclaimed rowboats around Father's Day. "Nice boats. You can get 'em real cheap." I thank him. He nods and jogs off on his ATV.

As I walk out, I see a stocky old man talking to an athletic-looking black fisherman. "I bet he told her the same thing he told me," the older man says, nodding my way.

"What was that?" I ask.

"That I can't be down here without my gear. I got a rowboat back there, I was just walking down to check on it. Thought I might go out fishing tomorrow."

The black guy is chaining his boat to a tree and stowing his gear in a camo-print backpack. He stops working and we shoot the shit about the DEP "trout police" for a few minutes. Then he sets a trio of shiny plump trout on his overturned boat. Two are still, one faintly gasping; he must have just taken them out of a bucket. "Wow!" I exclaim. "No wonder there's so many rowboats out there."

He laughs. "Can't tell nothing from that. They're out there 'cause they haven't gotten their three yet. That's why they're still fishing. I already got six. Threw one back, had to give two away."

I tell him they're fine-looking fish, though the sight of the gasping one troubles me. It's a long time since I worked on that boat, and I've lost my thick skin. I'm tempted to grab the poor trout and run down to the water, setting it free. Instead I walk back to the road with the old guy, who's puffing a bit on the very slight incline. "Haven't been fishing in quite some time," he says. "Too old. Too out of shape."

"It's a long walk," I say, hoping to make him feel better.

He nods. "Think I might go out fishing tomorrow."

Day 216. **April 17, 7 PM**

Suddenly summer-warm. I've already picked two crawling ticks off my neck and carried a dead garter snake off the road, clearly run over while sunning.

The reservoir's crowded with presunset walkers. The tattoo and beard count definitely spikes on the weekend. So do the Waldorf parent contingent and the too-loud talkers; there's a Venn diagram where all three intersect. I overhear conversations about painted turtles, Lyme disease, bedtimes, Bernie Sanders, senior center menus, Pilates, and lumber. Also a conversation in Urdu between a white-bearded man in royal-blue Nikes and a woman in a *salwar kameez*, wafting sandalwood perfume.

Trio on bikes playing Radiohead from a speaker as they pedal. Then a mother and daughter on pink tandem bike, singing "Ring around the Rosy" as they ride up the rise. *Ashes, ashes, they all fall* DOWN. Surely the creepiest song in the English language. But wait, there's more. "DAAAADD??? Sing the Fried Chicken Song!" And he *does*. Because everyone within earshot was dying to hear it.

Not all today's loudmouths are human. The spring peepers are starting to testify, and two Canada geese glide on the water, honking like kazoos.

A siren goes up from the Olivebridge Firehouse, winning the contest. The geese fly off, bugling sore losers. Two startled mergansers take off from the creek spill, wings beating twin Xs. The woods echo with revving large trucks and emergency horns gunning down 28A.

And then it's all over. I reach the stone bench just as the sun's rim slips behind the blue mountains. It feels Neolithic.

The sky cools and stills. A lavender hush descends. Peace.

Day 217. **April 18, 7:30 PM**

Pearlescent sky, sherbet colors. First little brown bat of the season, scooping gnats from midair. I'm delighted to see its acrobatic swoops. Hundreds of thousands of bats used to hibernate in the caves and abandoned cement mines near Rosendale, and a mysterious white-nose fungus struck down nearly all of them in the last decade, robbing the local mosquitoes of their alpha predator. Seeing a bat is great news.

Fish come up to the surface to feed, leaving concentric rings. A splash from an unseen leaper is so loud I jump. Sounds like somebody threw a whole ham in the water.

A bicyclist rides down the center line with just his left hand on the handlebar, holding a video camera in his right. I'm in his movie now.

That's okay. He's in mine too.

Day 218. **April 19, 5:45 PM**

Painted turtle crossing the road from one pond to another feels the vibrations of my oncoming car and draws into its shell. I pull over and carry it in the direction it's heading, holding it out to one side so it won't pee on my leg. Rites of spring.

Mares'-tail clouds, long and fibrous, like ghostly crochet hooks.

A strong northwest wind kicks up whitecaps. In the draws, trees unfurl the first tiny leaflets, a green so pale it doesn't look real. The platinum blonde of foliage.

A teenage girl wearing the triangle kerchief and old-ways long skirt of the Hutterian Brethren walks next to a tall young man in civilian clothes. High school friends, or an across-the-fence romance? Unlike many religious sects, the Hutterites send their children to local high schools. What is it like to shuttle between centuries, leaving the communal Bruderhof and daily prayer for the era of Snapchat and Instagram?

It's less windy up on the rise, where the trees offer shelter. Tips of branches are starting to leaf out, a tender lettuce-heart green. Soon there'll be no view of water between the bare branches; the woods will fill in. I catch a quick glimpse of an eagle flying through pines, and when I come around the curve, Eagle Guy the Older is on stakeout. He's wearing a heavyweight hoodie and greets me, "Boy, that wind is *fierce*."

I ask if he just saw an eagle take off from the nest, and he nods. "He's gone to get food. She's sitting the eggs." So they share nesting duties? He says they change shifts "about every two hours." Very feminist.

As I near the weir bridge, the eagle drops out of the sky like a thunderbolt. Seconds later, he flies back over the road with a gasping pierced fish and lands somewhere behind the guardrail. I speed up. When I reach the guardrail, he bursts up in front of me, giant wings beating the air in a clattering fountain of feathers and flashing scales, dragon-vast. The breath is knocked out of my lungs. He wheels over the path, swoops toward the nest, and veers off course, windblown. He takes his fish into the pine woods and doesn't emerge.

I catch up to Eagle Guy, rapt. "Did you *see* that?" He shows me the shot he took, close and crisp, of the eagle in profile. A foot-long trout gleams in his talons.

"Nice shot!" I tell him. My heart is still thumping.

"The eye's pretty clear. That's what you want, a clear eye," he says with reverence. So that's the trade secret, the Holy Grail of the eagle paparazzi. It seems like such a small thing to chase, day after day in wind, rain, and snow, but we all have our quests.

I tell him about my close encounter at the guardrail, and he says with a grin, "Don't you wish you had a camera?"

Day 219. **April 20, 5:10 PM**

Insanely full workday ends with a post-office run, dashing in at 4:59 as the Olivebridge postmistress clicks off the light. "Made it," she says. Yeah, with seconds to spare. I sit in the car and just breathe for a minute, watching the neighbor's goats graze. And that's what I need.

So instead of my usual walk, I park by the spillway and walk to the triangular marsh at the corner of Stone Church Road, a calm place if ever there was one. Red-winged blackbirds flit through tall backlit reeds. Distant beaver lodge. Three pine trunks gnawed bare at the bottom.

Frogs hop as I pass, plunking into brown water. A black-phase gray squirrel, ermine-sleek, runs up a tree trunk. A Canada goose mama broods her eggs while her partner stands by, looking uselessly male on a neighboring tuffet.

Bird calls: *pee-wee, pee-wee.* The squeaky-wheel *chaaawk* of a blackbird. Small woodpecker tapping. Tail-flicking wren at the edge of the swamp.

Up close, the sun-haloed reeds look shaggy and frayed. I notice how half-submerged logs first sprout patches of moss, then grass, then turn into long islands. Good turtle habitat. There are dozens on view, large and small. One of the bigger ones has a little one napping on top of its shell.

The sun warms my face. I am still and content.

Day 220. **April 21, 4:30 PM**

Sudden summer! Hazy and hot, with white air. Walkers in tank tops, bikers in shorts. Licks of yellow-green leaflets and lacy white flowering trees.

Day 221. **April 22, 5:20 PM**

What does it mean to take the same walk more than two hundred times? What will it mean when I miss one next week? I'm obsessed with this daily routine/not-routine and I still don't know why.

Leaves unfurling, a bit at a time. One deer grazing.

Tree falls in the forest. I hear it.

Day 222. **April 23, 8:20 AM**

Overcast, whitecaps. The mountains look unusually purple, a homegrown tribute to Prince. Nature in Cuban heel boots.

Random music of birdcalls, an orchestra tuning. Purple rain, stilled.

Day 223. **April 24, 7:20 PM**

Spandex-clad man and teen son, riding side by side:

"You liking that bike?"

"Seat's nicer than mine, that's for sure."

"It better be. That's a hundred dollar seat."

"Why would you spend a hundred bucks on a bike seat?"

"So your nuts don't fall asleep."

And there you have it, America.

I sit on the last bench till dusk. Holy silence, a sky like worn denim.

Day 224. **April 25, 6:55 PM**

I wake to the sound of helicopters, low and close, reporting for duty at the out of control wildfire in Minnewaska State Park. Photos online of the Shawangunk Mountains in flames.

It takes me all day to get down to the res. A ridge blocks my view of the fire some thirty miles south, but the air is uneasy. A streak of near-vertical cloud sticks up from the sun like Excalibur.

The woods are a singles bar tonight. Seven deer graze placidly on the embankment. Two more charge around them in circles, then chase each other into the trees. A couple of flickers give high-speed chase in figure eights, landing on tree trunks and taking off, pealing off calls that sound sort of like deejay scratches and sort of like "wheeee!"

And then there's the otherwise sane-looking woman whose freshly groomed poodle is wearing a navy dotted swiss swimsuit with pink ruffles.

Brindle sky. Setting sun drops into an eye between cloud and mountain, spreading a path of gold over gray water. There's a tall photographer next to the rail. Could it be the Sunset Man? I take a deep breath and turn to the sun, watching it drop out of sight before I walk toward him. Good luck charm.

Of course it's not him. Dark-framed glasses, a muttered hello. He walks back to his car, leaving me all by myself on the path. So I think.

And then I hear voices down by the shore: "Yeah! OH yeah!" Two dudes, Bill and Ted excellent, clowning around on the point where the eagles fish. They better not head for the nest.

I call out, "Hey, you guys, you'll get a hell of a fine if the DEP cops see you down there."

"We know!" Ted calls back.

"Just saying. Car usually drives by around sunset."

Well, sometimes it does. But it works. A few minutes later, Bill and Ted clamber back up the dike and climb onto their skateboards. As they glide past I hear one say, "Hey man, we gotta sleep out here some night."

"For sure!"

Day 225. **April 26, 1:40 PM**

Lovely weather for ducks. Cloud-lopped mountains, gray drizzle. Two swifts skim over the water, dipping down for quick baths on the wing.

Rain gets harder. I hope it'll put out the forest fire.

Day 226. **April 27, 12:30 PM**

Postcard-blue sky with comically small puffs of cloud, like a kid's diorama with cotton balls. My sixty-four-color Crayola box featured yellow green, green yellow, spring green, and sea green, among others; they're all out today. The country-club grass on the hillside is squashed down in two tire tracks: Louis CK, on the move.

Ten deer out grazing, a noon salad bar. They're scattered along the tiered hillside till two walkers stop to take photos. Then they run to the edge of the woods and resume grazing anxiously, jostling each other. One yearling stands briefly on hind legs to pummel another with forelegs. A few of the does look thick bellied. I wonder if there'll be more twins this year, since the winter was mild.

There's a cardinal singing: wolf whistle, *chee chee chee.*

I spot Eagle Guy the Gray and Eagle Gal the Scooter walking back from their post. Right behind their backs, an eagle swerves out of the woods and drops down to snag a trout. She lands hard in a nearby tree, and the sound makes them swivel. They both get some shots, but when I pass them and ask, "How'd you do?" Gray sounds dejected. "Mostly out of focus."

A runner stops on the Lemon Squeeze to talk to a man with a big dog. *Scofflaw,* I think, but as I get closer I realize it's a uniformed K-9 cop with a German shepherd. I join them and greet the dog, dark faced and muscular, with that lupine shepherdy musk. The handler tells me his dog is named Michael, after a K-9 cop from Oklahoma who lost his life in Afghanistan. Michael is trained for explosive detection. I hope he's just out for an exercise walk.

Day 227. **April 28, 3 PM**

Glum sky, gray ripples, two rowboats.

Oncoming walkers: a bearish man in a black suit and blazing white shirt, smaller woman in blue parka, skirt, and black tights. From half a mile away I peg them as Orthodox Jews. As they get closer, my hunch is confirmed by his beard and black yarmulke. He's a shambling, Zero Mostel–shaped man with a frizzy-haired woman who might be a young wife or grown daughter. There's a stiff distance between their bodies. As we pass, he averts his gaze in You're Not One of Us mode; I always think they can peg me as an apostate half shiksa. She makes deliberate eye contact, with a stilted "Hi, good afternoon."

I meet her eye and nod hello, wondering, *Does she mind?*

Two crows, one male bluebird, soaring from guardrail to crown of bare tree.

Day 228. **April 29, 8:20 AM**

Single small cloud topping Ashokan High Point like a wooly white hat. Water a rippling mirror.

Red-winged blackbird perched on a reed, flashing poppy-bright patches. Songbird village, tuning up for the day. The dandelions have morphed from bright yellow disks to fluffy white globes, and there's a goldfinch pair eating the seeds.

What is different today? Everything and nothing. My sadness at leaving for Maine, via LaGuardia Airport, finally breaking my unbroken streak. I love to travel, but this feels like leaving a lover. I turn at the end of the pathway for one last long look.

A red-tailed hawk buzzes my car as I wait at a traffic light near the train station, swooping from a Mexican deli with Cinco de Mayo flags to the pub sign across the street shaped like a derby hat. A raptor in downtown Poughkeepsie? I'd have to call that an omen.

Day 229. **April 30, 4:30 PM, Orono, Maine**

What does it mean to do something every day without fail? If you miss a day, did you in fact fail? Or is it a useful pause, a chance to pull back and reflect on the previous 228 days, or on the tyranny of all-or-nothing endeavors?

That's what I thought I'd be writing about on the first day I couldn't get to the Ashokan. (Orono really *is* too far; I've flown here for my online grad students' final workshop and reading.) I packed a copy of Bob Steuding's *The Last of the Handmade Dams*, which I've been dying to read, and I figured I'd keep my commitment alive by reading the history of the drowned towns and the dam's construction, and taking a walk along water—not hard, since UMaine's on a long island formed by the Penobscot and Stillwater Rivers. Orono is at one end and Old Town (of canoe fame) on the other, the campus sandwiched between the two. I'm staying in the graduate suite, across from a steampunk industrial plant with two massive brick chimneys, right on the Stillwater River. As soon as my workshop is finished, I go.

There's a dirt running path next to the river, uplifted in spots by thick roots. A fringe of trees separates it from the river: pine, white birch, cedar. Some of the cedars are massive, cracked open, like something out of a Grimm's fairy tale. An Old Town canoe drifts along the far bank: couple fishing. I flush out two mallards.

I miss the Ashokan a lot, but I have to admit it's delicious to set off into parts unknown. I don't know how far this path goes—all the way into town? It passes behind several frat houses, with homemade trails down the hill that probably lead from a kegger to make-out spots next to the river. There's a low plywood treehouse I take for a deer hunter's platform till I realize that it's topped with a Naugahyde couch. Par-tay!

The path starts to get squelchy. Not hard to see why: there are beaver-chewed stumps and toppled trees lying in shavings. At the edge of a wide swath of marsh, full of reeds, the path drops underwater. I can see it resumes a few hundred feet down, past the end of the marsh. What to do?

A second path veers to the left, with improvised bridges made out of old pallets. The pools on both sides are improbably filled with golf balls. Do the frat boys get drunk and whack shots off their hilltop? The path, which I'm hoping will circle behind the marsh on higher ground, turns out to meet stairs up the hillside, presumably leading to Alpha Tiger Woods Phi.

I turn back. The main path is hopeless; too wet. But what if I walk through the woods to the edge of the river? Its bank is a bit higher up. If

I stay parallel to the path, I could pick it back up again on the far side of the marsh.

There's a narrow trail down to the water's edge, made by what? Beavers? Deer? Students? I follow.

Within a few yards, it's tough going. The narrow trail isn't a trail anymore. I'm bushwhacking, bending branches and saplings aside. Are there Lyme ticks in Maine? Poison ivy? I haven't seen any telltale hairy roots climbing up trunks, but that doesn't mean it's not lying in wait, its slick maroon leaf buds still furled.

Also: bears. Black bears are the UMaine mascot. Are there live ones? Unlikely, this close to both campus and town, but I don't want to encounter a bear in this thicket. I peer through the undergrowth. I can see where the reeds stop, the end of the marsh. I thrash a diagonal through the thick woods. A small muddy stream cuts through, tumbling over wet rocks on its way to the river.

I hesitate. It's a natural boundary. I could just turn back, but a still, sure voice in my head tells me to keep going. I pick up a long stick to use as a staff and, feeling a little like Gandalf, pick my way over the wet rocks and up the far bank. It's clay-textured mud, full of deeply cut hoofprints—large and small deer—and something that looks almost feline, with a soft pad, four toes, delicate little claws.

I bushwhack a bit more and come out at a clearing. And there on the grass, backlit by afternoon sun, is a stunning red fox. We're not twenty feet from each other. His puffy tail gleams, pumpkin orange.

I look at fox. Fox looks at me. Then he turns with no trace of fear and trots into the reeds. I'm left gasping, hand pressed to my chest.

Day 230. **May 1, 11:11 PM**

One of my favorite students drives me to the Bangor Airport, and back home I go, via plane, subway, train, car, and reservoir walk. I'm tired to the marrow.

It's cold, dark, and raining. Fog curls around my ankles, and yes, I am a bit spooked. I've walked along the Ashokan at night many times, but never without stars and moonlight.

A plainsong of peepers. I'm home.

Day 231. **May 2, 5 PM**

Hudson River School sky over flat navy water, sun-silvered in patches. A break in the cloud cover spotlights Mount Tremper like Shangri-La.

Hippie family of five eating Fudgsicles. Sullen tween girl, bringing up the rear, twists both hands in the kangaroo pocket of her hoodie while clomping along in Doc Martens. Body English: I want *nothing* to do with these people.

Two boys with fishing poles sneak down to the edge of the water, Huck Finn and Tom Sawyer. I stop and look over the basin, trying to picture the valley beneath: the Esopus a swift-moving trout stream, the not-yet-drowned towns with their farmsteads and blacksmiths, the millwheel turned by Bishop's Falls. Then the desert of stumps being grubbed from the ground, the bodies exhumed, ancestral homes torched to their blackened foundations. Then mud, and the rising of water.

Birth and death at the hardscrabble farm. A red-and-white calf lies on a tuffet of hay among cattle and draft horses, licking new limbs. On the opposite side of the farmhouse, a red-tailed hawk disembowels a hen in a frenzy of yellow-gold feathers, beak bloodstained with meat.

Day 232. **May 3, 5:10 PM**

Haunted by yesterday's carnage, I survey the farmhouse field as I drive past. There's a large flock of chickens at the same spot. I'm startled to see the hawk in the center, still picking the carcass, surrounded by hens pecking seed. This strikes me as truly bizarre. That's their apex predator. Shouldn't they be, um, alarmed? It's like having a snack with the Zodiac Killer.

Birds are not us.

They're out in force at the reservoir. Songbirds sounding off, crows testifying, blue jays calling their squad. It's been raining all day, and they seem to be sharing the news of a lull.

Five mergansers swim away from shore in a V, single female followed by two mating pairs.

Low clouds felting the mountaintops, water rink-smooth. A couple of swallows dip low, speed skating over the surface, ice dancing with their reflections.

The path's lined with puddles, a few drowned pink worms, and a purple-tipped night crawler. There's a sudden upheaval of songbirds, shifting positions in treetops and trading alarmed calls. Then I hear it: the fluty *who-cooks-for-you* of a barred owl, down by the creek spill. Another swift predator.

A big driftwood stump in the shallows looks like a stag climbing out of the water. Above it, Xena is sitting her nest, white head barely visible over the wide wheel of sticks. She lets out a plaintive *skree skree*; sounds like *feed me.*

Day 233. **May 4, 4 PM**

Twin baby goats hop around their mom in the backyard pen next to the Olivebridge Post Office. They're insanely cute.

Inside, the talk is all fishing. Two local guys stand at the counter, one beefy, one wiry.

Beefy: "All these years, I never caught a trout."

Wiry: "You're kidding me."

Beefy: "Hundreds of bass, but no trout. Course I don't stay out for long. I don't catch something in half an hour, that's it, I'm done."

Wiry: "I smoked ten pounds already. I'm giving 'em away. I'm not even using the boat yet, just standing on shore, fishing spoons. I think the brown trout's even prettier than the rainbow. But my wife don't like trout so much—says it's too gamey."

Postmistress: "Bass has that nice white flake, with the fork."

Beefy: "They're best in the ice, or start of the season."

I head down to the res. I'm the only one walking today, and no wonder. It's cold and bone damp, with a needling rain that gets under your skin. The shoreline is a pointillist stipple of baby greens fading to white. No mountains at all, just a blanket of clouds. But the buds on the trees have unfurled into leaves, maples waving hello.

Day 234. **May 5, 12:30 PM**

Pathway conversations with neighbors. First Sarah Stitham, seamstress and Workday Wear clothing designer, who tells me she summited all thirty-five Catskill peaks over thirty-five hundred feet in seven months. I'm impressed. Sarah just shrugs. "The only way I'd find out which mountain was which was to climb them."

Next, Janet Steen, fellow writer and editor, out for a head-clearing stroll. "We're so lucky to have this," she says with a radiant smile.

Indeed. I stand still, listening to the music of whitecaps on driftwood. I close my eyes and instantly a sweet smell of green floods my nostrils, as if by closing off one sense I opened another. I breathe for a moment, drinking in tree smell, log music, and wind on my face. Then I open my eyes.

The mountains are purple, a stolid earth eggplant. Barn swallows and swifts make balletic spins. A cowbird pair sits side by side on the guardrail, like mismatched boots: him black with a chestnut head, her a dull brown.

Seven deer graze at the foot of the hill. Tall grass ripples like animal hide, seedheads swishing. I pluck a blade of new grass, stretch it between my thumbs, and blow into the makeshift reed, emitting a startlingly loud bagpipe blast.

The deer keep on grazing.

Day 235. **May 6, 4 PM**

Encounters with avian gods. Seven gulls are patrolling the Lemon Squeeze. A runner in yellow crosses the bridge, gulls swooping over her head like something out of Hitchcock. They circle and crisscross above, then resettle, five on one wall and two on the other. As I approach, they grow restive, eyeing me. Then they take to the air with a clamor of feline mews.

A huge bald eagle dive-bombs an interloper above Driftwood Cove, circling and banking, harassing the other bird until it flies off, a dark silhouette with slender curved wings. The eagle gives chase.

As I watch the duel, a compact, friendly man on a bike pulls up behind me. Osprey, he tells me, confirming my hunch. Then he takes out his iPhone and searches for a picture he took last month: a complete double rainbow, with closeups of one brightly colored span. "Disneyland," he says, grinning. "This place is amazing."

I tell him, "Enjoy your ride," and he answers, "Enjoy your . . . vision."

I do; I will.

Day 236. **May 7, 2:20 PM**

This morning as I'm washing dishes, two squirrels emerge from the navel-like hole in a nearby maple and run down the trunk, one after the other. Moments later, a much smaller squirrel face emerges. Checks all directions, sees parents are gone, and tentatively squeezes itself through the hole. Then it freezes, unsure how to move down the trunk. It finally clambers down a few inches, then scrambles back up, hanging onto the hole. An adult squirrel runs back up the tree, takes the baby in her mouth, and, instead of pushing it back into the nest, guides it down the trunk, letting it go and following after, nudging it on from behind. A Mother's Day parable for wistful empty nesters.

Variations on family all over the res. I arrive in the calm after rain. Newly washed air, the grass down the hillside a British Isles green. The water's blue platinum. A few rowers out in the distance, one slowly dipping his oars.

Group of seven adults with a baby carriage draped in a peach crochet throw. Young father of newborn: "Gramma? You wanna push her?" Gramma beams.

Two men walking together, one slight, with sloped neck and shoulders that suggest Down Syndrome. The taller man's body leans toward him, protective. Brothers, I'd guess. I say hi and they echo in unison.

Dad running behind a toddler in red cap and vest bombing along on a low red two-wheeler. Biker kid suddenly veers toward the stone bench, drops the bike on the pavement and plops down to sit. Dad follows gratefully. "Cool bike," I say. Kid looks at me like I'm from Mars and dad prompts, "Say thank you, Ida." So glad this confident, gender-neutral-dressed kid is a girl.

Only one ring-billed gull on the Lemon Squeeze wall. It glowers but does not take off as I pass. On the far side I spot something solid and brown hunkered under the guardrail. A groundhog? No. It's two Canada geese, side by side. They stiffen their necks, and I notice the female is holding one wing at an awkward angle. Is she injured? I sense movement, and as I watch, she twists her neck, yogi-like, onto her back. The male's neck stays tall. He's in sentry mode.

I sit very still on the opposite guardrail, willing myself invisible. A few moments later, a fuzzy pale yellow head pokes up from the female's wing feathers. Then a second.

A runner approaches. The babies pop under mom's wing, but the geese don't move. A bike passes, faster. They still don't move.

There's a couple down by the rise with a camera on a tripod. She's shooting his portrait. No one else on the pathway.

The two babies reemerge, followed by a third. There's movement beneath the arched wing. Are they jostling each other, or is there a fourth?

The photographer couple is finished, and they're walking toward me. The woman notices the geese and grabs her partner's arm. Without saying a word, they sit side by side on the guardrail a few yards from me, watching. She quietly sneaks a few photos.

Papa Goose relaxes and starts eating weeds. So does Mama, as baby number four pokes out its head. Papa stands. Mama does too, and babies number five and six tumble out. It's like a clown car. The yellow fuzzballs toddle around, never far from their parents, making soft little peeps.

Another biker glides up and brakes. He's wearing a neon-bright yellow jacket. "You checking out the baby geeselings?" he booms. "Is that what they call them?"

"Goslings," I tell him.

"Half of them'll be gone in a week. Eagles'll get 'em." And with that, he sails off. He may be right, but it seems pretty crass. The spell is broken. The photographer couple heads back toward their car and I walk up the rise.

Three does grazing, two visibly pregnant. They spot me and scatter, less zen than the geese.

The sky's clamping down, steely clouds rolling in. Six vultures spiral high in an updraft, and I feel my heart clutch. Then wonder why I value yellow chicks more than a trout—or, for that matter, a hungry vulture. Reservoir satori. Life is very big and we are very small.

An old woman stands staring out over the water. I say hi, and she answers me with a feeble hello. A teen girl walks over to join her. Her mother returns from her walk and all three generations head back to their car. The teen girl leans over the seat, helping Grandma fasten her seatbelt.

As I drive to the bridge, I pass a dead groundhog, belly fur yellow, four upraised legs stiff as an overturned hassock.

I feel very full, elevated and mournful at once. Something precious is flying past, too fast to catch. There are moments when you lay a finger alongside life's jugular and feel its pulse beating, a wild trembling thing. Life announces itself, waking you out of your everyday stupor and flooding your body with awe.

And then you turn onto the highway and drive down to Kenco to shop for a rain jacket, Mother's Day discount, 20 percent off! Which also is life.

Day 237. **May 8, 8:20 AM**

Air washed new, fragrant. Warm sun drying puddles. The mountains wear clouds like a shawl.

Day 238. **May 9, 6:45 PM**

Moonsliver. New wildflowers blooming: garlic mustard, bluets. After sundown I stand at the rail, staring down at what I think is a doe lying down with her newborn fawn for a patient ten minutes before realizing that it's just a patch of bare dirt. Behold the Great Naturalist! (Well, it was dusk.)

Day 239. **May 10, 7:40 PM**

On the way to the res I stop by my neighbor's to pick up a lightweight collapsible fishing pole. "That's a good poaching rod," he tells me, spinning a few of his own Ashokan adventures, including a time when he went skinny-dipping back in mellower, pre-9/11 days. Two DEP cops came by in a patrol boat, and he tried to convince them that he'd lost a lure and was diving for it. They laughed so hard they didn't fine him.

The sky is a stunner, with clusters of bottom-lit clouds in various textures. A whole school of mackerel sky.

Several people head back toward the parking lot, but I'm the only one walking out as the sun goes down. There's someone at the far end of the path, wandering back and forth between rails with a camera. It's the Sunset Man.

Of course it is. I feel my breath catch, that intake of hope.

"Oh, it's *you*," he says as he approaches. "Gorgeous night, huh?"

"It's just about perfect," I say, as we pass each other, grinning like fools. Was that *it*, after all these weeks? Gorgeous, perfect, so long?

We both slow down, stopping to look at our separate views. He takes a few photos. He waits by the guardrail. I start walking back, not too fast. He takes a few more. It's a tango.

The sky goes pastel, then tropical. The still water shimmers with color. And there he is, right at my shoulder.

"I knew this was going to be a good one," he says. "The way the clouds looked. And it keeps getting better and better." He asks my name again, reintroducing himself. Then he shows me his digital camera, flipping through photos he's taken: light, mountains, reflection. He has a great eye.

There's a lone rowboat out, a classic silhouette. "Like a Winslow Homer," he says, framing the shot. The sky's getting wild streaks of orange, deep purple.

"It's just about climaxing now," the Sunset Man says with a grin. He's joking, but um, that's one hell of a line. So's his next: "Was it good for you? I want to smoke a cigarette. It's that afterglow thing."

"I think it's still glow," I say. Batting it back.

And we talk. Sunsets, art, the Pacific Northwest. He remembers that I'm a writer, which I like, then compliments himself on remembering, which I like less. I ask him if he exhibits his photos. Not often, he says, but he posts them online and has won a few contests. The sky has grown darker around us, a cape swirling shut.

We walk back to the lot (when did it get decided that we'd leave together?), passing through the red glow of the safety light next to the barrier columns. Our cars are the only two left. He looks at my bumper, surveying its patchwork of slogans. "Good sticker," he says, and I wonder which one. Nobel Prize for Pete Seeger? Howl if you like City Lights Books? Or Adventure Awaits?

I vote for the third.

This feels like a cue to suggest a drink sometime, possibly now. But whose line is it?

We look at each other. As I try to find the right playful-but-I-really-mean-it tone, he says, "Well," pulls his keys from his pocket, and heads for his car. Lifting a hand in a brief, sudden wave, he gets in and backs up, taillights tracing a double red arc. It's so quick I'm left gasping for air, like a fish that's been hooked and thrown back.

Well, *what*?

Day 240. **May 11, 7:20 AM**

I wake up to bright sun and get right in the car. There's a pickup truck covered with decals in the Olivebridge lot, and as I approach it, I hear liquid birdsong and look for the source.

"That a Baltimore oriole?" calls a voice from across the lot. The truck's owner approaches. Grimy cap, long beard, Carhartts: central casting.

"I think so. Very orange. I can't see its tail markings."

He nods. "I know the birds. I get scarlet tanagers up on my mountain, but you don't never see them. They're too elusive. Stay up in the treetops."

No screenwriter making up dialogue would combine "don't never" and "elusive." He reaches into his truck and hands me a pair of binoculars. "Might be kinda dirty."

It is, yes, a Baltimore oriole, gray wings and gold breast. "You wanna see more of those, cut an orange in half and nail it to a tree," says the bird-watching mountain man. "That there's the female. That's her mating call."

Yes, well.

Two red squirrels run down a log. Two more court from trees twenty feet apart, rattling off a mechanical *chirr*, backlit tails flashing red in the sun.

Day 241. **May 12, 8:10 PM**

The sun's already down, but the sky is still glowing (I will not say after-glow). From the Frying Pan, a breathtaking panorama of mountains, sunset-gold water, the focal point of the arched bridge. In the foreground, three women with cell phone screens glowing.

Two are big happy girls wearing matching tie-dyed shirts, walking shoulder to shoulder and stopping for selfies. The third is a narcissist posed on the guardrail, tossing her hair as she skypes with her boyfriend *on speakerphone*! It's all I can do not to grab her iPhone and hurl it into the water.

Once I'm out of earshot of his overamplified voice, I hear something new. Crickets! First of the season. Like the spring peepers, they start thinly scattered, so I can hear individual insects, the pattern of call and return.

There's also a cloud of black gnats, swarming around me so I feel like Pigpen.

Small dark duck swimming solo, then a murmuration of starlings, swirling in recombinant patterns as they fly over the water. I stand at the rail for a while, watching night fall, and the tie-dye girls overtake me. We trade hellos, and as they walk on, one sings to the other, "Hello, hello-lo, hello, hello-lo" to the tune of "Hava Nagila." Her exuberance cheers me.

The moon is half-full. One minute I look up and it's all I see. The next there's a blazing star next to it. Hello, Venus!

By the time I get back to my car, constellations are forming. As I drive away, my headlights illuminate a pregnant doe next to the road. She gives me the same "Really?" look of disdain I gave to the girl with the speaker-phone. We're all someone else's intruder.

Day 242. **May 13, 5:25 AM**

No idea why I woke up at 5:10 a.m., but it's already light and the sky's thick with birdsong. Go!

There's a dead porcupine on the road to the reservoir. Bristles scattered, a smear of congealed blood, black leather paws clenched into little clawed fists.

The sun is a savage orange rising between banks of cloud. The tops of the mountains are briefly persimmon.

The hardwoods have leafed out in vivid fresh greens, no more lace. Most of the leaves are full size now but still hanging limp. When I pluck a yellow-green maple and hold it between my two fingers it feels like a membrane.

Day 243. **May 14, 3 PM**

I park near the West Hurley dike road, donning my who-are-you-kidding fishing gear: tan baseball cap, windbreaker, backpack with collapsible pole sticking out. The disguise is undermined by my Pete Seeger and City Lights bumper stickers (on a nontruck) and more essentially by gender. I've sometimes spotted a male/female pair out fishing; most often it's two old guys, two young guys, or one of each. But I have never, not once, seen a woman shore fishing alone.

Well, there's one now: me. Never mind that a closer inspection would find my backpack bait-free. I have my license and pole, and if a DEP cop stops me on one of these paths, I'm within my rights. Letter o' the law, bub. I'm walking the walk.

The waterline is so high there's no beach at all, so I follow an inland path, hoping to reach the wild point past the cluster of rowboats. Bluets dust the grass at the start of the trail, and there's a tangle of oily maroon poison ivy, which disappears as it gets shadier, yielding to mottled rattlesnake weed and a lone partridgeberry, red and round as a marble.

The trail leads to a pond that's been quarried on one end, leaving a pile of big bluestone slabs as an island. The water's clear, sparkling. It looks like a moose should be drinking here.

There's no clear path to the reservoir's edge, but I can see water through the trees. I follow a crumbling stone wall, which makes me wonder how long ago that pond was a quarry. Did it predate the dam? Was its bluestone used to construct the dike? I try to imagine these woods full of men in suspenders, loading stone onto carts hauled by mules.

I spot a dark curl of dried stool, full of berry seeds. Bear. But it's shriv-eled; not recent. One of my neighbors just saw a tiny cub fast asleep on a tree branch over Route 28A. Cubs mean vigilant moms, and I wonder if I should head back to my car. But I'm closer to the waterline now than the trail, so I push on.

The point is completely submerged, with dozens of small trees emerg-ing from floodwater. The drowned forest looks eerie, like footage from *Beasts of the Southern Wild*. I hear something banging against the trunk of a large tree and step closer to look. It's an enormous dead carp, rolling against the base of the trunk with every wave, so big it sticks out on both sides of the tree. Mouth open, a rigid white O, with white barbels on either side, stiff as porcupine quills. The scales look like huge dirty sequins, yel-lowish tan. The ridged fins are the size of my hand. It's a long time since my deckhand days, but I'd guess at least twenty-four inches and ten or twelve pounds, what we called a "money fish."

Monster goldfish, slamming a tree trunk. I can't look away. Then I think of that bear, of the pervasive smell of dead fish, and a voice in my head says, *Get out.*

I stumble along the drowned shore to the rowboats. The water's so high that a couple of boats are afloat, still chained to their trees. I see a tire, part of a Styrofoam cooler, a Rolling Rock can. What we leave in our wake.

Day 244. May 15, 2:30 PM

Cold and blustery with spatters of rain. I'm driving on Spillway Road, where there's whitewater coursing over the falls. For the first time in months, water tumbles down the wide concrete steps that funnel the

reservoir's overflow back to the creek. Whitecaps churn up the basin, with white veils of rain in the mountains. Of course I get out to look.

As soon as I open the door of my car, I smell pine sap and honeysuckle. There's a pile of fresh-cut white pine on the roadside, two big bushes blooming. The air vibrates with waterfall music. I stand on the bridge, feeling spray on my face as water spills over the curving cement edge and splashes down four giant tiers. It's exciting to be at eye level with the overflow, and I realize what it reminds me of: the sloshing seal pond at the Central Park Zoo. When I was a kid, there was nothing I loved more than watching their sleek bodies shoot past behind glass, sending cascades of water over the edge.

I walk down to the triangle marsh, where no turtles sunbathe; no sun. A lone red-winged blackbird sits at attention on a shredded cattail, flashing scarlet and gold epaulets. The water's clouded with specks of green algae and thousands of lily pads. The roadside is dotted with winter cress, clumps of fuzzy mullein, the spiked asterisks of bull-thistle leaves.

The aerator fountains are on, and their windblown spray looks like white curtains.

Day 245. **May 16, 7:15 PM**

High winds all day, tossing trees. When it clears in the evening, the sky is brilliant blue and smells like fresh laundry. Only one other person is out. I spot him ahead on the Lemon Squeeze, next to a tall metal frame that's not the right shape for a tripod. He's pacing a little, hand pressed to his ear.

As I get closer, I start to hear words. "I'm on the bridge . . . thought I had a spare tube, but I don't." I look at the shadow the object has cast on the wall: two spoked wheels. It's an overturned bicycle, standing upright on its seat and handlebars. He's got a flat tire.

I shoot him a sympathetic look, but he's lost in his phone call, his back to me, pacing.

I walk out to the weir bridge and back without noticing much but tall grass and a whole lot of goose poop. The sun's squatting on the horizon, blazing a gold path, and I think of Stonehenge. I hurry through the woods on the rise, hoping to get a clear view before it drops out of sight, but I'm distracted by shuffling in dry fallen leaves. After searching around for a moment, I spot the perp: a gray squirrel, scuffling for seeds on the forest floor. I look up and the sun's gone. I missed it.

The sunset is subtle, a pensive sky. I stand staring out at the water for a long time, lost in thoughts that don't gel. After a while, I realize there's a break in the pattern of waves, and something dark underneath. My first thought, irrational: a whale's going to breach!

But it's a log, as long as a phone pole, with a Y-shaped fork on one end that, for a blink of an eye, suggests a fluke. It doesn't look like a whale. It looks like a log. But how long was I staring at that stretch of water without noticing it? And suddenly there it was. Sometimes it's the things you don't see.

I walk back into twilight. And then I look up at the moon, as a great blue heron flies past it in silhouette. Just that one instant, no other.

Sometimes it's the things you *do* see.

Day 246. **May 17, noon**

The power flickers three times and goes out while I'm working at my computer. Two days of high winds; had to happen. Of course I head straight for the res. But as I grab my car keys, a flash of orange streaks past the window, grabbing my eye. It's a Baltimore oriole. *Two* Baltimore orioles, chasing each other around the wisteria, then tumbling onto the ground and smacking together, a bright thrash of yellow-orange feathers.

Orioles mating. As portents go, I'll take that over dead carp.

On the drive to the res, I notice a fresh yellow center line, dotted with orange safety cones so we'll know not to get our tires striped with wet paint. Just past the post office I catch up with a DO NOT PASS truck, which is driving slowly, lights flashing like a parade float. At the intersection with 28A, three more paint trucks sit, blinking, a toddler wet dream of construction equipment in all shapes and sizes. The driver of the largest truck is a middle-aged woman. Yes!

The sky is deep charcoal, which gives all the new leaves a yellowish cast, shades of pea soup and mustard. Butter and eggs—my favorite wildflower name—in bloom.

On the guardrail, a brown-headed male cowbird sits, flanked by three females. They fly off, but I see the same grouping twice more. Are they

Mormons, a cowbird ménage? Then I remember that cowbirds don't sit their own eggs but lay them in other birds' nests. Devious bitches. Real Housewives of the Ashokan.

Guy with Marine haircut wearing a tank top, SUNS OUT GUNS OUT, holding hands with his mother. He looks at me funny. Before leaving home I swapped my heavy coat for a smocklike red jacket, then realized it was colder down here and added a scarf and beret. I look like a caricature of a painter from the Famous Artists School in the back of old comic books, next to the Sea Monkeys and x-ray specs.

Driving home, I notice a yard that's been bulldozed flat. At the far end, a huge Buddha statue, cast in concrete. Not to quibble, but ripping out half an acre of living things to put up a Buddha seems to be missing the point.

A guy with a chain saw piles rounds of dead ash. A dummy deer target lies flat on its side with its head hanging loose.

These are perhaps some of the ten thousand things.

There's a newborn red calf in the pasture, a muddy cow scratching its neck on a fencepost. I realize that I notice other things more when I've been to the res. I slow down, pay attention, look around, and look up. For years when I've interviewed writers who teach, I've asked, "What's the most important thing you can give to your students?" I like David Means's answer: he tells them to go home by a different route so they'll notice new things.

That's good writing advice. (So is his colleague Amitava Kumar's: "Walk every day and write every day.") In its honor, I drive to Davenports Farm Stand, where I buy a Costa Rican chicken wrap and sit by the little dug pond to eat lunch. It's surrounded by yellow flag iris and mint runners. No koi this spring—too many kids tossing in food? There's a ghostly sense-memory of Maya and Zane playing tag here on warm afternoons when they were little. Now Maya's in college and Zane's a Marine, and they're both twenty-one.

I'm aware that the shape of my life is different than most people's. I could do this every day, take a reservoir walk at midday and eat lunch by a pond. But I don't. I wouldn't have come here today if it weren't for the blackout. No internet access, a mandated pause that feels like a gift from the sky.

It's part money pressure, the unending freelancer juggle; there are days when I leave my desk only to spread out a proofreading job on the dining room table, when I eat standing up, skimming books to assign for review.

Duty. Too much goddamn duty. And right out the door, all this *life* going on.

Day 247. **May 18, 4:25 PM**

Avian fuckers du jour: two slender gray catbirds. I spot them on opposite sides of the outhouse roof taking dainty hops toward each other. Hop, hop, hop, hop, and then suddenly wham, bam, thank you ma'am. It's over in seconds. He flies into a neighboring tree, and she sits on the outhouse roof, preening.

On the walkway, a pregnant young woman pushes a stroller. Scarlet tanager high on a treetop, a bold flash of red.

Day 248. **May 19, 11:50 AM**

Big-hair clouds. Stacked cumulus to the east, dense gray mass to the west. I arrive at the reservoir just as the rain does. However wet my clothes get, I'll have to drive to Manhattan in them. So I walk out fast under a dysfunctional folding umbrella, stand at the guardrail, and watch raindrops pock the water's flat surface. They look like pores on something alive.

The pink mitten is gone! It's the end of an era!

Day 249. **May 20, 6:30 PM, New York City**

I wake to jackhammers and sirens. New York morning wildlife: pedigreed dogs, grimy pigeons. On the upside, a small boy waits at the bus stop in top-to-toe Captain America costume, and nobody blinks. At the corner bakery, the customer behind me is a six-foot-three Asian male with waist-length black hair, pink glasses, and a black lace blouse. An elderly Jewish man asks the tattooed Latina at the cash register if she'll run away with him. "Aw, Jerry, you're sweet," she says, bagging his bagel and shmear. Morning ritual.

I'm supposed to head home "before rush hour," but the first parent minicrisis stretches that to "after dinner," the second to "I'll spend the night." Feeling burdened and sad, I tell my small, anxious parents I'm going to walk on the Central Park reservoir; I'll be back here in less than an hour, don't worry.

But I'm worried. This part of life is so hard. My parents are growing dependent as Maya becomes independent; I'm swapping one caretaker hat for another.

And breaking my daily commitment, again.

What's the point? If I've already broken my every-day vow, why keep going? I'm hearing the hoofbeats of failure. *Pack it up, kid, you're through.*

I try to tease myself into a new kind of stubborn. Maybe this is the lesson I need: not to go on without fail, but to go on despite failing. Persistence is victory.

It's worth a try. Because stopping at this point would break me. When I walk on the reservoir, I'm neither mother nor daughter. I'm not even walking a dog. I'm doing it just for myself, something women my age rarely get to declare.

My breath deepens as soon as I climb up the stairs to the path that circles the water. A flock of mallards wheels past me in magic-hour light. There are Canada geese, grebes, and buffleheads, all kinds of gulls. It's the Ashokan's big-city cousin, linked to the Catskills by aqueduct tunnels. A blocky WPA-era stone building at one end mirrors the ones on the weir bridge. I head toward it, following several Japanese tourists as disdainful runners stream past on our left.

I spot something gray moving down by the waterline. Rat, I assume. But no, it's a chubby raccoon with glossy gray fur and a bristling ringtail, trundling along the water's edge, stopping every so often to dip a paw into a clot of green algae.

It's *fishing*. A block from Fifth Avenue.

I walk next to the chain-link fence, pausing when the raccoon does. Dozens of overgroomed runners stream past, flashing headphones and gym-toned thighs, unaware that there's something wild six feet away. The raccoon finally scoops up a fish. I watch it chew, beady eyed and intent. Black cheeks and white eyebrows, a feral intelligence.

Red columbines, pink rhododendrons. Two overfed squirrels binge on sunflower seeds at the base of a tree; they have a benefactor.

As I leave Central Park, I pass a female weightlifter with magnificent haunches, then a Park Avenue matron pushing a very old dog in a baby stroller. I want to kiss New York City.

Day 250. **May 21, 4:15 PM**

I get home to discover a bear's torn the door off my garbage shed, strewing orange peels and bones down the hillside. I'll deal with it *after* my reservoir walk.

As soon as I step on the walkway, I feel like a masseur just laid hands on my shoulders. I take a deep breath. Then another. I stand watching barn swallows fly-catch and wheel.

The woods ripple with chipmunks. There's a revolting amount of goose poop near the bridge, as if hundreds of birds have bivouacked there for the night. Two families glide by, the first with six yellow goslings, the second with four midsize tweens, baby fluff morphing from yellow to brown. They veer ashore, clambering up the steep bank, chomping weeds. Some of the grass is already waist high, flecked with spittlebug foam.

Walking back, I'm approached by a chatty black family from Florida, tall rangy father, teen daughter and son. They've come north for another son's graduation from Marist College and decided to drive from "Pokippywhatever" to see the Catskills. They can't get over the height of the mountains, the number of trees, how few houses there are. "You *live* here?" The son sounds incredulous. "What do people, like, *do*?"

The dad wants to know when this road was built, and what used to be here before it was dammed. Having just finished reading *The Last of the Handmade Dams*, I fill him in on New York City's turn-of-the-century land grab, the two thousand people forced out of their homes. "Cities need water, cities take water," he says with a rueful nod.

On the pathway, I spot a mysterious speckled green sphere, brittle skinned, light as a ping-pong ball. It turns out to be an oak apple, a growth that forms around the larva laid in a leaf bud by a gall wasp. For centuries these galls were crushed with ferrous sulfate and gum arabic to make a permanent ink, in widespread use until the twentieth century. The oldest known Bible, the fourth-century *Codex Sinaiticus*, was written with oak apple ink. And I'm holding the source in my hand.

Day 251. **May 22, 4:40 PM**

The triangle marsh is clotted with silver-dollar lily pads and unfurling ferns. Indignant blackbirds chuck warnings, their wings flashing scarlet and gold: There's a *person* here!!!

Yes, well. Excuse me for staring.

Three beaver trees, stripped of low bark with gnawed waists. Biplane dragonflies landing on leaves. Stream of bubbles from something down deep in the mud. A great blue heron wings overhead, ready to take up its post.

I try to become heron-still, heron-patient. The dense, layered music of birdcalls and frogs separates into strands, and then individual voices: *this* bullfrog, *that* blackbird. A tenorish croaking. A deep, strangled gulp. Two mourning doves, not quite in unison. The monotone ratcheting of a gray tree frog.

And I realize, once I get still enough, that there are painted turtles on nearly every wet log, nestled on tuffets of moss and floating in piles, little turtles on bigger ones' backs. A green frog floats spread-eagled, perfectly still, with just its eyes over the waterline.

A black sedan speeds by at normal back-road speed—nothing hot rod, maybe forty-five miles an hour—and it seems insane. What passes for human "normal" is so far from nature.

I stop at the Olivebridge lot and sit on the stone bench for a long time, lost in thought, what they used to call woolgathering. Then I hear a siren-like voice from the parking lot, rising in inchoate howls of despair. *Yikes,* I think, *unhappy kid.* But when I turn my head, there's no child in sight. A small dark-haired woman strides toward me, fists jammed deep into pockets, her mouth a straight line. A few paces behind her, a pale woman, knock-kneed, in capris and white windbreaker, stomps down the center line. A few moments later she lets out a guttural howl, working her way up a scale of misery.

Oh. She's impaired. And her aide turns to snap, "Stop it. Stop. STOP!" like she's taming an animal. There's rage in her body. The pale woman moans again, louder. They're both at the end of their ropes, and I turn away to give them privacy, wondering if I should intervene or if it will make something worse. There's a moving reflection on burnished blue water. Then I see an eagle, strong wings working hard, heading home. What does it make of the woman's loud moans?

Driving back, roadside daisies in clusters. Four vultures butcher a roadkill deer in a ditch. Their naked red heads bending down as they tear.

Day 252. **May 23, 8:00 PM**

Road paving: FRESH OIL and LOOSE GRAVEL, petroleum stink.

The sun's already down, hiding out behind clouds with an orange deckle edge. Five light shafts fan upward like theatrical footlights, gelled in Follies Pink and Bastard Amber.

A great blue heron flaps over the water and lands on the curve of the beached-whale log. There's a pause. Then the great wings extend and he lifts off again. He lands at the waterline, wades out with deliberate steps, and stands still as a lamppost. I think of the Hermit tarot card.

It's twilight now, but I head for the woods, which are dark and silent. No leaf-scrabbling chipmunks, no birdsong. Then a loud, sudden cry from the eagles' nest, sharp staccato and then an extended *skreeeee* that I translate as "STELLLL-LAAH!"

I'm the only one left on the walkway. I let the dark fall around me, a swirling gray cape. I've felt raw all day long, and the evening calm soothes me. I start to hear voices, and make out an uneven silhouette moving through granular dusk.

Two men, holding hands. They're surprised when they see me loom out of the darkness. One says, "Suddenly, a person."

Day 253. **May 24, 10:20 AM**

Morning birds hallelujulating. One cormorant bobbing, one walker, one bike (older woman in white, sitting tall in the seat, gliding with hands clasped behind her back: Look Ma, no hands!).

Old hippie walking old dog. Gray beard and gray muzzle.

Day 254. **May 25, 6:10 AM**

Spotted fawn crossing the road on spindly new legs. Mother waiting in woods, backlit by morning dapple.

The rising sun is white gold, too bright to look at directly. The reservoir ripples like blue sateen sheets on the world's largest waterbed; Barry White should be crooning.

Bright orange blaze of a Baltimore oriole, winging from tree to tree. Backlit high grasses and cobweb strands. Richard Serra textures on the guardrail, constellations of rust.

A scrap of white paper, right on the pathway. I unfold it, hoping for mystery. It's a receipt for $10.58 from Ming Moon Chinese takeout in Shokan.

It's morning. It's hot. There are birds going crazy in treetops. I hear a rusted-hinge *craaawk* and the great blue heron glides overhead, long feet pointing back like a rudder.

Coming around the last curve on the rise, I spook two young deer just about to jump over the guardrail. They nudge each other—*I will if you will*—then turn tail and run down the hill, flag tails bobbing.

Two Canada goose heads crane up through high grasses like periscopes. They've bedded down on the shoulder. As I get closer, two more heads pop up, then two more. They look wary, and then I see why: there's a tuffet of fuzzy gray down on the grass, like an exploded sleeping bag. A dozen or more goslings, sleeping together like a pile of puppies. Their heads all face inward, so it looks like a downy gray tutu with multiple heads. One of the adult males gets up to play bad cop, snake-necking at me with a hiss. The inside of his beak is bright pink.

I stand still until they get calm. The other adults get up and start munching crown vetch while Mad Dad stands guard. Two big goslings follow, stretching their stubby wings, and the rest rise all at once. Blinking and stumbling on rubbery feet, they sort themselves into a loose line between the adults, and the whole group marches across the pathway. I count nineteen babies, in batches of three different sizes.

No wonder there's been so much goose poop.

I start back, squinting into hot sun. The exercise walker approaching is reading a book, gazing down at its pages. I've seen her before, and I'm always astonished. What world would she rather be in than this one?

Day 255. **May 26, 7:40 PM**

Every year there's a heat wave that slingshots you straight into summer, ready or not, here it comes. It hit ninety today, no hint of a breeze. Even now, close to late sundown, heat bakes off the pavement. The egg-yolk sun drops through the slot between cloud and horizon, laying a triple reflection across mirror water. As it does, a hundred swallows shoot out from under the bridge, like bats coming out of a cave. Their swooping reflections double the number, an airborne ballet.

Day 256. **May 27, 5:35 AM**

Pastel sunrise, rays, halo, and all. It could be a gospel album cover.

The hill is a sea of grass, tall and unruly. A doe looks up with a mouthful of greens, sees me coming, and high kicks it into the woods.

Lone rowboat off Brodhead Point. There's a Milky Way swirl of yellow pine pollen dusting the shallows. It has an ominous look, a flaw in the water. Xena glides past, barely flapping her wings. Morning stroll.

Three vultures in a roadside ditch, gorging on a dead deer. When I slow down to rubberneck, one flaps its wings at me. The fourth set of black wings has a black head as well. It's a crow, picking bones.

I gas up my car, circling back via Boiceville, where I spot a sign with a graphic icon of a round-headed *L* bent over an open book: Library.

I want one of those. It can go next to the sign that says NOTICE.

I cross the bridge over the rushing Esopus Creek, tailgated by a large truck. After several curves, I pull over onto the shoulder to let him streak past. I'm about to get back on the road when I realize I'm right next to the gate of a former estate. Two crumbling stone pillars with lichen obscuring carved letters: ESTELINA. Stone railings fan off to each side.

Oh, come *on*. Got to. I park.

An abandoned driveway winds uphill into the woods. It's rutted and ancient, covered with moss and dog violets. A stream runs alongside, its banks muddy. I see several deep hoofprints, one hiking boot. There are hemlocks and wrist-thick grapevines; whatever ESTELINA once was, it's been decades since anyone drove there. But there might be an old stone

foundation or even a ruin, like the burned-out hotel near the summit of Overlook Mountain.

I walk up about half a mile. The driveway grows fainter and disappears into a flat glade of ferns that would make a great trysting place. I bet Onteora High School truants come here to smoke weed.

If there are ruins, I don't find them.

I drive past several logging operations with huge stacks of pine trunks in muddy bald gashes. Why are they clear-cutting here, on protected lands? I taste bile at the back of my throat. Stumps like vandalized graves.

Someone's named their driveway Vision Path Road. Just past it, the haunted-looking Snyder's Tavern, unpainted for decades, with sumac obscuring the porch and Budweiser neon on one peeling window. There's an octagonal Victorian turret with sinister lace curtains that may have been hanging there since the place opened, before Prohibition. But there's a new-looking truck and a REPEAL THE S.A.F.E. ACT sign, so it isn't abandoned. It's just giving the finger to curb appeal.

Watson Hollow, West Shokan Post Office, Olive Free Library, Calvary Baptist, FORMER SITE OF BRODHEAD BRIDGE sign, and then I'm at Brodhead Point, where manly men fish. Six burly late-model pickups. Woof!

Day 257. **May 28, 9:40 AM**

Fourth day of this infernal heat wave. Sky looks like skim milk.

Today's news is butterflies. Yellow and black tiger swallowtails, cabbage whites, fluttering sulfurs. Also grasshoppers, earning their name. Inchworms twisting from trees on long silken threads.

Racing team: whippet-thin riders on whippet-thin bikes.

Solicitous mom, to squinchy-faced daughter in hot-pink bike helmet: "Why are you so cranky today?"

Daughter (cranky): "I'm *not cranky!*"

Mom (dripping empathy): "Just having one of those days?"

Daughter (eye rolling): "Yeah mom. One of those days."

Mom (chastising): "Watch where you're going!"

Well, there went *that* Bonding Experience.

At the triangle marsh, the first pond lilies have opened, fat white corsages the size of peonies. There are dainty blue flag water iris, turquoise dragonflies swooping from plant to plant, lace wings iridescent. A huge snapping turtle floats with its head on the surface, its massive shell arched like a knobby brown pumpkin. As soon as it spots me it dives for the mud.

Day 258. **May 29, 8:15 AM**

Already hot, hazy, and obscenely humid. Two racing bikers stand in the shade of the DEP cop hut, eating bananas.

Tall grasses in full seedhead, studded with wildflowers: oxeye daisies, hawkweed, cow vetch, crown vetch, yellow sweet clover, peppergrass, bladder campion, lavender aster, English plantain, yarrow, buttercup, butter and eggs, daisy fleabane, sweet everlasting. The names are a poem.

Two fireplug-shaped guys in motorcycle boots, one wearing a vest with a POW/MIA patch, the other with a faded, tobacco-stained American flag bandanna, walk past speaking what sounds like Croatian. They both nod politely.

Day 259. **May 30, 1:20 PM**

Sneaking one in between overnight rain and afternoon thunderstorms. Lots of high clouds loom over what I will forever think of as calico-ass mountains.

Light breeze swishing high grasses: amber waves of grain. So many flags out for Memorial Day. Flags on flagpoles (including a yellow Don't Tread On Me), rippling from fenders of Harleys, mounted on houses, tied to fence posts, planted in window boxes and tubs of petunias. I remember Papa hanging a forty-eight-star flag from our roof gutter when I was a kid. Larry, David, and I dressed in blue shorts and red-and-white striped shirts to wave little flags at fire trucks and drum majorettes and old men saluting in VFW caps. There were Fourth of July town picnics. Each kid got a strip of coupons: Good for One Hot Dog, Good for One Cotton Candy, Good for One Straw Hat, Good for One Pony Ride. Fireworks at dusk. We curled up on a bedspread to ooh and ahh.

Then Vietnam, then Kent State. I stopped reciting the Pledge of Allegiance and wore a black armband to school. I dated a Jerry Garcia look-alike with an upside-down flag sewn on the back of his work shirt and played Jefferson Airplane's "Volunteers" album till every groove crackled.

A country-western Falstaff struts past with a beer, crooning a song to the bottle-blonde woman he's with. Her smile is embarrassed.

An extremely old man in flat plastic sandals, one leg in a stretch bandage, limps next to his oversolicitous daughter.

Eleven Hutterites in traditional dress: older man in full beard and suspenders, women in kerchiefs and ankle-length skirts, younger man in a plain white shirt and dark pants, little girl in pastel blue dress and straw hat. Every one of them greets me, except for three women who stop to lean over the Lascaux wall, watching barn swallows while their long skirts billow.

Three big birds ride air currents on outstretched wings. A bicyclist with a church-lady hairdo tells her companion smugly, "Well, *that's* a very American thing to see on Memorial Day." She may speak the truth in the era of candidate Trump: they're not eagles, they're vultures.

Day 260. **May 31, 7:55 PM**

Why I love nature: it does not give a shit about money.

Day 261. **June 1, 5:50 AM**

Sun up, slanting low, carving dark shadows on emerald mountains. The tree line goes all the way up now. All green.

Day 262. **June 2, 1:30 AM**

So-late-it's-early walk under the stars. I've driven home after the Bennington Video Picnic where Maya screened a hypnotic short film. While we walked across a wide lawn to the outdoor screening site, I interrupted her twice in midsentence to point out a baby squirrel, then a great blue heron flying overhead. She told me, "You're getting *distracted* by nature."

First fireflies! Yellow semaphore, ghostly.

My brothers and I used to catch them for milk-bottle lanterns. The heavy glass bottles were delivered every morning to a tin box outside the kitchen door. Our backyard had a rose trellis and two unpruned apple trees next to an overgrown hedge. I loved sneaking outside after dinner. Already in my pajamas, I'd hunch on cool grass in the hedge's blue shadow, watching the fireflies pulse, the warm glow of the house's lit windows. The summer night smelled like roses and mown grass. Nobody knew where I was, and the thought of that thrilled me.

Still does. Spontaneity takes a back seat when you're raising children. Getting to see Maya, savor her work, and drive to the reservoir all by myself on the same summer night feels like a rich gift. Connection and freedom, the best of both worlds.

Day 263. **June 3, 9:40 AM**

Rainy morning, foggy res. No mountains.

Birds singing anyway.

A new wildflower: tall spikes of vivid blue flowers with long magenta stamens and buds. I look it up when I get home and the name is as cool as the plant: viper's bugloss.

Wild phlox and white roses everywhere, first mountain laurel. June.

Day 264. **June 4, 9:45 AM**

The Cheerfuls, on bikes! Living up to their name! Good morning, good morning!

Teal water, milky blue sky. A slender green inchworm reels in silk by twisting its whole body into a hook. I look up. It's at least twenty feet to the nearest branch. That's a long rappel.

Eagle Guys Elder and Younger, stalking the nest. Elder tells me there's only one eaglet this year, born in March, and I spot a smaller head sticking up out of the nest. Flying lessons start soon, Elder says, squinting up at the nest. "It'll be gone by August. They don't stick around too long once they can fly."

Seven rowboats out. Trout floating belly up; some fisherman thought it was too small and threw it back, killing it anyway.

Driving home, I stop at the Tongore Cemetery, where there are lots of VFW Memorial Day flags. Tombstones with local names: Brodhead, Davis, Krom, Bishop, Winchell; one says "A Giant of a Man." I think of act 3 of *Our Town*: "Do any human beings ever realize life while they live it? Every, every minute?"

Day 265. June 5, 9:40 AM

Today is the Ride the Ridge bike race, the Tour de Krumville. It's been raining all morning, now down to a drizzle. The thirty-mile loop leaves High Meadow School at 9:30 and winds uphill toward the res, so I figure I'll walk out into quiet and come back as the first racers arrive.

Two walkers ahead, moving slowly and stopping to stare at the view. They turn out to be young Pakistani men. One asks, "Do you live near here?" I tell him yes, expecting tourist questions, but he says in reverent tones, "I live in Kerhonkson, but on the main road. This is . . . SPECTACULAR!"

Yes.

The mist is a cool, breathing thing, rolling uphill and over the bridge. The tall grass is rain flattened, cowlicked in whorls. Two deer dash across the path ahead, vanishing into the mist like something out of a fairy tale.

Ominous throb of an approaching helicopter. All black, it parallels the path, circles over the reservoir, and returns. No one my age can see helicopters without thinking of *Apocalypse Now*. They remind me of vultures, and sure enough, one shows up on cue, tarry pinfeathers spread and bedraggled. Last time I looked, the roadkill deer in the ditch was picked clean, a twist of bleached ribcage and spine on the side of the road. I have an old-country urge to spit over my shoulder, *puh, puh.*

A man and a woman sit on the third bench, a short distance away from each other. They're utterly still, and as I get closer I notice their hands are folded; they're praying. I get it, sort of, but they have their eyes closed. Why come to this place of magnificent beauty and not look at God?

That might be the definition of faith.

My holy is mountains and mist.

First thirty-mile racer is female, a sturdy, determined blonde, way out ahead of the pack. She is kicking ass.

After the first solo racer, the riders start arriving in pairs and clumps. Many chat as they pedal; the vibe is relaxed. I spot a few eighty milers in team jerseys, speeding back through from their much longer loop. They slick past on blade-thin tires, calves bulging with tribal tattoos.

A couple of High Meadow moms on the thirty-mile course dismount, pulling out iPhones to snapshot the view. One of them says, "Now one of you with your bike. You'll have memories."

Day 266. **June 6, 7:30 PM**

The woods near the Secret Cove are covered in pinkish-white mountain laurel. Toting my backpack and pole, I walk into the woods where the laurel is thickest and head for the cove.

There's a woman shore fishing, alone! Then I spot the life-size inflatable doll, face down on the gravel.

The *what*?

I tell myself it must be an illusion. I'm a good hundred feet away, and my view's screened by branches. It must be a mounded-up beigey-pink tarp or some kind of inflatable gear. But no, it clearly has legs on one end and a head with bright yellow hair on the other, and it's lying right next to the woman. Is it some bizarre sex toy, or one of those Resusci Annie first-aid training dummies? Whatever it is, why the hell did she take it out fishing?

I want to move closer and get a clear view. Then I spot a man fishing about fifty yards farther down and get instant cold creeps. If I'd seen him first, with that David Lynch movie doll lying facedown on the beach, I would have turned tail and fled. I'm grateful the woman is there, looking normal in a purple t-shirt and chinos. The man appears normal too—blue jeans and gray sweatshirt, short hair, a local-firehouse look.

Did he see me spying on them through the branches? I don't wait to find out. I melt back into the woods and walk toward the point, trying to make sense of what I just saw. Maybe these two just did an EMT training and didn't want to leave the doll in the back of the truck because it might freak someone out? (Um, it *did*.)

Or was it some sort of on-site rescue practice? *Okay, we're done, now let's go grab a few trout. Turn her upside down, wouldya?*

It's also entirely possible that I invented the doll, the same way I've convinced myself that a bare patch of ground was a doe lying down, or a stump was a bear. But I'm sure it had legs. And a wig.

I am *not* going back there to check.

I walk toward the Rock with a View at the tip of the point, but somebody's fishing there too, an old-timer wearing a classic tan fisherman's vest. I watch as he spin casts, his arm making graceful effortless arcs. Blue-collar zen.

I head down to a stretch of rock beach that I've never explored and work my way back down the far shore, gazing over the water. When I reach the trailhead, a DEP cop car sits idling as a cop gets out to unlock the gate. It's Officer Bald.

I can see that he doesn't remember me, or busting me right on this point many months ago. I give him a friendly hello.

"Got your stuff with you?" he asks politely. I hand over my fishing license and reservoir access pass. He looks at both, gives a satisfied nod, hands it back. "No luck, huh?"

I tell him I got a tangle. He looks at the reel on my poaching rod, which is indeed tangled. "Looks like you're gonna have to cut off that lure and rethread it," he says, then asks, "Anyone else out there? Were they fishing too?"

That "too" makes my day. So does the image of Officer Bald walking up to the couple with the inflatable doll to ask, "Any luck?" I walk back to my car, grinning hard.

Day 267. **June 7, 8:40 PM**

The sunset looks so spectacular from the supermarket parking lot that I drive straight to the res, Do Not Pass Go, Do Not Unpack Groceries. It's starting to fade by the time I arrive, and the wind is surprisingly stiff, whipping up whitecaps. It's a Sunset Man sky, and I wish he were here. I'm ashamed to admit I look for his car every time I pull in, though I barely remember what color it was. Gray, silver, blue? Something bland. I couldn't pick it out of a police lineup.

Day 268. **June 8, 9:25 PM**

Gusty wind churning up whitecaps, scudding clouds, rattling trees. Post-sunset sky looks like an angry bruise. First few stars, and for one thrilling moment a gap in the clouds frames a pale crescent moon.

Day 269. **June 9, 4:30 PM**

Sailboat weather. Clear blue sky, high waves. The sandbar off Driftwood Cove has almost reemerged, so combers break on unseen shoals. It looks like surf.

Scattered branches and leaves blow over the pathway. The air's fresh and clean, like sheets on a line. Rustling leaves singing wind songs.

Black double-winged dragonfly, samurai kite.

At the hardscrabble farm, a hen stands poised with one foot in the air, waiting to cross by the sign that says

CAUTION CHICKENS

ALSO COWS & HORSES

PEOPLE TOO

Day 270. **June 10, 8:15 PM**

My birthday's not for five days, but a Friday night potluck and sunset walk seems like a good way to celebrate. Cast of characters: both parents; brother David; and dear friends Alan, Shelley and Bill, Lily, Mourka and Miky, Sarah and Geoff Harden, Nicole and Paul Quinn, Jana Martin, Teresa Giordano, Carol Goodman, and my childhood friend David H., who's taken the bus from New York.

Eighteen reservoir walkers, the stalwart remains of a much larger group who gorged on food, wine, and Lily's astonishing cake—a sumptuous confection topped with fresh flowers, berries, and homemade whipped cream—at my house. The sun has just set and the colors are ripening as we meet in the parking lot. Our group fills every available parking space, including a handicapped space for my parents. Papa's on his cane and Mom on her walker; David guides them along.

Jana herds us all into a group at the guardrail and picks up her Nikon. "Say 'Nina,'" she says, and the group bellows "NEEEEE-NAA!" making me wince. This happens twice more, and I beg, "Please quit braying." David answers on cue, "I DON'T BRAY!" channeling Liz Taylor in *Who's Afraid of Virginia Woolf?*

Alan, a teacher who leads lots of workshops, tries to get everyone to hold hands. Several people are already too far ahead; the rest clasp hands, looking vaguely embarrassed. David croons a sardonic, "Someone left the cake out in the rain . . ." and after a few steps, Papa pleads, "Can we stop now?" The remaining hand holders start chanting, "The people / United / Will never be defeated!" and then we break up.

We fan out according to pace. I'm in the bring-up-the-rear group, walking at an elderly-parent amble with David, Alan, David H., Shelley, and Bill. Ahead, clumps of hikers, strollers, and chatterers move at varying speeds down the walkway.

Papa is the first to fade. I take his hand, asking if he can make it to sit on the first bench, about fifty yards farther. He agrees, but changes his mind, saying he needs to get back to the car. My brother and disappointed mom escort him back; jet-lagged Shelley and Bill join them. By the time we've all hugged goodbye, the hiker pack (Hardens and Quinns) is hopelessly far ahead, and the strollers and chatterers lean over the Lemon Squeeze wall in clusters, admiring the view.

I walk fast, hoping to catch up. My old friend David H. sprints forward to meet me. We walk arm in arm for a while, then pause to let Alan catch up.

By the time the three of us get to the Lemon Squeeze, the hikers in front have turned back at the rise. As we walk toward each other, an eagle flies overhead, giving its blessing.

We start walking back. Suddenly Mourka starts thrashing and drops to her knees, croaking, "Can't breathe!" Epileptic seizure?

We gather around her. Nicole says with calm authority, "Hands in the air. It opens the pipes." Mourka complies and we support her until she starts breathing easier. Turns out she swallowed a bug that got lodged in her throat. Tears streaming down her cheeks, she exclaims, "Some drama for your book!" A Russian baroness born in a German displaced persons camp, Mourka just published a memoir; it takes a true writer to talk about books while choking.

We head back, and again I lag with the slow walkers, drinking in this place I love in the presence of people I love. Venus comes out by the near-crescent moon, followed by Mars to the east, then a scatter of stars.

Lily's white linen jacket and long white skirt shimmer in twilight like a Victorian ghost.

Day 271. **June 11, 5:15 AM**

The summer sky's already lightening when the alarm goes off at 4:30 a.m. By the time Alan and I get dressed, make coffee, and share a small wedge of leftover cake, dawn's swirling around us in pink, gold, and apricot.

It's already started to fade by the time we arrive at the res. Alan's disappointed; we should have left sooner! I tease him with a mock tantrum, balling my fists and stomping my feet, "It's not *perfect*!" But it's pretty damn gorgeous.

Two club-kid deer drift off the foot of the hill, vanishing into the woods. Seagulls and barn swallows weave. Xena buzzes us twice, coming and going. The great blue heron makes a long circular swoop over the reservoir, then flies back alongside the path at eye level, so close we can see every feather.

The sun lifts above the horizon, bright gold. The far mountains are carved with deep shadows, trees pulsing between green and orange.

Bumblebees drift through sunlit wildflowers. "If you watch for a while, you can see why Impressionism had to happen," Alan says, breathless. "The light changes every moment."

It does, it does.

Alan and I hit the Olympic Diner for breakfast. We still have an hour to kill before his birthday "surprise" (which he's figured out that I've figured out, but we're playing along and not speaking the actual words). We stroll through the Kingston Farmer's Market, where Alan tries a free sample of lavender ice cream while I buy golden beets. His verdict? "Too lavender."

It's clouding up as we drive north to the airfield next to the Kingston–Rhinecliff Bridge. I guessed right: he really *is* taking me over the reservoir in a small plane! It's silly, extravagant, perfect.

It takes us three tries to find the main office. It's not in that house. It's not in that hangar. We gripe about signage. The third time we repark the car, Alan says, "I hope the pilot is hot. Sam Shepard hot."

We finally find the right building and enter its lobby. A woman looks up from her computer to tell us our pilot is out with a student; go wait in the lounge. It's a corner alcove with dull gray walls, a coffee machine with no coffee, and conjoined BarcaLoungers facing a TV atop a fake fireplace.

Alan gets impatient fast. "This looks like a funeral parlor." He picks up the remote, tries to figure out how to get cable, gives up. We doze in faux-suede BarcaLoungers.

After a weirdly long wait, a young pilot, blandly pleasant and geeky, joins us in the lounge. He asks whether we'll both need headsets. Alan says, "It's not really a flying lesson, we just want to fly over the Ashokan Reservoir. Can we do that?"

The pilot hesitates. "Well, there's some weather moving in. I was going to stay close to the airport in case we have to turn back. But we can probably make it as far as the reservoir."

Probably? What about making it *back*? Is that probable too?

As we step out the front door, the first splatty raindrops start. Alan and I exchange glances, an instantaneous mind-meld NO WAY. "Um, can we reschedule?" We can. And we're off.

In the car, Alan gloats, "Well, this worked out great. I get to be a hero for having the idea, and I don't have to pay for it!" Twenty years ago, when he still lived nearby, he saw a small plane land right next to the bridge. On impulse he drove to the airfield and flagged down a pilot (yes, Sam Shepard hot) who gave him a joyride for thirty-five dollars. *That* was what he had in mind, not this corporate flight school in crap weather.

I drive Alan to Rhinecliff, where he'll catch an earlier train. As we wait by the tracks, I point out that the Kingston–Rhinecliff bridge is already invisible, socked in with fog. By the time I drive back across it, it's a white-out carwash rain.

Maybe we'll try again in September, and maybe we won't. This was not meant to be, but the thought was a gem.

Day 272. **June 12, 2:30 PM**

Reservoir mystery: Two white sneakers, one in the road and one on the shoulder. A mile or so later, a blue denim shirt on the center line. Fast-lane strip poker?

The wind has come up like a beast. I park by the West Hurley dike and head out toward the moose pond. Trees toss, creak, and groan. It feels thrilling and vaguely unsafe to walk into the wind-roiled woods. Were there this many blowdown trees over the trail before?

Something massive explodes out of one of them, practically into my face. It's a red-tailed hawk. Cinnamon tailfeathers spread, it coasts down the trail at eye level, directly in front of me, like a guide. I follow it, rapt.

When I get to the pond, now dotted with lilies, I flush out another huge bird: a heron. It circles around, straining to balance in high wind, then heads through the woods toward the reservoir. I follow again.

The drowned forest where I saw the dead carp is still underwater. Whitecaps lash at the tree trunks like surf. The wind's loud as traffic.

I walk out onto a small point, surrounded by water and wind. It's the first time I've stood still, and it underlines how far from still everything else is. Trees bend sideways, gusts tearing at leaves. Is this a hurricane? A blue jay shrieks. Spooked, I start walking back fast. A bulky man stands on a rock with his back to me. He's not fishing—this wind would make casting impossible—but holds something I assume is a camera. I don't wait to find out.

Something skitters across the path, windblown. I pick up the end of a blown-apart paper wasp nest, a tornado-shaped funnel.

Day 273. **June 13, 6:40 PM**

There's a candlelight vigil for the Orlando massacre victims at Kingston's LGBTQ Center tonight. Though part of me yearns to mourn in a shell-shocked crowd, surrounded by love and community, I go to Reservoir Church instead.

It's windy, sky mottled with all kinds of clouds. I sit on the first bench and take forty-nine yoga breaths, slow deep inhale and exhale. It takes a long time, longer than it took forty-nine people to die in a hell of gunfire.

At breath forty-two, an eagle wings over the cove, majestic. The sun rays out from behind a dark cloud, casting parallel fingers of light before it emerges, a searing white disc.

I walk out under a marvel of cloud textures: cotton ball, mattress pad, salmon ribs, bubble tea. How can the world be so gorgeous and terrible at the same time?

The heron stalks slowly along the base of the dam. I walk parallel, watching him balance on steep wet stones, stilt legs knock-kneed. He places his large feet deliberately, sometimes spreading out one wing for balance. His long neck rests in an S curve, stretching out suddenly straight to spear a small fish from the water's edge. His amber beak is surreally long. He tips his head back to swallow.

He lifts off in a sudden slow glide, retracting his neck and angling into the wind as the eagle returns. For a moment, they're side by side, wings carving wind.

On the rise, a doe stands on tiptoe, antelope-necking low branches and dropping back down to chew mouthfuls of leaves.

I walk back into roiling cloud drama and pass Sarah Stitham, who calls in astonished delight, "What a *crazy* sky!"

I sit cross legged on the stone bench to watch sunset play out. The clouds are a true bluebell blue over indigo mountains. To the east, clots of cumulus ombre from charcoal to gold.

Sarah heads back to her car. I'm the last person left, and the sky's getting better and better; Sunset Man's missing out. I crane my neck as stippled gray slowly morphs from a faint glow to flamingo, lavender, coral.

The last color left in the turbulent sky is a vibrant Stonewall pink, and a song comes into my head unbidden: Hosier's "Take Me to Church."

Day 274. **June 14, 5:20 PM**

Last day of my fifties sure stunk up the joint. Let's see if this walk will help.

All the way out I'm enveloped in gloom, with an inner brat snarking, "Something you've never noticed before? Yeah, *right.*"

But of course there is. Nothing dramatic. The usual suspects are doing the usual things: deer chomping, crows sounding off, chipmunks dashing through leaves. But there is a moment when I stop by a hillside of sun-haloed daisies. The light reminds me of a painting in Maurice Sendak's *Mr. Rabbit and the Lovely Present*, and I think of his uncharacteristically radiant interview with Terry Gross, where he says, "There's something I'm finding out as I'm aging, that I am in love with the world . . . Live your life, live your life, live your life." And just like that, I'm smiling through tears—that most Russian of all stage directions—with the sun warming my face.

And there *are* things that I've never seen before. A deer and a wild turkey graze at the edge of the woods. I watch for some time, and they keep moving together, maintaining a distance of ten or twelve feet. It looks like the deer has a pet.

Two more deer stand at the creek spill. It's so still and clear I can see them above their reflections, moving in unison. One is taking a drink at the water's edge. The other wades into the water and stands there shin deep, like an old Jewish lady at Coney Island.

A Canada goose family stirs by the guardrail. Vigilant parents, two goslings approaching adulthood. When they run, they hold up stubby wings like baby birds in a cartoon.

I'm in love with the world.

Summer

Day 275. **June 15, 7:30 PM**

I'm starting the last of four seasons today, and it's my birthday. Road markers, stone cairns on the passage of time.

Soft cloud layers swaddle the sky, the sun a white halo. A woman is down on her knees at the guardrail. Stretching, or worshipping?

Busy tonight, summer carnival crowd. An elderly couple has brought folding chairs, sitting at the guardrail with glasses of wine, like the people who gather in Key West to applaud the sunset. I went there twenty-two years ago, when I was pregnant with Maya. Sunrise, sunset.

On the stone bench, two young hippies with beards and tribal tattoos. One of them plays the recorder, softly and not very well. His buddy lolls, grinning the grin of the stoned.

A couple leans over the Lemon Squeeze wall, peering down at the water. The woman calls out, "There are four great big fishies if you want to see." I go over to look. Four whopping brown trout hang out next to the dam. They're joined by a smaller one. "Look, it's a bay-beee," the woman croons.

I hear a sharp voice snap, "Get down!" and turn to see a girl hanging over the wall with her feet a good foot off the pavement. A thick-legged young mother strides toward her with two other children in tow. The girl on the wall doesn't budge. "I'm *looking*," she says in eye-rolling tones.

The crowd thins out as I reach the rise. Then I hear exuberant singing, three clowning male voices. Three teen bros on skateboards kick-step up the hill. As they round the bend, I hear one say to the others, "No seriously, I don't even like Bob Dylan's *voice*," and I think, *Oh, fall in.*

A slender blonde and a larger brunette in a jaunty fedora cross the Lemon Squeeze hand in hand. As I get closer, I recognize Sarah Stitham with her partner Kate McGloughlin, an artist who paints the Ashokan again and again; her ancestors have lived in the Esopus Valley for twelve generations, and some lost their homes when the dam was built.

"Reservoiristas!" I greet them.

Beaming, Kate asks, "So are things being good to you?"

"Some yes and some no," I answer a little too honestly.

Kate says, "We're all in the same boat. Ars longa, vita brevis." She throws out both arms, indicating the sky's glowing mesh of clouds and crisscrossing contrails. "We're *millionaires*, all of us. Millionaires!"

Yes, we are. And I'm sixty fucking years old.

Day 276. **June 16, 7:10 PM**

Bloomsday. I drive past a spike-horned young buck, a black squirrel, and a tight pack of racing bikers, riding so close they look like one long organism, a bright caterpillar with wheels.

I turn into the Frying Pan, saying out loud (yes, I talk in the car; doesn't everyone?), "I want a bear. A beautiful, glossy black bear. I don't want to go through this year without seeing a bear on the res." Then I get facetious, pretending to channel: "I'm calling you in, Bear. I'm *summoning* you."

There are lots of parked cars, and I don't feel like joining a crowd on the walkway, so I grab my backpack and prop fishing pole, heading down a short path to the beach. The water's still high, so I hug the tree line, watching my footing on uneven stones. I see several dark feathers—Canada goose; must be molting season. Then I spot a much wider, rounded-tip feather lying on a flat rock as if on an altar, downy white at the base, gray brown speckled with white near the tip. It's shiny and perfectly smooth. I've never seen one before, but I know instantly that it's an eagle feather. I also know it's illegal to own one, even if you pick it up in the wild, unless you're a Native American with a permit for religious use. That's a sacred object on that flat rock: it *is* an altar.

The feather radiates power. The sight of it thrills me. Is it illegal to lift it up, just for a moment, and hold it against my heart? Because that's what

I do, in a sort of improvised atheist's prayer, taking a deep breath and closing my eyes. When I open them, there's a bear cub on the beach.

My heart drumbeats. It's not just the beautiful sight—is there any color as rich as a black bear's fur?—or the danger. I know seeing a cub means there's a mother nearby; that generally conflict-averse black bears may charge when they sense a threat to their young. But beyond that mind knowledge is something that feels exactly like magic. I called in a bear—and yes, I was *kidding*, but I spoke the words—and it came. While I was holding a sacred feather.

I don't believe in this stuff. I'm offended by white pseudoshamans who try to appropriate Native American culture. I don't know what made me pick up that feather; I did it on impulse. I do live near Woodstock, which might tar me with the woo-woo brush like secondhand smoke, but if I heard this story from somebody else, I'd think they were full of shit.

But there's a *black bear cub* about fifty feet from me, framed by an arch of white birches. Its body is partially screened from view by a low-hanging pine bough, but it's probably about the same size as my golden retriever. I have a clear view of its face. It looks back at me without fear, bright eyed and curious. It looks like Sendak's Little Bear.

I dip my head—that's what you're supposed to do; no direct eye contact—and crane my neck slowly from side to side, scanning the woods for its mother. I don't see her. Not on the ground, and not up a tree. The cub seems to be on its own, maybe lost. It may be a small yearling, cast out by its mother before her next heat to protect it from suitors' aggression. I know it's the wrong thing to do, but I'm yearning to move just a little bit closer, to get a clear view past that pine branch.

We stare at each other, enthralled. The cub is the first one to move. It takes two steps toward me, and thrilled as I am by its trust, I've got too much Alaska training to let it approach when there might be a mama bear just out of sight. Even if it's alone, I can't be its new mother, and it will be safer if it keeps its distance from humans. I back away slowly. Keeping my head low, humming softly to sound reassuring, I make my way back down the beach and back toward my car with careful steps, trying to make my whole body unthreatening as I pass through the thin strip of forest and back to the Frying Pan circle. I have to remind myself that I should breathe.

I open my car door and sit in the driver's seat, feeling my heart beat with miracle. Something has happened that I can't explain. I'm not who I thought I was.

Bear!

Day 277. **June 17, 8:10 AM**

Flock of baby-lamb cloud puffs. Deep blue water, green mountains. There's only one other walker, tiny and determined, with a canted torso and one shoulder much higher than the other.

Sweet spice of wildflowers in blazing sun, including the first periwinkle-blue "cornflower" (a childhood misnomer for wild chickory) in full bloom. It's my mother's favorite flower and grows wild along Littlehales Lane, the dirt road to the summer cabin my family rented for decades on Skaneateles Lake. How many jars of Queen Anne's lace, black-eyed Susan, red clover, and goldenrod did I pick for that picnic table?

Chickory flowers don't keep well in water—they shrivel when cut—but I always put one in the mix, just so Mom would exclaim when she saw the bouquet. She has the gift of seeing familiar things as if they were new every time. How many sunsets did we watch from that porch, always "the best one yet?" How many meals of charcoal-grilled chicken, farm-stand tomatoes, and corn on the cob, while the dinner boat made sunset rounds, honking out "shave and a haircut" so Ed Littlehales could toot back "two bits" from his deck?

We finally had to give up that cabin—path too steep, too many stairs down to the beach—and now Ed is gone.

Orange butterfly. Summer.

Day 278. **June 18, 11:05 PM**

Blue moonlight, fireflies, ring around the moon. Seven white lights on the water. Night fishing!

Day 279. **June 19, 7:45 PM**

Haying at the hardscrabble farm. I drive very slowly behind a piled hay wagon shedding green straw. Chickens free-range through the fragrant stubble. A red rooster jumps a hen, pinning her down with his wings. She shakes him off, ruffling her feathers, then crosses the road to peck at some rodent roadkill, coming up with a beakful of bloody intestines.

A scatter of white catalpa blossoms blows over the road. Families eat barbecue at picnic tables. Father's Day in America.

The light of the setting sun spills over banks of sweet clover and daisies. Sun sinks behind mountains, yellow to blue.

A biker in blue spandex stops to say hi. It's Tim Moore, a musician from Woodstock. He just saw twin cubs ("the smallest bears I've ever seen") on Route 28A. He pulled over for a closer look and heard grunting and chuffing: the mother bear bluff-charging out of the brush. He jumped back on his bike so fast he ripped open his shin.

I look east and there's the moon, suddenly risen. It isn't officially full till tomorrow, but it's round as a coin. Prestidigitating moon. Rippling water like tangerine silk.

Day 280. **June 20, 8:20 PM**

Dead blacksnake flattened and sun dried on asphalt, looks like a leather belt.

It's summer solstice and a full moon, June's Strawberry Moon, together again for the first time since 1948 (or 1967, depending which website you visit).

The sun's already sunk behind Cornell Mountain—it must start inching south as summer sets in—and water and sky are a tie-dye of silvered pastels. There's a fisherman out at the tip of the point, wrist-flicking fishing line into the water.

The western colors intensify as I walk out, brindled purple and orange. It's one of those Maxfield-Parrish-was-a-realist sunsets. I keep looking over my shoulder at soft pink swirls to the east. That's where the moon will rise. When?

All of a sudden I see it, so subtle it's like a mirage. It's the same seashell pink as the cloud it's against, a ghostly breath of a circle, like a hole punch that hasn't let go of the page. As it levitates up, it solidifies, growing brighter and pinker until it's the same vibrant shade as the sunset across the horizon, as bright as a quince blossom. I've never seen a moon this pink. It's a '50s lipstick moue, a hot-coral shade that belongs on a drag queen.

As it continues to rise, it turns pumpkin, then amber. A muscular black man rollerblades by, doing backward crossovers, impossibly graceful.

The moon rises into a small patch of cloud as I walk back toward the DEP roadblock posts (apparently they're called "retractable bollards"). I hear something crunch through dry leaves on the hillside below. Too big for a squirrel; maybe a fawn? I veer over to look.

On the opposite side of the guardrail a small black face rises, sharp nose and round ears. A bear cub, standing on its hind legs.

I blurt out, "Hello," and it looks at me, startled, drops to all fours and scrambles back down the hill. I hear rustling leaves farther down in the woods; might be mom. I speed walk to my car, stirred and a little bit spooked. What am I, the Bear Whisperer?

Is it the same cub I saw down by the Frying Pan, two and a half miles away, on the other side of the bridge? Or the one Deborah saw fast asleep on a tree branch, or one of Tim's twins? Is the reservoir hosting a cub jamboree? (The group name is a sleuth of bears, like a murder of crows, or a murmuration of starlings.) Excuse me, Officer, there's a sleuth of cubs by the retractable bollards.

Day 281. **June 21, 6:20 PM**

It's my mother's birthday—her ninety-second—and summer solstice. It's always seemed apt that she was born on the day when the sun stays out longest.

A cottontail dashes across the road, zigzagging from some imagined predator. The triangle marsh is scummed over, no turtles in sight. A tall stalk of fuzz-leaved mullein is just starting to bloom, a spiral of small yellow blossoms.

A midsize gray bird flaps over the marsh and lands on the top of a spar tree. It's silhouetted against the clouds, but the thick short neck and long bill peg it as a black-crowned night heron. Its call is comically unattractive, like somebody with a bad cold saying "grok." The Harvey Fierstein of herons.

His glam cousin the great blue preens, twisting his neck in impossible curves to groom the base of his wings between his shoulder blades. His gray feathers bristle in rock-star spikes.

Sudden clatter of wings as hundreds of starlings land all over a neighboring tree, pause a moment, then take off all at once in a wheeling formation.

Day 282. **June 22, 7:50 AM**

I wake up tired and burdened, totally not in the mood for a walk. But I have to go down to New York, so it's now or never.

Roadside daylilies. Empty hay wagons on crewcut blond field.

Teal water, the usual paradise. Cliff swallows parasail.

The prettiest thing is the grasses, seedheads bleached silver and stalks green gold, nodding in a light breeze. A homegrown *Christina's World*, minus the chick.

Day 283. **June 23, 7 AM, New York City**

Away game report from the Jacqueline Kennedy Onassis Reservoir in Central Park. I've just walked my father (not quite retired at age ninety) to his medical office, his heavy briefcase perched on the seat of the walker he folds up to hide from his patients, and I'm moved by the sight of an ancient sycamore, trunk massive, bark peeling, still here.

A white egret flies over the water and lands with a ripple of wings. A merganser dives, coming back up with a fish, which it swallows in one giant gulp.

The morning runners are more organized than the sunset crowd. Everyone's northbound. I transgress five ways: I'm walking, I'm walking south, I'm wearing street clothes, I have a large purse over my shoulder,

I'm NOT THIN. One wedge-shaped dude in sweat-drenched shirt and sunglasses would rather run me over than swerve. I have to step up onto the fence curb as he hurtles toward me.

Many hours later, I drive from the train station to the Ashokan, where I'm greeted by cool night breeze, fireflies, and constellations. I'm wiped; won't be much of a walk. I take two steps onto the path and a falling star plummets. I gasp, I laugh.

On the drive home, a sudden red fox.

Day 284. **June 24, 9 AM**

I'm walking today with a recent ex–New Yorker of my acquaintance. She was skittish about getting lost on back roads, so I drove out to meet her on Route 28, our landmark the huge Adirondack chair outside a store called Big Moose. Since I'd spotted a mower denuding the shoulders alongside the Olivebridge Dam, I drove her instead to the Frying Pan side.

The Recent Ex–New Yorker pulls on a white mesh jacket with SPF protection and mosquito repellent, which she bought when she went to Costa Rica at the beginning of the Zika virus scare. She also has lightweight binoculars, and I'm not surprised when she tells me that she was a Girl Scout. Be prepared!

She tells me that the Catskills are not really mountains. (Wikipedia corroborates: "Geologically, the Catskills are a mature dissected plateau, a once-flat region subsequently uplifted and eroded into sharp relief by watercourses.") We talk for nearly the whole walk, but she's struck by the quiet. Having spent yesterday in the city, I get what she means. It's the larger quiet, the surround; in movie sound it's called ambience. Room tone without a room.

The Recent Ex–New Yorker is enjoying her first Catskill summer, and the profusion of new things blooming in her yard keeps surprising her. "Suddenly there are red flowers where there was nothing. Nature moves so quickly."

The pavement is littered with Canada goose poop and dozens of feathers, and the culprits bob on the water in two large flotillas. Adults molt when their young are not yet ready to fly, so the whole family is earthbound (and water bound) for five or six weeks. By August, they'll be fully fledged.

The teen eagle is almost ready to fly. It's sitting on Fabio's posing branch above the nest, and I spot an adult halfway up a large pine. My guest whips out binoculars, thrilled.

Rounding the curve, we run into the mowing machine, idling on the path. The driver is perched on the guardrail, cell phone in one hand and a Coke in the other. "I hadda stand up, my legs were starting to hurt," he explains, sitting down.

Day 285. **June 25, 6:10 AM**

Honeyed dawn light, carving shadows on the mature dissected plateau. One rower, metal oars glinting.

Fuzzy bumblebees working the lavender thyme, an industrious hum. There's a scatter of drying loose hay on the pathway. Cowbird couple gleaning.

Red-winged blackbird and robin on fence. Unseen warbler warbling.

Two young bucks thunder out of the woods, see me, and skid to a stop like horses on reins. Their antlers are velvet, curved prongs with the start of a second point. We look at each other. I watch the lead one flinch, torn between asserting his dominance and wariness of this strange two-legged mammal. I give ground, walking on, and they graze in the ferns.

Cobweb stretched between bull thistle thorns. What a way to go.

Noisy car pulls in, red, needs a muffler. Hungover young couple (up all night?) stumbles out, both smoking cigarettes. She: *Flashdance*-cut oversized tee off one shoulder, green streaks in black hair. He: baseball cap, hoodie, toe-walking in sneakers. They lean on each other. Affection, or gravity?

Ghost half moon, setting.

Day 286. **June 26, 8:25 PM**

Muted sunset, the day's heat still baking up from the asphalt. Something I've noticed before: the riffle and shimmy just after the sun goes down. Amid the textures, a long narrow snake of flat water. It looks like the ghost of the creek that was dammed up to make this great basin. I picture the houses and farmstead, the mill with its paddlewheel working. If you squint, you can see the white buoys that bob on the waves as the tips of church steeples.

I cross the Lemon Squeeze and stand gazing down at the geometry of terraced steps flanking the creek spill, with its grassy land bridge and Japanese scatter of trees and reeds. A large bird wings out of the woods like a shadow, flying low over grass and water. Blunt head and powerful wings: great horned owl.

The grass on the embankment has gotten so tall that deer disappear in it, visible only as movement, a glimpse of brown rustling through stalks. Except when one runs and leaps: head, whitetail, head, whitetail, head.

Day 287. June 27, 7:20 AM

I'm seized by the urge to walk out onto the sandbar that juts into Driftwood Cove now that the water's so low. I take my fishing pole and bait bucket as camouflage.

It's already hot as I cross the beach. I see footprints embedded in mud: deer, a few bootprints, no bears. The flat stones are dusted with reddish dried mud, which reminds me how recently all of this was underwater. I have a shivery, fleeting sensation of walking down a dirt road that leads to the Drowned Towns.

Day 288. June 28, 1:30 PM

Thunderstorm gathering. Thick, humid air, shifting wind. Clouds swallowing mountaintops. Something wicked this way comes.

The DEP's mowed the whole hillside since yesterday. It looks like a plucked chicken. The air smells of green. Swallows swoop overhead, restive and chittering. Two vultures soar, stiff winged, lurching through turns like a couple of drunks.

Across the Lemon Squeeze, two giant mowers rumble in a relentless geometry, angled into the hill. The mowed rows are not unbeautiful, in their patterned way, but nothing moves. The uncut strips riffle with every breeze, bowing and tossing. I close my eyes, hang my head over, and hear the wind blow, a great susurration of grass. When I open them, there's a single orange butterfly dancing.

The rise is much quieter. Between the eagle's nest and the strand, I spot a doe lying down. She's licking her groin and her sides bulge. She raises her face, and something in her eyes—not fear, but a sort of pleading—lets me know she's about to give birth. She's chosen her spot well, away from the mowers and hidden by big clumps of vetch, so she's invisible from everywhere but the exact spot where I stand. I can see her sides heave.

I don't want to alarm her, so I walk on, thinking about my own labor and Pamela Erens's amazing novel *Eleven Hours*, which I've just finished reading.

It's started to drizzle. The mowers have called it a day, and a flock of blackbirds is already gorging on fallen seedheads. Fast food.

Roadkill groundhog, fur bristling, its innards raw meat. A rancid dead-creature musk blows through my car window. Nature doesn't coddle.

Day 289. **June 29, 7 AM**

I'm meeting actor and writer David Smilow at seven for a walk, and when I pull into the parking lot at 6:59, he's standing by his car in aikido t-shirt, shorts, and sunglasses, arms folded ironically. He's already been here for twenty minutes.

It rained hard last night, and the air smells like wet hay. There's fog rolling up over the Lemon Squeeze, a fringe of low clouds periwigging the High Peaks.

We walk at a clip. David's curious about a fast-swooping brown-and-white shorebird I haven't identified yet, and I spot some tiny magenta flowers called Deptford pinks.

As we enter the Lemon Squeeze, I spot something dark and still on the far end. Is it garbage, a stone? We approach.

It's a young snapping turtle, its shell the size of a catcher's mitt. It's only a few yards onto the long, shadeless bridge, and looks exhausted; whether it clambered up the rocky dam or the newly shorn hill from the creek spill, it's already made a long uphill trek. When you rescue a turtle crossing the road, you have to carry it in the same direction it's heading, or it'll make the same journey all over again; territorial imperative. So when David offers to move it onto the grass at the end of the bridge, I tell him it has to be the *other* end.

He picks it up carefully, setting both hands at midshell, out of reach of the snapping jaws. The irate turtle hisses, pisses, thrashes its clawed feet, and twists its neck around, trying to bite him. Its mouth is wide, moist, and shell-pink inside. "Little dinosaur," David says, admiring its moxie. He carries it all the way over the bridge, and it never stops trying to do him damage. When he puts it down, he steps back quickly, but it doesn't move.

We walk on. David says, "We'll see if it's waiting for us when we come back."

I pause to look down at the spot where the doe gave birth. The grass there is flattened, a perfect circle.

The teen eagle pokes his head up from the nest. No grownups in sight. He looks like he's itching for car keys.

We turn back at the weir and walk back, and the snapper is gone. David probably saved its life. In the *Aesop's Fables* version, there would be payback.

We drive to the Pineview Bakery, an unreconstructed '40s-style eatery close to my heart. With its knotty pine wainscoting, lunch counter stools, and glass case of white-flour breads and white-sugar pastries, it looks like the Catskill luncheonettes we used to stop at when I was a kid. The griddle smells of frying bacon.

We order eggs over easy, home-baked sourdough toast, coffee. One of our fellow diners gets up to pay at the register. He's wearing a black t-shirt with a pirate cartoon, an IATSE union logo, and the words "Mercenary Stagehands. When the money's gone, so are we." David laughs long and hard. Life is good.

Day 290. **June 30, 7:45 PM**

Water an ominous battleship gray, so still I can see a trout stalking a minnow.

Sunset starts pastel and slowly turns to flamingo, persimmon, tandoori salmon, hot lava. Everyone on the pathway stops moving to watch.

A family approaches on bikes. Young mom snaps, "It's not a fuckin' video game! Drive straight. You're gonna hurt someone! Don't cut Daddy off or I'll take your bike and throw it right into the water. I'm not kidding, I'll pay the fine. You drive like that, somebody's gonna get hurt."

She catches up to me and flashes a toothy smile. "Beautiful, huh?"

Day 291. **July 1, 8:45 PM**

A cracking Catskill thunderstorm just rolled through, and the ozone is bracing. Low clouds lounge on top of the mountains, a giant pajama party. The shaved hillside is littered with straw. There's wild thyme in pale purple bloom. I crush a sprig between my fingers, a whiff of Provence, and spot a low bush of black raspberries. Most are still red, but a few are ripe. I pop one into my mouth, savoring the burst of juice, rich, dark, and tart on my tongue. I think of Anne Gorrick and Peter Genovese's homemade blackcap jam. "It tastes like the Hudson Valley," Anne says, and it does.

Apricot glow on gunmetal water.

There's a family of three on the bridge. Both parents lean over the wall, looking down at the water. Tween son leans beside them, straddling an orange banana bike and wagging its back tire back and forth in midair like a giant round tail. I walk past; we trade genial hellos. When I hear them behind me, I pause at the guardrail, letting them pass. The dad is talking about a hospital procedure: incision, IV, something pressing against the scar. The mom makes sympathetic low clucks. I keep my gaze on the distant horizon, giving them privacy. When I turn, they're a hundred yards past me, parents walking abreast, son biking beside them, hand in hand in hand.

Day 292. **July 2, 8:20 PM**

I drive past Vly Pond at sunset. My great neighbors Don and Linda Driekonski stand at the edge, watching a beaver swim past like he owns the place. Don says he's building a dam by the culvert. Two orange koi the size of sub sandwiches lurk in the shallows.

Just up the road, an owl swoops down to pluck something—a squir-rel?—off the roadside. I can't see what she's got in her claws, but its weight makes her lurch. Brutal beauty.

The clouds over the res are the color of creamsicles. Two guys stand in midpath, flapping their jaws about Hillary Clinton. One has two cameras strapped across his chest like bandoliers, the other a curly black dog on a leash. Behind them, red sparks from an early-bird firework.

Day 293. **July 3, 4:50 PM**

Stretched white clouds, sultry air, midsummer too-hotness. Walkers with hats. One of the larger hats, white with black stripes and a floppy rolled brim, looks like a prop for "Ascot Gavotte."

Day 294. **July 4, 8:35 PM**

I'm leaving the Omega Institute, exhausted from teaching the first session of a five-day writing intensive. So tempted to stay in my sweet little faculty cabin tonight, but the reservoir calls.

I arrive just after sundown. *I'm home*, I think, walking past a flattened Poland Spring bottle some helpful soul has left on top of a bollard. In case the owner comes back for it? A mini Claes Oldenburg sculpture?

The sky is ablaze with the twilight's last gleaming. Tie-dyed furrows across the horizon, a purple lenticular cloud. The fiery sky turns the water bright orange.

It's one of those sunsets that goes on and on. As it fades, I recall nine-year-old Maya, hiking back from the massive Big Cedar on the Olympic Peninsula's Rainforest Trail, turning toward me with shining eyes: "That was so undisappointing!"

A few backyard fireworks go up. Useless bangs, green and gold spar-kles. After the sky's grand finale, they look so dinky.

Day 295. **July 5, 7:20 AM**

Rain all night, walkway still shiny. White sky and low fog. Mirror water. Mulchy smell of wet hay.

Two other walkers, including the Reader. One morning-after deer. I take a last look and head back to Omega.

Day 296. **July 6, 4:00 PM**

Ninety-five and humid. Heat like a wall. Hard to take a deep breath. You could fry an egg on the sidewalk. Or me.

The thin strip of wildflowers along the guardrail looks exhausted. The chickory's sun-bleached, the daisies hang limp, and the yellow sweet clover is dying. The DEP has lopped all the shrubs growing up through the dam and left them on the stone slope to wither. Their leaves curl in the heat, turning khaki. Farewell, honeysuckle, witch hazel, young birch.

Sweat streams down my forehead, pooling under my eyes. I remember the eagle turning lazy circles over the lake at Omega an hour ago and wish I were still there; it's my afternoon off. The heat is oppressive, and when I see a greyhound-lean runner streak past, followed by a racing biker in black spandex, I feel like slapping them both. Showoffs! Narcissists! Male anorexics!

I want an ice cream cone.

Day 297. **July 7, 7:20 AM**

Air steamy, wildflowers glorious. The chickory that looked so defeated last night is a vibrant Marian blue, kissed by dew and surrounded by goldenrod spires, lemon hearts, and Queen Anne's lace unfurling small dainty parasols.

Three older Chinese people are doing some kind of exercise with a lot of vigorous arm circling. Qi gong? It's too fast for tai chi.

As they finish, they remount their bicycles one at a time. First the woman, then the dark-haired man, and finally the white-haired man whose arms were so fluid and graceful. On the bike, he's knock-kneed, uncertain. He wobbles off after the others, his body transformed from master to beginner.

Mountain Man arrives as I'm leaving. He sits on top of the picnic table, feet on the bench, drinking coffee. His sleeves are cut off at the shoulder, exposing some faded tattoos. His face is squinched, quizzical.

From the weir bridge, I spot the teen eagle, circling above the nest. Fledged!

Day 298. **July 8, 3:30 PM**

First reservoir walk in a damp swimsuit and sundress. I'm wearing my water sandals, my big toe swathed in an oversize Band-Aid. The Omega workshop ended at noon, and before I left, I grabbed a quick swim at the lake. For the first time all week, one of the kayaks was free. I took it out, gliding through lily pads and water hyacinths, and paddled back to the beach feeling blissy. As I stepped out, I saw blood gushing from my big toe and a pool on the kayak floor; must have gashed it on metal. It didn't hurt then, but it's throbbing now, making me limp. Instead of attempting the two-and-a-half-mile walkway, I stop at the triangle marsh.

It's clotted nearly solid with lily pads. Cattails turn brown from the bottom up. Whir and crunk of frog song.

A water snake races down the steep bank. Dark, nearly black, it slips into the water and disappears, leaving no ripple.

Some of the lily pads are big as dinner plates, flat on the water or raised up on stalks, folded in like cocktail glasses. Large flowers, white with yellow stamens, on separate stems.

Thunderstorm brewing. Dead air, locker-room humid. The charcoal sky gives the greens an unearthly glow. A black squirrel ripples by, ermine-glossy. One high-stepping crow.

Day 299. **July 9, 4:30 PM**

Drizzle and mist, mountains lost in a whiteout. A silver-nitrate glow along the horizon.

Loud voices behind me: "Whoa. This is cool!"

"It looks like the Pacific Northwest, you know, *Twilight*?"

"Totally."

Okay, that tears it. I slow down to let six teens pass me. They stop to take selfies, and one of them turns. "Ma'am? Would you take a picture of us?"

Nothing makes you feel older than being called "ma'am."

Yeah, fine. I set down the grumpy and put on my friendly, taking a group shot against the misty background. Then they ask me to take one of all six of them walking away. "The rock band shot," I say, and they laugh.

"Walk cool," says the tallest boy as I frame their backs.

After they leave, I go to the guardrail where I saw the minks and spot a tiny silk spiderweb strung between leaves. It glitters with miniature raindrops. As I turn my head, I see dozens more, each with its own microbeading. If I hadn't stopped, I would never have seen them.

Day 300. **July 10, 8:45 AM**

Twenty-two years ago, I was speeding to Columbia-Greene Hospital, barreling north on the Thruway. Happy birthday, dear Maya. My daughter is twenty-two, unavoidably, irreversibly adult. Old enough to be away from her mom on her birthday, first time in our lives. And here I am, doing my best to reclaim what a solo life looks like. One step at a time, in the literal sense.

I arrive at the res in the pause between rainstorms. It's a weekender crowd. Man jogging with Portuguese water dog, wiry black coat with white T on the chest, flaggy tail, lolling tongue. Didn't get the "No dogs, dipstick" memo. Looks happy.

Two boys play a Pokémon game on their iPhones while their dad exhorts, "You don't have to look at the screen every minute. When one of them's near, it'll vibrate. Look *up*. Look around. Look where we *are*, or I'm gonna take those phones away. Look up like a normal person!" The boys look up, because they've been made to. Their backs show frustration. A minute goes by, then: "Dad? Can I just *check*?"

Woman sits atop the Lascaux Cave wall, hugging bent knees. How did she get up there? What if she fell?

Creek spill a lake of clouds.

Twenty-two years. Three hundred walks. Tick tick tick.

Day 301. **July 11, 7:30 PM**

Woman walking with friend: "The marketing spin is that they're supposed to whisk away sweat. The question is, where does it *go*?"

Day 302. **July 12, 8:40 PM**

After-dinner walk with my brother in shimmering dusk. The heron glides across, wingspan mirrored by pearlescent water, and comes to a stop at the foot of the dam.

David stands at the guardrail, a sigh in his exhale. Then he says, "The local sublime."

Day 303. **July 13, 7:50 PM**

Summer storm blowing in. The sky looks like an outer-space photo of Earth, aswirl with streaked clouds. I'm so tired I keep yawning. When I reach a bench, I get the urge to lie down on it.

Why not? No one out here but a magical wind. Flat on my back, I gaze up at clouds shifting in layers, a blue-and-white lava lamp. A glinting plane threads through the fast-moving clouds like a needle.

A few swooping swallows. Fresh air on my face.

And I fall asleep. Not sure for how long, but I wake to the sound of a bike creaking past. Then two women's voices approaching. One of them spots my crossword sneakers and says, "Is that Nina?"

Busted. Reservoir napper.

On the way home, a huge dark bird swoops past my car and lands on a dead tree. I pull over and find myself face to face with a great horned owl. She looks me right in the eye. Intense gaze. Then she swivels her head, looks at me again with stern amber eyes, and lifts off, silent on giant wings.

Day 304. **July 14, 8 AM**

Rainclouds, not raining. Air like soup.

I am sick of this walk. There, I said it.

What is holding my feet to the fire, insisting I come back here day after day? Stubbornness ramps up the guilt, saying, *You can't stop now!*

Yeah, fine. But that's part of this too, right? Learning to push through the everyday sameness and find something new?

And here it is: The weeds along the Lascaux wall are covered with Japanese beetles in clusterfuck. Some leaves chewed to lace, others bent under the weight of hard-shelled iridescent couplings. Plato's Retreat, Gregor Samsa edition.

Day 305. **July 15, 3:30 PM**

Six-point buck posing on the road, new antlers in velvet.

I'm driving high into the western Catskills with photographer Franco Vogt for a profile of poet Cheryl Clarke and sidebar on Hobart, Book Village of the Catskills.

It's wilder up here. Roadkill: fox, porcupine, blacksnake, two shaggy raccoons. Sleepy mountain towns along feeder streams of the Delaware, fading Victorian houses and peeling-paint barns, and I realize this is exactly the way the Esopus Valley would look if the dam I walk on had never been built. As if proving the point, a bald eagle flies past.

I get back to the res in midafternoon baking sun. Waves of heat rise off the pavement. It's silent. No other walkers, no birdsong, the water too still to lap. Thunderheads starting to gather. Two black helicopters buzz overhead, shiny as Japanese beetles.

Biplane dragonfly, translucent yellow-and-black chiffon wings, perched on the tip of a dying sweet clover. It doesn't look real.

Day 306. July 16, 7:50 AM

A chipmunk runs under my wheels, too late to react. I hear/feel the small thunk, and clutching my throat doesn't help.

Six wide Harleys with six wide riders.

Cobwebs between grass seedheads, full of dead gnats. Canada geese grazing under the guardrail, the younger ones now the same size as their parents. Their black necks are flexible as garden hoses.

The mowed hillside is already starting to green, with clover and Queen Anne's lace springing back up. Everything cycles back, ripens, and falls. That small boy stunt-walking from bollard to bollard might grow up to marry the Asian toddler with a Minnie Mouse purse on the handlebars of her princess bike. Or that sullen preteen with black spikes on his helmet.

A bicyclist raises his arm in an extravagant wave. It's my neighbor Andy. "What number walk?"

"Three hundred and six."

He tells me his favorite vanity plate is parked on the Frying Pan circle: "Rolling Estonian. Have you seen it?"

"I've seen an Estonia plate, but it didn't say *rolling* Estonian."

Andy grins, triumphant. "On the license plate *frame*."

Attention to detail.

Day 307. **July 17, 8:45 PM**

Gibbous moon rising, the color of buttermilk. There's a guy unpacking a tripod and other gear next to the guardrail, and I'm curious (*unpacking, now?*) but I don't stop to ask.

Several walkers and bikers, all incoming. The last people I pass are two jocks piggybacking their girlfriends. The blonde's being giggly about it, but the brunette drapes herself over her young man's back like a horse-crazy girl hugging the neck of a stallion, pure dreamy erotics. She'll remember this moment forever. His muscular shoulders. His Nike swoosh t-shirt.

And then I'm alone. Teasing breeze, almost cool, sound of waves. First deer grazing the hillside.

I hear a rusted-gate *crawk* and turn to see two great blue herons flying together. A few more calls and they separate, one flying west and the other east.

The first stars appear, Venus, Mars. Astronomical twilight. The guy with the gear is still at it. A red LED glow marks the feet of his tripod, and he's unfolded a table for his blue-lit laptop. Some kind of time-lapse night photography?

As I get closer, I realize the tripod's not holding a camera, but high-tech binoculars. "Want to see Mars?" he asks.

I look through the two lenses. Mars looks a bit bigger and redder than it does to the naked eye, but honestly, it's still a dot, no great shakes. I say something polite. He shows me Jupiter, using his laptop to guide the telescope, and I'm reminded of the two boys playing Pokémon Go.

Jupiter's also a dot, though I can make out the oblong smear of its rings. "How about the moon?" he says, refocusing.

This time he hits pay dirt. The moon's image fills the whole screen, and it's so detailed I can see craters and shadows in three dimensions. "Wow!" I exclaim. He tells me it's 49x magnification, that he has a bigger telescope at home; his laptop app "only has twenty-seven million objects."

He wants to talk, but he's kind of the Paul Giamatti character, and I'm getting impatient. I wish him good night and set off, passing two young Asian girls as I head for my car. The last thing I hear: "Want to look at the moon?"

Day 308. **July 18, 5:40 PM**

Rumbling thunder. Clouds stacking in weirdly still air. One vertical mass looks like Greenland, gray and immense.

Two lightning bolts, ten seconds to thunder, then eight. The last few walkers scramble back in, hoping to beat the storm. I sit on the first bench. I'm wearing a sundress and kayaking sandals—if I get soaked, so what?

Gray slant of rain moving over the water. The wind comes up fast, and I'm suddenly inside the storm. Rain lashes the pavement, obliterates mountains. It's falling in sideways sheets, forceful and stinging, just this side of hail.

Skin-soaked in moments and starting to shiver, I head for my car. The rain's pounding down like a carwash, too fearsome to drive in. My windows steam up from inside as rain sluices over the windshield.

After a few minutes the rain starts to lighten, and so does the sky. When the sun reemerges, there might be a rainbow.

What the hell. It isn't as if I could get any wetter.

Hair and dress plastered, I walk out into the last of the rain. There are white shreds of clouds stuck on top of the mountains, like stray tufts of wool. The horizon is silver.

The first shaft of sunlight slants through, and all of a sudden I see a vertical curve, stripes of color surreally bright. Then I spot the opposite end rising up, and a faint pastel sketch of the arc in between. As I watch, it fills in from both ends, and a second arc forms just outside it, not quite as distinct.

Two crows sit on the guardrail. I'd swear they were watching the rainbow.

Day 309. **July 19, 9:15 PM**

Two bats skitter and loop. It's finally cool, and so quiet I can hear fluttering leaves. One grasshopper chirps. The peepers have finished their spring mating choir, so there's just an occasional bullfrog *glunk* from the swamp.

The full moon clears the trees, then rises through filmy clouds, making them glow from behind, like gray burnout velvet.

I'm completely alone. It feels private, romantic. The moonlight's so blue it looks fake, like the day-for-night moonlight in movies. It casts shadows of trees on the mowed grass below. A few fireflies twinkle.

Then I see a light coming down off the rise. A bicycle headlight? It's moving too fast for a walker, and I can hear voices, a gravelly rolling. The light seems to glide.

It's the three skateboard bros, fanned out into a wedge. The boy in the front wears an LED headlamp. They glide by in silence.

Big Dipper, Orion's belt, Cassiopeia's chair. Summer camp constellations.

Day 310. **July 20, 8:15 PM**

Peachy little mare's-tail wisps in a robin's-egg sky. One long diagonal brushstroke.

All for sale at the same house: brightly painted guitars, farm-fresh eggs, wedding officiant.

Day 311. **July 21, 1:10 PM**

Heat dome! Corn sweat! There's a heat mirage shimmering over the pavement. Baked air, no breeze. Wildflowers stand still at the edge of the path, morning chickory blossoms already closed into tight little fists. The only things moving are a few cabbage-white butterflies.

A cormorant sits on a buoy, drying its outstretched wings. Sunburnt bridge workers huddle in shade drinking Cokes.

The line of cars ahead of me slows along Route 28, drivers rubbernecking something on the shoulder. As I pass, I see a father and son standing somberly in front of a makeshift memorial of wreaths, bows, and plastic flowers.

Every minute matters.

Day 312. **July 22, 8:05 AM**

Roadside attractions: scurrying groundhog, two wild turkeys with seven small chicks strung out in a line like Madeline's orphans.

Katydids ratchet from trees.

Sweat-sheened woman runner returning.

Bees landing on purple thyme. Dreams of ice coffee.

Day 313. **July 23, 6:40 PM**

I've been seeing other reservoirs.

Sarah Harden invites me to walk with her at Woodstock's Cooper Lake, a water supply for the city of Kingston. Today spiked up to ninety-three degrees, but now there's a riffling breeze and the clouds are spectacular. So are the Catskill foothills in the background, kneaded shapes with precipitous drops. White pine and paper birch, understory of wild rose, burdock, goldenrod, blackcap, and blueberries.

On the berm, Sarah shows me scooped hollows a friend told her were snapping-turtle egg nests. She was skeptical until one day she and Geoff were walking there and saw a tiny snapper with mud on its back, scrabbling toward the water.

We pass a couple that looks like a magazine ad: blonde young mother in lacy Victorian whites, dark-bearded husband with sleeve tattoos carrying a tiny blonde baby in a blue striped romper. "Her first lake," says the mother when we stop to coo.

I stop at the Olivebridge parking lot on my way home. A Mexican family stands at the guardrail, exclaiming. One of the women has a thick curtain of hair that falls past her waist, cherry red dyed over black.

One shore fisherman clambering over damp driftwood.

Ashokan, hello.

Day 314. **July 24, 6:15 AM**

This is the time to sneak under the heat dome. The grass is still dewy, the air's fresh and cool, and there's enough breeze to whip up little whitecaps. The first thing I see when I step on the path is an eagle, gliding high. No white head, but the T-shaped wingspan and wedge-shaped tail are unmistakable. It must be the newly fledged teen, on a joyride.

I pick up a dead click beetle, shiny and black, with circular white fake eyes on the carapace. What predator falls for this scam? It's the Nigerian prince of camouflage.

A seagull lifts over the rise, free floating on air. Then a second eagle, white headed and tailed, glides alongside the path. Snaggled wing feather; Xena.

Two baby squirrels chase each other across the path, wrestling and flipping. They see me and streak for the trees.

The bull thistles are backlit by rising sun. Their spines shine like long silver needles. The buds are covered with coarser but less painful spikes; even the emerging mauve flowers (Crayola shade: thistle) are bristly as scrub brushes.

Some of the mulleins are tall as my head, tips branching in prongs like saguaro cacti, leaves felted and fuzzy.

Wild grapevines droop with clusters of unripe fruit the size and color of peas. Behind one of the vines I spot a deer tearing into a giant shelf fungus. She presses it against a log, shifting it into position, then picks up the whole thing in her mouth and munches, cheeks mumpy.

A woman in a coral t-shirt straddles her bike, watching Fabio pose by the nest. "What is it about those birds?" she says. "I saw another one on my way out. Two eagles. That's a good day."

I don't tell her I've seen three—sounds competitive—but that is a *great* day.

Day 315. **July 25, 7:20 AM**

One pickup truck parked at Brodhead Point, white with Tennessee plates. I hesitate, but the driver is probably out in a rowboat. I need some cool woods today.

Sunlight cathedrals through pines. I spot a few mushrooms along the path: white with gills, mustard colored, shiny tan. A few early hickory nuts, hard and green.

The beach is a shock. There's way, way too much of it: hundreds of feet of exposed rock and dirt. I walk down to the water and see recent footprints. That would be Tennessee Guy.

And there he is, spin casting. He sees me too, so it would be rude to turn tail. "Morning," he greets me.

He's silver haired, fit, squinty eyes, push-broom mustache: Sam Elliott, tenor edition. "I been out here since the crack a dawn. Saw the sun rise.

Beautiful morning. Beauty-full. Woulda been nice to get a few fish on the stringer, but that's what it's all about, am I right?"

He's right.

We chat about how low the water is ("down four feet since last *week*") and how high the Lower Basin is since the last water release. ("I don't know what they're doing. *They* don't know what they're doing.") Then I head up the beach, climbing across bluestone crags and around the point.

I stand on a rock lapped by water and survey the High Peaks, summer green, the whole view ringed by a tonsure of dry rocky beach. I look for my throne by the mossy stream. The stream has dried up and the log sprouts new seedlings.

I walk back down the highwater stripe at the edge of the woods. Tennessee Guy has propped up his rod. He calls out, "You're s'posed to fish down by the water."

"Not fishing. Just walking back to my car," I tell him. He asks me if I'm from around here. "Lotta people think I'm not, on account a my accent, but I lived here till I was nine. Then we moved downta Tennessee. Still like it here best." Okay, now he's fishing for company. He's friendly, and I like that he savored the sunrise, but the odds he's a Trump voter seem pretty strong (red state, fish-and-game lobby, good ol' boy). He bids me goodbye with "Enjoy your day, darlin'."

Walking through woods, I see a red dot move on spindly legs. Daddy longlegs. Instantaneous memory of Birch Brook Day Camp, half an hour from my childhood home. We changed into swimsuits in a tent that always seemed to have daddy longlegs climbing up its canvas walls. Janie, a girl in my group who was white-blonde albino, was terrified of spiders, so I used to catch them and take them outside. When I picked one up by its leg and the leg *came off*, I freaked.

Birch Brook's swimming pond was marshy, with cattails and frogs by the sand beach where the Buddy Board hung on a tree. We ate pink baloney on Wonder Bread and drank Dixie cups of Hawaiian Punch. Larry and I rode to camp on a yellow school bus; David was too young. The tough kids in the back bellowed, "On top of spa-ghettti, all covered with cheese, I lost my poor meeeatball, when somebody sneezed" and "Great big gobs of greasy grimy gopher guts, mutilated monkey meat, carcerated chicken feet."

Two groundhogs on the roadside, about six feet apart, munching in unison. They look like a theatre-class mirror game.

Day 316. **July 26, 8:20 PM**

Horizontal ropes of cloud glow postsunset orange, like tiger stripes on the western sky. To the south, dusky rose cotton candy. It's a Sunset Man vista, and I can't help wondering why I haven't seen him again. I remind myself that I've walked here three hundred–plus times, and we've had two conversations. That isn't exactly a pattern.

I remember the way I felt after the first time I met him, blithely assured that our paths would cross soon, and realize something has shifted. That bright cloak of SOMETHING WILL HAPPEN has vanished like mist, leaving me vaguely embarrassed at getting my hopes up. When I picture the last time I saw him, the phrase that pops into my head is "beating a hasty retreat."

An abrasive voice booms over the Lemon Squeeze: "What the fuck? There's bugs, that fuckin' boat hasn't moved, it's just sitting there. This fuckin' SUCKS."

Two teen boys, unhappily out for a walk with their mother. The one who's not bitching does some sort of wannabe parkour, jumping up onto the end of the cement wall. The top is angled, not flat, and his balance is poor. After flailing his arms a few times, he jumps down on the far side—the crumbling shelf over the increasingly steep drop down the terraced hill—and starts running along it. My heart's in my mouth. When he realizes that in a few steps he'll be more than a hundred feet from the ground, he vaults back over the wall. Their mother says nothing. His brother says, "Fuck! I just swallowed a fuckin' bug."

I pause on the far side to take a deep breath, and a man who's walking his bike so he can look at the sky better says, "I don't know where to look. Everywhere you look, there's beauty."

Well, maybe not *everywhere*.

It helps, though, and so does the sky, getting brighter and wilder. An eagle wings by, heading back to the nest. Next comes the heron. The evening commute.

Day 317. **July 27, 5:35** AM

I wake at first light and get out of the house within minutes, feeling proud of myself. Then I drive past my neighbor Judie's house. The lights in the stable are on and she's feeding the horses, and I realize that she has not only been up for hours, but does this *every morning*, and then goes to work.

At the hardscrabble farm, four horses wait by the gate in unmatched pairs: white draft mare shoulder to shoulder with smaller Norwegian mare. They stand stock still and ghostly in predawn light.

I get out of my car to a cool breeze and whitecaps, a slice of fading half moon. Blessed quiet. A few early songbirds, a crow or two, but no human sounds, which is just what I need.

The teen eagle soars away from the nest, surfing wind currents.

The first rays of sun hit the mountaintops, red as a safety light. I'm surrounded by woods when it clears the horizon, blazing between trunks of white pines like a special effect.

I walk onto the weir bridge. There's a NO PEDESTRIANS sign, but it's on the far side of the WPA-era pumphouses, and I've seen other people walk out there with cameras. Why not?

Cliff swallows loop, and I watch one emerge from its dried-mud nest under the eave of the pumphouse, with its ersatz Mayan stone frieze. In all the times I've driven over this bridge, I never noticed those nests. Five cormorants bob on a buoy.

I spot a young doe eating grass near the top of the dike, just a few feet away. She sees me and freezes, then turns and walks down toward the water. I walk onto the pathway along the Lower Basin, rising sun in my eyes. There are two small backlit shapes up ahead, in the grass near the guardrail. Canada geese?

I lift a hand, squinting. One of them moves, and I recognize its pointy ears and long neck: a fawn, poking its head up to see what I am.

Twin newborn fawns, curled up to sleep in the grass. The doe must have left them while she went to graze. Not the safest of spots; teenage mother.

I inch closer. The second fawn raises its head. I'm so near I can see the white hairs on their chins, their wet noses and translucent ears. They look at me, wary.

The first fawn struggles to stand. It's the size of a beagle on wobbly stilts. Its spots are unevenly placed, with dotted lines over a spatter of freckles, a solid white line on the side of its neck. The second fawn stays put, craning its head, anxious.

The doe is grazing back toward them. The standing fawn dashes to meet her. The shyer fawn gets up and follows on wobbly legs. I leave the three nuzzling, mother-and-child reunion.

The beach past the rise is wider than I've ever seen it, including a flat stretch of sand. I'm astonished to realize some of the stones form a rectangle: an exposed foundation. My heart beats too fast. I remember seeing foundations and even some cellar stairs once in a drought year, under a foot or so of water, but this is completely exposed, on dry land, and I've walked past that pile of rocks *how* many times without seeing its shape? Some of the big stones have tumbled out of place, but there's one partial wall and two straight-edged corners. Whatever it was, it was small: a one-room cabin or outbuilding. But it's been there since people lived in this valley, a ghost building from the Drowned Towns.

Day 318. **July 28, 9:10 AM**

Sky like skim milk, steamy air. I'm walking the circular path at the aerators next to DEP headquarters, below the dam. I used to bring Maya here when she was little. She and her friends could zoom around and around the circle on trikes, and they'd never be out of my line of vision.

The fountain is a tall central jet ringed by lower ones, rising out of a tumble of large bluestone chunks. A breeze I can't feel wafts a sheet of fine mist in my direction. It feels good on my skin. Sixteen Canada geese graze on the lawn, patches of purple thyme amid vivid green grass. Many pines, some with thick twisted trunks, some tall and straight. There's a sad colonnade of dying blue spruce and a short run of cedar. Cones of all sizes litter the path.

It's a shift of perspective to stand *below* the embankment, looking up toward the spot where I've often stood looking down. I see the guardrail and, every so often, the bouncing head of a runner or a gliding bike helmet.

The aerator building has giant arched glass-brick windows and riveted doors like the entrance to the Emerald City. Above, a stone lintel carved CITY OF NEW YORK CATSKILL WATER SUPPLY, A.D. 1915 with a carved shield of beavers, barrels, and windmill blades. Signs everywhere: NO ADMIT-TANCE. The parking lot holds enough DEP cop cars to restage *The Blues Brothers*.

Day 319. **July 29, 11:30 PM**

I stop for a midnight walk after a lovely performance at Maverick Concert Hall. There's a car parked in the lot, which gives me pause, but when I step out and look up—amazing sky, star filled and moonless, full Milky Way!—I can make out two soft female voices ahead. So I walk past the red safety light and onto the dark pathway under a shimmering ceiling of stars.

As I get closer, I realize they're not speaking English, but a melodious Slavic language. I can't see a thing but a faint glow on the guardrail, but it sounds as if they're lying down on the pathway, not too far ahead. I don't want to scare them (or worse yet, trip over them) so I call out, "Hello."

"Hello," they answer in accented chorus.

"Are you looking for shooting stars?"

In chorus: "Yes."

"Have you seen any yet?"

They haven't. We talk for a minute—the Perseid meteor shower peaks later, in August; it's a lovely sky anyway; yes, very beautiful. It's odd to converse with strangers you can't see. I have no idea how old they are or what they look like; I don't know if they're lying on top of their jackets or sharing a blanket. I wish them good luck and walk on, looking up.

There's Cassiopeia, the familiar W shape, and the tight cluster of the Pleiades. And *whoosh*, there's a meteor!

It doesn't streak far, but it feels like good luck. "Did you see that?" I blurt, but I'm too far away, out of earshot. And it's already gone. I hold still for a moment, framing a wish, then turn around and start back.

Soon I hear the two voices rising and falling and a ripple of laughter, and I realize this stargazing outing is really about something else: two friends enjoying a conversation in the dark. I wish them good night and head back to my car, feeling blessed.

Day 320. **July 30, 6:30 PM**

Two opossums skitter across the road, looking spooked. Black marble eyes and bare rat tails, their giant pink feet.

Something I've never seen before, right in the parking lot: a black Jeep with a hunting arrow stuck in the socket where the antenna should be.

Day 321. **July 31, 4:25 PM**

View from the bridge after all-day rain: tarnished-silver sky, low clouds bisecting mountains. I'm heading back to the spot where I saw the bear cub, and though I know I'm unlikely to see it again, my pulse quickens with anticipation.

The wet rocks are slippery. I pick my way carefully, resting my hand on a rowboat stern stenciled *Prowed Mary*. It's not far to the point with its arching white birch trunks, and I wonder again at that little bear coming so close to the rowboats and parking circle. There are patches of moss at the edge of the woods, small fronds poking up in green asterisks. I see several flat rocks and wonder where I found the eagle feather.

There. That birch archway, screened by that pine bough. There's no cub in sight, but I feel the same carbonated sensation of miracle stirring, like hummingbird wings in the belly. I look at the nearest flat rock, and there's a goose feather stuck in a crack. If I had any doubt, it evaporates. That's the altar.

I'm seized by the impulse to stand where the cub stood and see what it saw. I walk under the birch arch and turn. From this side, the arch looks even more magical, with the mountains and distant weir bridge in the background, like the entrance to another world.

The rain's coming down harder, so I walk into the woods. I see several chewed-up mushrooms, some tan and some reddish, and a pristine flat white one that might be a poisonous amanita.

Bears know.

Day 322. **August 1, 2:20 PM**

Third day of rain and it's green as feckin' Ireland. The water is textured gunmetal. One slash of sun scatters glints of silver like chain mail.

Two moms with a young girl on a lavender scooter. One points to a pothole and says soberly, "That was a meteor from *outer space*." Girl looks dubious. Mom goes on, "We used to see those a lot when we hunted for dinosaurs."

Clouds closing in from all sides. Air feels heavy and ominous. Treetops dead still.

Day 323. **August 2, 5 PM**

After three days of rain, the scintillation of bright sun on water is hypnotic, like a disco ball.

Grasshoppers taking surprisingly long leaps, ratcheting miniature drumrolls.

Puddles line the path. A decapitated Queen Anne's lace head floats in one, then another, then a third and fourth. Installation artist at work?

On the Lemon Squeeze, a man pushes his adult son in a wheelchair, mother walking behind. Below them, a vulture takes off from a tree, its giant wings spreading. A second follows. Their long shadows glide over treetops.

Day 324. **August 3, 6:55 PM**

On the drive down, I spot a small, lean, elegant hawk on the power line. Straight tail, brown-and-white breast, compact head: Cooper's hawk?

The Queen Anne's lace bomber has been here again, leaving a floral doily on one of the bollards. I pluck another and leave it on the next bollard. Artists in dialogue.

Heron, still as a post on the creek spill below.

Dragonflies and cliff swallows swoop like maniacs, snatching gnats out of the air. The dragonflies look like miniature helicopters. One flies into the side of my head, a startling sensation of flutter and *smack*, my hair tossed, chirring wing sound right next to my ear.

A slender, straight-backed Chinese man walks out barefoot, carrying shoes in one hand. He's wearing a white shirt and warm-up pants. We exchange smiles as we pass.

Moments later, I hear someone singing behind me. I turn, and he's standing in the center of the Lemon Squeeze, facing the setting sun and singing a full-throated prayer that sounds like Chinese opera.

Walkers circle around him; he's utterly unselfconscious, his voice shaping sound. I walk back and stand listening, leaning both hands on the warm cement wall and watching the amber sun. Five ducks swim across its reflection, and the combination of this impassioned, exotic music and birds silhouetted on shimmering water is so gorgeous my eyes brim with tears.

The man finishes singing. He bows to each of the four directions—west, east, north, south—then raises a hand to salute the sun. He picks up his shoes and walks back very slowly. As he passes, I thank him for his song. He says, "You love sunrise? Very good for you!"

I stay at the wall until the sun's blazing disc disappears behind mountains, raising my hands to my heart. The air cools around me, an instantaneous whisper of pink in the clouds.

Driving through Olivebridge, I see the same hawk on a different power line and have the bizarre sensation the man I just saw has retaken his avian form.

Day 325. **August 4, 5:55 AM**

I wake with the light, pull on my clothes, and head down to the res in apricot predawn. It's actually chilly, a welcome sensation. The air feels rinsed clean. There's dew all the way down the hillside.

The sun clears the trees, fiery gold. An eagle glides out from the rise in what seems like slow motion. Then a seagull, its white wings warmed by dawn light.

On the rise, a backlit young buck, twin prongs in new velvet. I cross the weir bridge to walk down the east path to the Frying Pan; I haven't completed the whole five-mile loop since it got so hot. A low-slung fog steams off the water, rising in twists. Four cormorants fly in a widely spaced line, one after another.

I pass a bearded man in quasi nineteenth-century garb (brown felt hat, collarless linen shirt, quilted tan vest) gripping an Evian bottle. When we pass again on the way back, he's stripped down to a tie-dyed tank top.

Familiar faces approach: Look Ma No Hands, Eagle Guy the Gray, Big Bird, Krampus, the Reader. What are their nicknames for me?

Day 326. **August 5, 8 PM**

The air is still, humid. A turtleneck sweater of clouds.

Nothing moves but one bat, looping over water. I catch a split-second glimpse of a platinum strip of new moon, just as clouds close around it. It's like a mirage, so startling I gasp.

Sounds of leaping fish, katydid drone.

Day 327. **August 6, 7:50 AM**

Two middle-aged locals:

"Lotta people today."

"There've been, lately."

"Summer."

"Yeah, well, it's one of the best views in the country. In the whole *country.*"

Amen to that, but today I'm preoccupied with the iced coffee I spilled on my last unstained shirt, and saggy old socks that keep sliding down into my shoes. Never mind that the sun's fanning radiant columns of light between backlit gray clouds. Sometimes it's all about coffee and socks.

Monarch on tall purple joe-pye weed. And crossing the road, unimpressed by oncoming traffic, a plump skunk in lush black and white.

Day 328. **August 7, 9:30 AM**

Turquoise water, slight whitecaps, sun, breeze. Sky vibrant blue. It's not crowded: I hit the sweet spot between the early exercise crowd and the families with bikes.

Lovely walk. Nothing of note but perfection.

Day 329. **August 8, 7:40 PM**

Tonight's guest star: Beckett Nathaniel Dixon, age four, and his parents Nelly Reifler and Jonathan Dixon, both writers.

The man of the hour rides a bright plastic three-wheeler he's almost outgrown, bombing onto the pathway with loud shrieks of glee. His parents convince him to take it down a notch, but the long straight drag strip is irresistible. Walking behind him as he hunches over the handlebars, knees pumping hard, it's impossible not to think of *The Shining*. Eventually he steers to the left, dismounts, and walks over to see what the grownups keep stopping to stare at. He peers over the guardrail that's been blocking his view of the water and gets very still. Then he says quietly, "Wow."

Jonathan: "One of those places that makes you feel really insignificant."

Nelly tells Beckett the reservoir's water goes all the way down to New York, to the faucet in their friend's apartment, a hundred miles away. Beckett says "wow" again. He can't stop staring. I love him for this.

By the time we get to the rise, it's getting dark and he's getting tired. Jonathan's brought a rope to pull him along on the trike, but Beckett wants to be pulling, not pulled. There's a lot of rope tangling, a little clashing with dad, a few tears in mom's arms, then a compromise plan.

The first stars emerge, near an almost-half moon. Beckett says the moon is a star too. Nelly corrects, "The *sun* is a star too." Beckett: "So is the moon." She does not push the issue. Overtired four-year-old; let him have it. Good mom.

When we reach the parking lot, I ask Beckett how he liked the reservoir. He's monosyllabic, too tired to expound. I bet he'll sleep well tonight.

They get into their car, and I walk out again as the sky darkens, cools, and fills up with stars. I see two of them fall.

Day 330. **August 9, 9:20 PM**

No stars, shooting or otherwise. Dark shapes, black on charcoal. Dark mountains, dark trees, dark beach, dark water.

Papa's been spitting up blood. I have come up here to clear my head. It's not working. Numb clutch at my heart.

Katy did, katy didn't, katy did, katy didn't, into infinity.

Day 331. **August 10, 4 PM**

Papa is okay. Residual bleeding gum from a dental cleaning, complicated by the blood thinner he takes. Dentist treated it with a coagulant made of aluminum chlorohydrate and kaolin clay. Bleeding stops. We all breathe.

I walk during a hot, humid stretch between storms. More thunderheads gathering, tall and gray over High Point, but a merciless sun beats down on the path.

Three mergansers tip underwater in unison, synchronized swimmers. Curly-haired dude with a bushy mustache sits on a bench with his camera. His rust-colored t-shirt says IT'S NOT ME, IT'S YOU, a poor choice of slogan for chatting up female walkers. He tells me he's hoping to catch a shot of a rainbow. "One of those days I can just hang out, chill, and relax," he beams as I nod, smile, and extricate.

By the time I get back to my car I am drenched in sweat. Rivulets run from my forehead to eyes and down the small of my back. I'm funky in yesterday's clothes, can't wait to get back to my house for a shower.

Papa is okay.

Day 332. **August 11, 5:30 PM**

Insane heat and humidity punctuated by violent cloudbursts. I just interviewed Sunil Yapa, author of the remarkable novel *Your Heart Is a Muscle the Size of a Fist*, and my head is still buzzing with talk about the power of human connection, darkness, and light. So the partial rainbow I see from the bridge, glowing bright against gunmetal clouds, seems like a big ole metaphor.

I drive to the Frying Pan. The wet pavement exhales steam. I set out in flip-flops, then kick them off and go barefoot, splashing through puddles.

Distant thunder grumbles over the north peaks, with steely gray clouds to the east, blue sky and sun glowing in from the west. I keep looking back over my shoulder; no rainbow. Then I spot it, pale and translucent but still the full spectrum, a rainbow's wan ghost. I watch as it fades.

Day 333. **August 12, 3:10 AM**

I wake from an unplanned nap in my desk chair with lights blazing all over the house. I go downstairs to turn them off and see stars out the window. I step onto the porch. Sure enough, there's a break in the clouds that have hidden the Perseid meteor shower all week. Tonight's the peak night. Feeling lightly insane, I pour cold coffee into a thermos and drive to the res.

There isn't one car on the road. Lots of blown leaves and ripped branches from earlier thunderstorms. There are puddles. And bats.

As I open the door, a moth circles the dome light, casting a dark moving shadow. I'm spooked, but the fillip of thrill wakes me up. I step out of the car.

It's dead quiet. The sky's clear overhead, still covered with clouds to the east. I can't see Cassiopeia, where the shooting stars are supposed to originate.

I set out in the dark. Within seconds I see a short streak, and yes, I do gasp. A small voice in my head says, *Okay, you can go home now.* A larger voice tells it to shut up.

Distant flashes of heat lightning. Cool night air moving around me, a soundtrack of bullfrogs and katydid scrape.

Another small streak. I stop walking and crane my neck, scanning from side to side. I tell myself I'll go home after ten shooting stars. Or twelve. I just want to see one really big one, one dome-to-horizon white trail.

Streak, streak, one after another: nine, ten.

Okay, maybe twenty. Then I get this crazy idea to stay here until I've seen *sixty*, for my sixtieth year. The clouds are beginning to break up; the newspaper said there could be up to two hundred per hour.

Sixty meteors sounds impossible. But when I get up to thirty, I realize I'm going to do it, come stiff neck, come boredom, come yawns and long pauses. Every time I think, *This is stupid, you've seen enough*, I spot another.

I hear a trout jump. A barred owl calls over the water, again and again. Then another owl, higher, a tenorish purr.

Constellations and stardust. It's not about meteors, is it? It's about being part of the universe. Letting things go. Because loss is enormous, but love is infinite.

I count sixty-four meteors in just under an hour. Number fifty-seven is the best.

Day 334. **August 13, 6:20 AM**

Sun's already up. I pass a big flock of wild turkeys scurrying down the road shoulder in Olivebridge. Mama hustles the young ones away from the dangerous object I'm driving.

The newly washed air smells like linen. One fisherman rowing, his flashing oars catching the light.

I stop on the Lemon Squeeze to look down at pockets of mist in the draws. They look like Blue Ridge Mountain hollows. Then I spot someone walking on top of the guardrail, tightrope-style. He's not totally grace-ful—he has to swing out a leg or both arms to counterbalance—but he's making good time. I notice a tall silver cylinder in his left hand. Is he chugging a breakfast Colt 45?

I walk out far enough to look up at the eagles' nest; nobody home. As I turn back, the guardrail walker rounds the curve, ducking low-hanging branches. He loses his balance, hops down. "Stage fright," he says, sheep-ish. He's got a goatee and glasses, wears a backward baseball cap and tiki necklace. The Colt 45 is a steel water bottle.

On the way back I spot Look Ma No Hands on her bike with both hands clasped behind her, her spiky white hair and girlish "good morning."

Then Meekman, smiling meekly, and Eagle Guy the Gray, heading out to shoot on a day that's supposed to hit 95; "real feel" with humidity 112. I'm impressed.

On the ramp to the bridge, a roadkill spotted fawn, its slender neck stretched back and eyes still bright. I breathe out "Oh!," involuntary and useless. Might be one of the twins I saw sleeping, not ten yards away.

Day 335. **August 14, 9:40 AM**

Air washed clean by last night's apocalyptic storms. The sky is clear blue, stippled with small wisps of cirrus, mares' tails, and mackerel sky.

I drive to the Frying Pan. The stream to the right exhales mist, celes-tially backlit; a river runs through it. The undergrowth on the approach road is bayou lush: neon-green grasses, moss-covered logs, deep puddles. Where's my little bear?

The sun beats down on my bare shoulders. The default wildflower on this side is not Queen Anne's lace, but butter and eggs, laced with crown vetch, wild thyme, and chamomile. It's all pastel yellow and lavender, Easter egg tints.

I spot a walker bent over a book and think it's The Reader, but the shoulders seem broader. As we get closer, I see it's a very buff man with earbuds and sunglasses, toting a slipcovered library hardcover. He sees me look, so I ask what he's reading. "Baldacci." He tips his sunglasses back onto his forehead. His eyes are sky blue. "I started it on the treadmill, but it's good for places like this, where you won't get run over. I like multitasking, I guess."

I guess. And have I got a girl for you, I think as he replugs his earbud and drops down his shades. They could read during sex.

Driving back, I notice that one of the dead-end spurs is called Brown's Station Road, a name I remember from *The Last of the Handmade Dams*. I turn onto a suburban cul-de-sac of '60s split-levels and ranch houses, backyard playsets, petunias, a Trump sign next to a boulder topped by a Tonka truck.

This is where the camps for the laborers were, full of drying spaghetti and laundry lines. I wonder if that Trump voter knows he lives on the spot where they housed the hundreds of immigrants and southern blacks who hand built the reservoir dike that his house is below. It's an act of faith building a house here. If the dam ever broke, there'd be one hell of a flood.

Day 336. **August 15, 8:10 PM**

I missed the sunset, which happens much earlier now. Missed the damn afterglow. The sky is dull gray, and I drive to the res with a thrill-is-gone irritability. Let's get this over with.

Three oncoming planes, lights bright as UFOs. I'm thinking about alien abduction stories, why so many people cling to the same scenario, with transporter light beams, metal examining tables, and anal probes. (Especially the anal probes. If their civilization is advanced enough for space travel, why would they need to know what's in our bowels?)

I suspect I'm not paying attention.

I go to the guardrail to gaze at twilight. Something moves down at the base of the dam, by the waterline. Is it a bear?

It moves again, and I realize that it's two shapes: a couple, making out furiously. He's lying on top of her, heads mashing together, feet practically in the water. I'm shot through with envy. Not just for the passion, and partner to share it with, but the youthful defiance, the flouting of rules.

I wonder if they're going to take their clothes off and do it. Philip and I would have, back in the day. We christened more than a few outdoor sites, including a ruined castle alongside Loch Ness.

It feels creepy to watch, so I take a step back from the railing. The angle's so steep that they're out of view instantly. Picked a good spot. I try to imagine how reckless they feel, how madly in love.

I went to the dentist today, had my teeth cleaned, did errands, sat in my desk chair, and typed a lot. Where is *my* reckless in love? How did I dwindle into this sixty-year-old solo woman whose life is so dinky?

It happens to many of us as our lives arc toward twilight, toward autumn, but sometimes that sense of loss cuts to the bone. What is added as time hurtles by, taking so much away?

Patience, I think. I could never have gone to the same place every day for a year when I was young and eager. It's taken this long to learn that a life is a series of moments, no more and no less. The forest *is* the trees.

The moon glows through clouds. There's a pale ring around it, like an areola. I walk past the rail where I stood with the Sunset Man, months ago now, and wonder again why he came on so strong and then slipped away into nautical twilight. Did some look in my eye scare him off? Did he have someone waiting at home? Some men like to flirt, and it doesn't mean anything. That's what they tell themselves.

Call it a reservoir mystery.

This is why I write fiction. Because you get to *make up the plot.*

Day 337. **August 16, 5:25 PM**

Sweltering. The long-horned Highland cows at Vly Farm stand chest high in their small muddy pond, cooling off.

Storm clouds over the mountains. Water like satin. The air sweats.

A Y-shaped branch sits on the center line like a divining rod. Monarch butterfly drying wet wings atop a dead weed. Did it just hatch? Is it wounded? Just as I start to wonder if it might be dead, it closes and reopens its wings, very slowly. It sits still a few moments and lifts off, fluttering, dipping, then swooping down onto a Queen Anne's lace blossom.

A young woman reads local news off her phone to her boyfriend. "A bear broke into the Phoenicia Liquor Store!" They both burst out laughing. Drunk bear!

Charcoal clouds roll in like a special effect, lava-lamp changeable. One of them beckons to me like a big 3-D hand, then dissolves in a swirl.

Another cloud is three pronged, wicked witch flying out of the west. This is the one with the payload—it's blotting out mountaintops as it comes closer. The beach looks exactly like the book jacket of Billy Collins's *Picnic, Lightning*: glowering sky, ominous yellow foreground.

Kate and Sarah walk out on the dam. Kate gestures upward. "Now *that* is a painting!"

"That's about twelve paintings."

She nods with her native enthusiasm. "How are you? Are you very very well?"

This time I just say yes. "I love that there's a sunset going on somewhere behind all of that."

"That's the metaphor, isn't it?" Kate says. "For this whole election cycle. There's a sunset going on somewhere behind all of this."

Metaphor for more than elections, I think.

Day 338. **August 17, 6:30 PM**

Tonight's walking companion is my beloved nephew Jeff, on a visit from Paris. Jeff lived with Maya and me during his freshman year of high school, so he's sort of like my second kid, the one I haven't seen for so long that he's now a scruffy-bearded young man, a rock drummer and aspiring filmmaker who ties himself up in more knots than he has to. He tells me about his apartment and work woes, the floods on the Seine. I tell him some things I've seen out here during this year. Then we both fall silent and stand looking out. Calm water. Brindle clouds.

A brisk white woman is leading a group of what might be Fresh Air Fund campers. One of the boys says, "Wait. Now we have to walk all the way *back*?" and she answers, not unkindly, "How else do you think we could get to the car?"

Two deer on the beach by the rise. Jeff sees something move inside a thorn bush. A female cardinal flies up, flashing cherry-red tailfeathers. I didn't spot her. Good eye!

Day 339. **August 18, 2:50 PM**

West Hurley Dike Road. Too many trucks.
    Sign: CAUTION—DRIFTING SNOW AHEAD (possibly not today)
    Flora: Queen Anne's lace, black-eyed Susan, Daisy Fleabane; girl flowers
    Beach: Two old-timers hauling a rowboat
    Sky: Cauliflower godhead

Day 340. **August 19, 8:00 AM**

Two pickup trucks stopped side by side on Vly Road, owners chatting through open windows. No rush, guys. No, really. If I hadn't stopped here to wait for you, I wouldn't have noticed this ditch full of jewelweed, that first flaming branch of red maple.

I'm meeting my friend Robert Burke Warren at the Olivebridge lot. He's a lean and handsome man who once played Buddy Holly on London's West End. I'm five minutes early and he's twenty late. I've brought two thermos mugs of coffee; I finish mine and start drinking Robert's. Runners and bicyclists come and go.

Robert arrives agitated, says he got lost. He's talking and not really looking. Downloading.

On the Lemon Squeeze, Robert looks down and sees something swimming. Dark head, concentric ripples. Is it a young beaver, a muskrat, a mink? We can't identify it from this height, but watching it slows us both down, gets us into a rhythm of looking at things.

As we reach the rise, Xena flaps over the tree line and lands on a pine. Robert's thrilled, and I say, "You've been blessed." Xena preens briefly, then sits like a newel post. And sits. She shall not be moved.

Robert wants to see her take off. He calls, "Hey! Over here!" I wince.

On the second yell, I ask him not to do that. As we walk away, he says with a mix of defiance and shame, "I knew that was obnoxious."

A second eagle calls out from the woods, and Xena calls back. Then a *bibbity* song, which I've come to think is the way eagles purr. When we turn to look at the nest, there's Fabio on his posing branch. He spreads his tail. He shimmies a little. He lifts off and flies. Robert says "Aaaah!" and we watch in rapt silence as he soars past, crosses the water, and finally drops out of sight.

We spot a flotilla of red-headed ducks. "Beautiful family," says Robert, sounding a bit misty. His son Jack is leaving for college next week; Robert and his wife Holly are already reeling.

Over coffee and eggs at the Pineview, we talk about books, about kids leaving nests, seeing eagles. Robert says, "You have no idea how much I needed that. Seeing an eagle—*two* eagles—that's not quotidian. I'd have to call that a religious experience."

He tells me that I've got a glow on since I started my reservoir year. Then he says, "Jack thinks my eagle fixation is funny. He doesn't get that when we were growing up, bald eagles were endangered from DDT. I thought I'd never get to see one in my lifetime."

Blessed.

Day 341. **August 20, 7:20 AM**

Two solo fishermen, one in a turquoise rowboat.

Eagle beelining toward Driftwood Point. I watch it drop down to the water. The fish gets away.

Another eagle ascends in a corkscrew spiral, photobombed by a crow. Lots of *skree* and *caw*. Crow gives up. Eagle soars.

I'm leaving for a multigenerational family reunion in the Finger Lakes, and I can't bear to leave the Ashokan. I'll miss two consecutive walks. I'm annoyed about that; they're annoyed that I'm planning to drive home midweek so I won't miss more. We are family. We get annoyed. Comes with the turf.

I forget which anonymous charcoal-gray rental is mine; have to locate it by the iced coffee and Bert Jansch CD on the front seat. "The time has come / For me to go."

Day 342. **August 21, 5:20 PM, Skaneateles Lake**

Away. I've come to this lake every August since I can remember. There were a few Cape Cod vacations when I was a toddler, but my first memories of living near water are from the series of cabins we rented on Skaneateles Lake, year after year after year. The long drives in the car, pre-Thruway, three kids pounding each other and screeching with boredom between stops at roadside attractions like Petrified Creatures, the Musical Museum, and Corning Glass Works. Car games: counting license plates, Twenty Questions, Papa's improvisational Polly and Billy stories. Wintergreen Life Savers (if we were good).

The long glacial hills lined with cornfields and dotted with dairy cows grazing. Then finally a view of the teal blue, string bean–shaped lake and the clamor of "I saw it first!" (Winner got a Wintergreen.)

August was freedom. Playing for hours by the lake, running back to the cabin for picnic-table lunches where our wet swimsuits left saddle marks on wooden benches. The dusty uphill walk to Fesko's IGA for Creamsicles and penny candy. Picking wildflowers on the way down, the same late-summer mix of Queen Anne's lace, goldenrod, black-eyed Susans, daisies, red clover, and chickory I see on the reservoir.

My parents rented several more and less funky cottages (one had an outhouse called Little Ol' Sunset Lodge) before we found the one that stuck, a pine hunting cabin with an outbuilding housing three cots for the kids (our own *house!*), an outdoor shower, and a row of Adirondack chairs on the cliff overlooking the lake.

Years later, when the cottage was sold, we started renting Ed Littlehales's cabin, two docks north. Pinewood was a rudimentary rectangle with a porch along its full length, with a couch-size green swing in the shade and a picnic table in the sun. The view of the lake, screened by vertical tree trunks at sunset, is etched on my brain as the definition of summer vacation.

A few years ago, the steep staircase down to the lake got to be too much for elderly parents on walkers and canes, and we found a new rental across the lake, in a cluster of houses below an insanely steep first-gear hill. It's right between two other houses, just steps from the lake. It isn't the same, but the water—deep green, cold, and silk smooth on the skin—is as lovely as ever.

I'm walking up that insanely steep hill. I start panting by the first curve. My legs feel like I'm trudging through drying cement. Plus I've got my back to the lake view, which just feels wrong.

And yet. There's a deep ravine with a burble of running water, the run-off stream from a waterfall three miles above. It's ringed with primordial ferns, dripping hemlocks, and kelly-green moss.

There's a spill of dirty black feathers on the steep bank. It's a desiccated dead crow, nothing but wing feathers joined at the bone. There's no smell of rot. As I prod with a stick, the head rolls loose, beak still in place, black fluff of cropped feathers still stuck to the skull.

I want it. It gives me a dark-hearted grave-robber thrill.

Two live crows fly overhead, raucous. Chipmunk streaks across the road, tail held vertical.

Mowed field full of seagulls, all facing the same way, so regularly spaced that they look like miniature drive-in speakers.

When I walk back down the steep grade to the lake, the sun's raying across it, the water a miracle blue. If I squint, it could be the Ashokan.

Day 343. **August 22, 11:55 PM**

I leave Skaneateles, pulling away from a picnic table full of relatives enjoying the dinner I cooked. It's the longest drive I've ever taken to get to the res, four hours on mountain roads. I stack up CDs on the seat: Bonnie Raitt, Little Feat, Neville Brothers. I *will* stay awake. At 9:59, I'm the last customer to enter the Roscoe Diner, a minute before closing time. Coffee to go and a black-and-white cookie. Back on the road.

Long Delaware County hills. Seen in the headlights: three raccoons on the gallop, a fear-addled cottontail, roadkill skunk. Rising harvest moon, like a huge pumpkin muffin. A few days past full; rim looks charred at the edge.

That moon follows me right up to Olivebridge. Sky full of stars. I walk out and breathe, standing in moonlight so bright I can see my own shadow.

Day 344. **August 23, 7:40 PM**

Past sunset, small waves and big sky. Canada geese honking, sudden first stars. Summer's winding down. It feels as wrong to be here as it did to leave. A big chunk of my heart is at Skaneateles Lake with my family. We've been saying for years it may be the last time we go there. This summer we all know it is.

Larry and his family came from France, David from Philly; Maya's coming from Vermont to drive back there with me. It's a gathering of tribes. Even with one of us taking Papa's arm as he walks to the dock with his cane, with two of us steadying Mom by the elbows as she inches her folding aluminum walker into the lake, it's too much. The days of Mom snapping her bathing cap under her chin and slipping into a brisk side-arm crawl, of Papa floating on his back, sighing with deep satisfaction, "It takes all the rottenness out," are behind us. We all know what's ahead.

I look out at this place where I've grieved for friends, and the world feels as fragile as silk.

Day 345. **August 24, 7:25 AM**

Goldfinches, goldenrod. Fall palette incoming.

Three mergansers dive. Big flock of Canada geese on the beach. Eagle Guy the Gray tells me he saw eight giant flocks in flight yesterday, all heading south.

Scatter of pale-pink wild phlox. Tall lemon cinquefoil. A bumblebee climbs out of a flower, so close I can see yellow pollen sacs on its hind legs.

I drove all the way home in mid–family vacation, partly to pick up Maya in Troy, but also so I wouldn't miss a whole week so close to the end of my reservoir year, and I've seen nothing unusual. Nature is teaching me lessons.

Shadow of chickory blossoms thrown across rough cement wall. Leafless, they look dead in shadow. But they're covered with blossoms in vibrant Delft blue.

Metaphor, metaphor, metaphor.

Day 346. **August 25, 1:20 PM, Skaneateles**

Today's walk by water is to Carpenter's Falls, a narrow sheer drop off a jutting rock slab, a few miles up the roadside ravine. The approach trail starts in hemlock forest, then edges along a gully with a near-vertical drop. Most of the way there are rocks and roots to provide a safe footing, or small trees to grip, but on one stretch you need to goatfoot over a slanting path with nothing between you and air, running on sheer adrenaline and faith that you won't slip and fall.

My nephew Jeff is a confident mountain goat, Larry and Laurie a little more cautious. I flunk. I get partway across the first bare patch and panic, unable to move either forward or back. Finally I just sit down and inch back on my butt, heart pounding, brow covered in flop sweat. Two ridiculously agile local boys hotfoot under the waterfall's curtain and scramble back up the sheer cliff face as if it were nothing.

The view from the rock where I wait is magnificent.

Never again.

Swimming in cold clear lake afterward much more my speed.

Day 347. **August 26, 2:20 PM, Skaneateles**

I drive to the lake's eastern shore with Maya and my nephews Jeff and Marc, who all grew up going to Ed's Pinewood cabin in August.

The road's so familiar I could drive it blindfolded. We pass the Borodino firehouse, with a sign for its annual Pancake Breakfast, and turn onto Littlehales Lane. Deeply rutted and crisscrossed by water bars, it's what used to be known as a "corduroy road." Once we pass the invasive McMansion halfway down the hill, the view is the same as ever: cornfields and wildflowers, green pines and blue lake.

We park at the bottom and walk back up the dusty dirt road. Piney woods on the right, golf course on the left, screened by scrubby wild sumac. I remember how endless this half-mile walk used to seem when

Larry, David, and I trudged up to the now defunct Fesko's IGA, with its plank floors and rattling coolers, to buy penny candy. Mom chaperoned us in a sleeveless housedress, her brown hair pulled back in a ponytail clip.

The golf course is abandoned now, covered with seagulls and Queen Anne's lace. Single crow in a dead spar tree.

There are dozens of small copper butterflies on the road, Monarch Mini-Mes. Their small triangular wings are orange on top and light brown underneath, so when they fold them and rest, they can pass for dry leaves. I step forward into sudden bright spirals of orange.

We turn back just below the McMansion. Before we get back in the car, we sneak down the driveway still marked with Ed's routered brown and buff Pinewood sign. We stand looking down through the trees at the roof of the cabin where three generations of memories live.

Marc is the first to turn away. Jeff is the last. I turn and see him with hands on hips, gazing back for the last time. Maya takes my hand and we stand still as mourners.

Day 348. **August 27, 6:40 PM**

I reach the Ashokan in magic-hour sunlight. Snakeskin crinkle of water.

I walk out on autopilot after six hours of driving, including a detour to drop Maya off. Too tired to observe other walkers. There are some. They walk.

Three small Vs of Canada geese fly low to the water, above their reflections. Five, seven, five: a haiku of geese.

Day 349. **August 28, 10:10 PM**

Star-gazing walk, setting out from the Frying Pan, first time I've been on this side late at night. There are no other cars, no red glow from the safety light. The pathway approach is so dark I can't see the bollards till I nearly walk into them. I'm aware of the dark woods behind, of my breath, jittery and excited.

I walk with an unlit flashlight clutched in one hand, jingling keys in the other (bear warning, just in case).

Cool breeze blowing sleeveless dress. Katydid scrape and tree frog ratchet. A single bat swoops overhead, dark against darkness. House lights on the hillsides across shadowed water, headlights crossing the weir bridge a mile away.

I stand still on the path for a long time, looking up at passing planes, blinking satellites, patchy stars. Then a flicker of lightning, so far to the west I can't hear any thunder. Another. A single long lavender bolt snakes down in a livid flash, spotlighting faraway clouds.

Day 350. **August 29, 7:35 PM**

I stop by my parents' "retirement house" to pick Mom up for the sunset walk I've promised, but she's fallen asleep. I'm afraid she'll be disappointed, so I wake her gently. Of course she still wants to go, and of course it takes her so long to get ready that we miss the sunset.

We walk out in twilight, and she exclaims over every pink-tinged cloud and contrail. The great blue heron flies over, a dark silhouette against water and mountains. Stopping and starting as she rolls her walker, we make it out to the first bench, where she sits and looks, catching her breath. On the way back, she says, "I'll carry this in my heart."

Day 351. **August 30, 9:10 AM**

The barn on the corner of Vly Road is stripped for rehab, three tall ladders leaning against exposed post and beam. Across the road, Highland cows graze, rust-red fur hanging over their eyes. Punk-rock calves, cave-painting bulls.

The sun's already high, and it's getting hotter by the minute.

Bumper stickers: WATERBOARD WASHINGTON. ROSENDALE ROCKS. I AM NOT ROUNDUP READY. Hillary sticker plastered diagonally over a Bernie sticker; I'll vote for her, but I won't like it.

Wildflowers look exhausted, more dried than blooming. Red-seeded tall grasses, stretched webs full of gnats. Bright stands of purple vetch plied by industrious bees. A lone spike of purple loosestrife.

Cedar waxwings swoop, sleek tan with dark masks. Couple on bikes wearing open shirts over swimsuits. She has a dense curtain of waist-length blonde hair, topped by a white hat with a black ribbon. They pass me riding, then lean their bikes on the guardrail and walk on in flip-flops. A mellow triathlon?

Sun-wizened old man with a t-shirt tied around his head like a turban, sunglasses, neon-green sneakers, shambles onto the pathway and starts an improbable mini-jog.

One white seagull midlake, just floating.

Day 352. **August 31, 5:30 PM**

Another reservoir mystery: two dog dishes left at the end of a parking space. One's full of water, one's full of multicolored bone-shaped treats and happy ants.

Light drizzle matches my mood. The Cheerfuls glide by with a unison "Hi." Their permasmiles make me feel lonely and weird, that teenage girl dressed in black sitting under the table.

It starts to rain more as I walk, and I mutter, *Okay, give me a sign I should keep getting wetter, or I'll turn around.*

Almost immediately, the head and neck of a cormorant pop up where I didn't know one was diving. It looks like a periscope. As I stare at it, something large flies behind it.

It's an eagle, flying so low it's nearly skimming the surface. It lands on a rock at the water's edge, near the drowned barn.

I walk fast but steadily. When I'm about fifty feet away, it turns and looks at me sharply. I freeze. We stare at each other for several long minutes. Then I venture a small step, and it spreads its wings, taking off in a lazy low flight around the back of the point.

I keep staring as something brown moves. There's a deer on the beach. She heads down to the water to drink.

Cormorant, eagle, doe. It feels like a sign, but they're not here for me. The birds and the animals are here all the time, all around us. The grace is in learning to move slow enough that you notice.

Day 353. **September 1, 4:50 PM**

September again. Calendar circling around to the start of this year-of-walks project, and I'm obsessed with all the things I haven't done yet: night fishing, seeing the res from a rowboat, a plane. If the plan was to contemplate cycles of time, I guess it's worth noting there's never enough of it.

Lone maple turned flame overnight. More to come.

I'm walking with my brother Larry today. He's thrilled by the cool wind and whitecaps and long stretch of driftwood, exclaiming, "It looks like the Aleutians!" He describes the difference in the way cold fronts move through quickly in North America, rain yielding to crisp windy weather, as opposed to the changeable French *ciel de traîne*. Larry likes to expound, his voice lecture-loud as we walk.

The deciduous greens are beginning to dull; if you squint, you can see what color each tree's going to turn. Larry calls it "a salad bowl mix." Mesclun forest.

The Cheerfuls ride by. Then an Orthodox family, dad surrounded by small sons in yarmulkes, followed by mother and toddler daughter, walking a few yards behind. Then a squat white-haired Indian auntie in patterned white sari.

Larry beams as we pass through the bollards. "This place always makes me feel good. I'd come here again tomorrow."

Day 354. **September 2, 3:40 PM**

Larry is good as his word. We're baaaack.

We stop at Olive's Country Store to get him a one-day fishing license. The clerk doesn't bat an eye at his French driver's license; her mother's from Strasbourg, near Larry's hometown of Houdemont. What are the odds?

I buy Larry's license. He buys me a blue landing net from the tackle rack. I'm not sure why I need a landing net, since we're not actually planning to fish, but I like its style.

I park at the fishing gate near the steep trail that spooked me when I was alone. We don props and costumes—caps, backpacks, fishing poles, landing net—and walk along the cracked roadbed, passing bluestone cliffs riddled with roots, a NO TRESPASSING sign that's been there so long that the tree's grown around it. When we reach the railroad tracks with the high view of the abandoned quarry, Larry stops, inhales, and says, "Well!"

I spot what looks like a hedgehog on an old railroad tie. It doesn't move, and as I get closer, I realize with a macabre thrill that it's a porcupine scalp, bristling with quills. The skull's nearly intact, missing one side of its jaw, so there's only one curving incisor, the color of pumpkin. On the railbed, more scattered bones: a length of curved spine, a femur, a couple

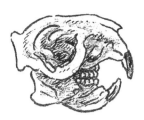

of ribs, a patch of quilled skin. What would dare rip up a porcupine? I've heard the fierce fisher cat will sometimes attack them, flipping the spiked body over to gut it. Respect to the tough.

I lift the skull carefully, setting it off to one side of the trail. We cross the tracks and step onto the trail that winds downhill to the quarry.

There's an immediate problem: both sides are lined with a lush growth of poison ivy, and the trail is so narrow it's almost impossible not to touch it. If you lost your footing, you'd fall face first into berrying vines. We turn back.

I retrieve the stashed porcupine skull, and Larry recites, "We left old Crego's bones to bleach / On the plains of the buffalo," which makes me laugh very loudly.

We drive down to Basin Road, park again, and walk out on the dike. The grass is chest high in some places. Terrific, we'll trade poison ivy for Lyme ticks.

I've been here before too, but I turned back when I spotted an unidentified man in a truck. This time we go farther, passing several bays with Maine coast–like islets. A great blue heron lifts off, and we watch till it flies out of sight.

The embankment's too steep to get close to the water till we reach a grassy path to a pine-covered point with a scatter of rowboats. We thread our way down to the shore.

Larry picks up a flat slice of bluestone and skims it, a supple flick of the wrist we were both taught by our Uncle Lou at Skaneateles Lake. Skip, skip . . . skip. Timeless.

Day 355. **September 3, 9:10 AM**

Raucous convocation of crows on Driftwood Cove point. They mesh with the katydids, ambient sound.

The Cheerfuls ride by, beaming as ever. He says "Hi" as she says "Good morning." Marital strife!

Day 356. **September 4, 9 AM**

Sky, water, blues. While I was out walking, Papa fell, knocking Mom to the floor. He's all right; she isn't. She banged her knee, hard, but refuses to go to the ER despite wincing pain. Our family is meeting Laurie's for breakfast, twelve strong. Mom will get to that diner come hell or high water. Sometimes she's such a damn Yankee.

Day 357. **September 5, 6:20 AM**

I close the car door, and an eagle glides overhead.

Sunrise, glowing basketball. It's cold—fifty-four degrees—and low cloudlets cling to the mountainsides.

Crows on the move. I count thirteen on the way out, including a Gang of Four that flies over three times, discussing the news of the day.

Shovel Cove is socked in with fog, just beginning to lift. I don't see a soul till I reach the weir bridge, where a carpentry truck pulls over. The driver (green eyes, nice smile) leans out to ask if I can give him directions to Brodhead Road. Yes I can, though I'm tempted to jump in and show him the way.

Seven cormorants play musical chairs on the usual buoy. Maximum number seems to be six. One hops on and another jumps into the water, again and again.

Driving home, I stop at the hardscrabble farm's self-serve cart for fresh eggs and homemade maple syrup. Two roosters are having a crow-off, bassline of moos from the paddock.

As soon as I open the door, the phone rings: Mom had a bad night, leg in spasm, knee swollen from yesterday's fall. We need to take her to the ER for x-rays.

Deep breath.

Day 358. **September 6, 11 AM**

It's not broken. After several hours on a stretcher, groaning through painful x-rays, Mom was sent home from the ER in an Ace bandage and leg brace to immobilize her knee. A muscular orderly with tattoos and a gentle West Indian lilt lifts her into my car's back seat; breathless, she calls it "a hug."

Back at the house they've never fully retired to, she pushes her walker with small, mincing steps, like someone with bound feet. The stiff leg brace hurts her. I unbuckle it so she can ice her knee, and go grab a quick res walk while my brother takes over.

It's windy as hell, tail end of Hurricane Hermine. Clouds, trees, and wildflowers churn. Hair whips over my face as I walk. It's like being a sailboat. The world's in upheaval.

Crows flapping like black paper scraps. Great blue heron blows past in a drunken swoop, riding gusts sidesaddle.

On the pavement, one small scarlet leaf.

Day 359. **September 7, 7:40 PM**

Exhausted from New York round trip. Mom's knee is better. David's on duty today and tomorrow while Papa's at his office, and I'll go down Friday and Saturday when he goes back to Philly. Tag teaming.

Twilight on the Lower Basin. Mountains in long silhouette, black against blue. Tooth-white crescent moon.

Only seven walks left. One thing I've learned: a year starts as a drizzle. Then the days pour.

Day 360. **September 8, 5:50 PM**

I'm walking with nature essayist Susan Krawitz today. The path to her classic white farmhouse is flanked by rudbeckia. Two hens escort me to the door, heads bobbing in tandem like synchronized swimmers.

It's humid and hot. Susan comes to the door wearing sandals and shorts. We're going off road, so I'm dressed for poison ivy, high grass, and ticks: long sleeves, long pants, sneakers and socks. I suggest a change. Susan says she's not allergic to poison ivy, she can see if there're ticks, and "I'm not doing boots, nope."

As we're leaving, she asks me, "Do I need my purse?" and I say no; faux fishing license my treat.

However. Faux fishing license requires a photo ID, which is in Susan's purse. It's too close to dusk to drive all the way back, so we head to the car feeling bummed by the prospect of walking the usual pathway in blazing late-afternoon sun.

"Or," I propose. "We could poach."

"What's the fine?" Susan asks. I don't actually know, since I've never been fined. But what are the chances of a zealous DEP cop patrolling an obscure fishing path late on a weekday afternoon? We decide to go outlaw.

We turn left at Boiceville, crossing the Esopus Creek, which runs wide and flat over loose stones. A groomed dirt road snakes through the woods, edged by meadow and burdock. I'm hoping it leads to the headwaters where the Esopus enters the reservoir.

The creek is fast flowing but tranquil, the path in deep shade. Susan can't get enough of the tree trunks. Beech, red pine, hemlock, white oak: giants. Some of them might be two hundred years old, rare in a landscape that was largely razed at the turn of the century. In a break of meadow, where the path turns river-bottom sandy, she identifies the bunchy white flowers next to the seven-foot ragweed as "pussytoes," a wonderful name. We step over old railroad tracks overgrown by tall grass and head deeper into the woods.

Both of us notice a lot of small holes drilled down into the dirt, about an inch wide. Susan says they're probe holes made by woodcocks digging for earthworms. I bend down for a closer look, flushing a bird. Camouflaged by dead leaves, the woodcock explodes in my face, flying off in an indignant clatter.

We swivel to watch, and there in midpath is a cottontail, frozen in silhouette, doing its best imitation of Easter candy. The sun hits its pose like a spotlight. As we approach, it zigzags ahead in a frenzy, crisscrossing the path. We're both relieved when it finally dives under cover of weeds.

We come to a mossy seep, which some thoughtful hiker has bridged with three logs. The creek's gaining momentum, tumbling over stone in a whitewater chorus. Both of us feel like we're in the Adirondacks, or Maine. The path winds up to a promontory overlooking the Chimney Hole, a spectacular, trout-heaven bend full of eddies and whirlpools, stirred up by three feeder streams. Improbably, there's a picnic table. Also a large wooden sign set into the steep bank below. We can just see its back, so I clamber down and turn back to read it.

A red line splits the sign in half. The right side is lettered ESOPUS CREEK; the left, ASHOKAN BASIN. We're at the borderlands. Somewhere just ahead, this mighty creek is refilling the reservoir basin with mountain spring water. But the path ends right here. Should we bushwhack?

We pause for a moment, scooping cool water into our hands and pouring it over our faces. We're both drenched in sweat, and I'm tempted to grab an illegal swim. But the sun's dipping low in a sky full of painterly clouds, probably no more than half an hour till sundown. So back we go, through the forest primeval.

Dusk falls. As we wind along Route 28A, a huge blocky owl flies in front of the car, angling into the woods. Not a barred owl; too big and heavy. Great horned, or great gray? We both vote for great horned; dark feathers.

We stop at the Olivebridge lot for the view and walk out to the first bench, watching the charcoal sky flicker with heat lightning. We get back to the car just as the first raindrops splatter its windshield. "I think your reservoir year made you magic," Susan says as the downpour begins.

Day 361. **September 9, 9:20 AM**

Steamy air and still water, a fluctuant mirror. I can see everything swimming or surfacing. The Family Merganser shoots around under the surface, then glides along it in stately interlocked Vs, a flotilla. A diving mink swims to the foot of the dam, ripple-walks along stones, and sits grooming itself like a kitten.

A small dead fish, floating, its white belly turned to the clouds. Severed Queen Anne's lace head on the pathway, a basket of tea-colored lace. One dead cricket, shiny as licorice.

On my way to New York City, heavy with summer's-end grief.

Day 362. **September 10, 11:50 PM**

These are the walks I won't miss. There is no way in hell I'd come back from New York, bone tired from caretaking elderly parents, and drive to the reservoir at midnight in a muggy drizzle unless I was keeping a pact with myself.

Every day for a year. *Every goddamn day.* Right.

I walk out in city shoes saying, "Okay, yeah, I'm here. Can I leave now?" But the place casts its spell over crabby exhaustion, and I stop to survey a mysterious sky. Blurry rainclouds to the north and west, a break of stars to the south, a titter of heat lightning. Katydids. Crickets. Oxygen.

On the way home, a barred owl soars right over my car. That's the third time that's happened. Whatever it means, I believe it.

Day 363. **September 11, 6:55 PM**

Fallen leaves on my windshield, a date that still haunts. Wild turkey herding four young ones away from the road. Dead red eft.

The water is restive. No whitecaps, but wind/water music, beating on stone. There's a chill in the air. Walkers head back in their shorts and sundresses, arms drawn in tight.

Dragonflies hover above amber grass, silhouettes of dried flowers. Down the hill, deer melt out of the forest, one, two; then three, four, and five. A sudden herd, where there was none.

Half moon rising. Thin ropes of cloud, glowing coral.

The world feels fragile, a lace shroud of beauty.

Day 364. **September 12, 3:10 PM**

A discordant clang of metal on stone. Unseen behind trees, a man yells at a woman somewhere on the beach. "What the FUCK are you doing? Are you fucking CRAZY? Why would you walk me right into that rock when the path's OVER THERE?" She mumbles an apology, but he won't be soothed. Apparently she made him drop his end of the rowboat. "You did that ON PURPOSE," he rages.

Their voices clash, carrying over the water. Then I see the man row out fast, his whole back clenched in fury. The woman stomps back up the beach by herself. Good for you, I think, willing her strength to keep walking away.

The afternoon sun bakes my shoulders. A hairy yellow-orange caterpillar inches across the hot pavement. Not sure if its spikes sting, I dustpan it onto a curled leaf and ferry it onto the grass, whispering, "Go transform."

Day 365. **September 13, 4:30 PM**

Three hundred sixty-five! Are we there yet? Not quite. It's a leap year, which always feels lucky, like getting a tip.

Maya and her friend Fred are visiting from Bennington, and we walk from the Olivebridge lot. When we reach the Lemon Squeeze, Maya leans over the wall, staring at sun-sparkled waves. "Look how the water's all walking in the same direction! It's so pretty," she coos, only half-ironic. "Pretty pretty pretty!"

I drive them to Brodhead Point, with its wide beach and reverse-angle view of the dam we just walked on. It's a well-trafficked place, not the safest of stops without fishing licenses, but we'll keep it on the down low. Fred looks for flat stones to skip, and Maya kneels down to dip her hand into the water. "I grew up here, and this is the first time I've ever touched the reservoir," she marvels. "The water is *perfect*. Feel this water. I really, really want to go swimming. I want to get into this water so much it's like being an addict."

Fred skims a stone in a remarkable arc—a long first hop followed by twelve or fifteen smaller splashes—and lets out an unbridled whoop of joy, immediately clapping both hands over his mouth with a guilty "oops" look that makes Maya and me laugh.

We wander a bit. The Andy Goldsworthy found-object sculptor has been at it again, with a tall installation of driftwood and stones on the beach and a new weave of branches between several trees. At the water's edge, Maya's collecting small stones and Fred's throwing them. "We are such different kinds of little kids," she tells him.

As we head back, she slips her hand into mine and says, "I get it, mom. I totally get your obsession." Just like that, something locks into place. Instantaneous amber, the jewel of connection, a moment frozen in time.

Day 366. **September 14, 5:50 AM–11 PM**

My year's-end walk is an all-day ramble around the Ashokan with multiple stops, starting at my home base, the Olivebridge lot. It's dawn, with a
pewter sky starting to warm the horizon. The first thing I see on the path
is a headlight, too bright. Are you kidding me? A DEP prowl car *now*,
before dawn?

Then I realize it's a single bright headlight: a bicyclist, out before
sunrise.

One bat, silhouetted. No trace of a breeze. It's so quiet I hear individual crickets. Then the crash of three deer grazing high on the hillside,
spooked by my presence and galloping down to the safety of woods, white
tails flagging.

The clouds start to glow, draping the shoulders of High Point. But the
sun doesn't clear the horizon till I'm past the rise. As usual, crows are the
heralds:

Here. It. Is.

Two more deer graze on the edge of the walkway. The doe raises her
head, wary. Her fawn is now nearly her size, its baby spots fading.

The whole Lower Basin is lavender. Low fog swirls over the water, off-
gassing steam like dry ice.

The sun rises fast, and the morning gets hot. I spot the prayer-bench
couple sitting in silence. He clears his throat, and they open their eyes and
get back on their bikes. They say, "Morning." So do the stocky Latino dude
in the black hoodie and the silver-haired L. L. Bean lady in green. Just
"morning"; the "good," I guess, goes without saying.

I'm disappointed not to see an eagle on my last sunrise walk, but just
as I'm thinking, "They're eagles; they don't take requests," I spot a broad-
winged silhouette. No mistaking the great curving M of its wings or the
long trailing feet: it's the heron. They don't take requests either. I know it's
just heading off to fish, that its sudden appearance is not in the least about
me, but I still feel honored.

A skitter of shorebirds runs across sand near the ruined foundation.
I stare at its blocks, trying to raise the house's walls in my mind's eye, the
steep pitch of its Dutch roof, efficient small windows, a curl of smoke over

the fieldstone chimney. Farm wife sweeping the porch, daughter gathering eggs in an apron as hens squawk and scold. Farmer hitching his team to the plow. A homestead amid other farms, in a deep fertile valley of creek-bottom land. Gone, gone, gone.

It isn't just here, and it isn't just New York City's long-ago land grab that's drowned out that past. It's the pace of our lives, the SUVs, earbuds, and iPhones that keep us from seeing and hearing and touching the place where we live.

As I sit in the parking lot, Mountain Man pulls in and parks his truck, radio blaring. A Bottini Fuel truck parks behind him, idling loudly; the driver beelines into the Call-a-Head. After they leave, there'll be birdsong. And after I leave, there'll be eagles. They live here. We're just passing through.

My plan for today is to circumnavigate the reservoir by car, stopping and walking at various points where I've never been. I want to see the Ashokan from every direction. First stop: Pineview Bakery. As I enter, a grizzled guy in work boots and a camo cap slouches up from the counter, and his buddy deadpans, "What, *you*? Go to *work*?" The regulars sit in a row with empty stools between them, like barflies, and the fry cook knows everyone's name. The comfort of daily routine.

There's an artsy couple outside on the porch, hanging out with the baker. The man has a groomed beard; the woman a downtown haircut, dark nails, an ironic leopard-print jacket. They're being Authentic. When they get up to leave, a guy at the table behind me says, "That's the one with the pig. She's got a pet pig."

His companion says, "*With* her?"

"Well, sometimes."

The fry cook enacts a Three Stooges routine for the deadpan waitress, then asks, "Did they have the Three Stooges in the Philippines?" She shakes her head.

I pay for my breakfast and pick up an illicit cinnamon sweet roll for later, as Gloria Gaynor sings "I Will Survive."

My next stop is a fishing gate I've never tried. It's on Route 28A and my Reservoir Angler Map shows it leading to something called Bridal Veil, which I hope is a waterfall.

The trail winds downhill through hemlock and pines. Downed trees crisscross the ground, a fertile aroma of rotting wood. There are dense glades of ferns, a dry streambed. I follow it down to a pristine wild beach. Red grass grows between bluestone shards, dotted with purple asters and lady's thumb. To the left, a perfect sitting log, angled toward the High Peaks. Not a built thing in sight. It's the prettiest waterfront view I've seen yet, and I found it *today*, after 365 walks.

I head down the shore. There's a tiny dry twist of snakeskin between jagged rocks, baby's first shed skin. Beyond it, a cliff rises over an ideal swimming hole, deep green and private. This must be where the waterfall drops in spring melt. I'm tempted to strip off my clothes and jump into the water. Who'd know?

A shadow flies over. I look up sharply; broad wings silhouetted by white-hot sun. Vulture? Then I catch a glimpse of the fanned white tail. It's an eagle! It spirals above me again and again, rising higher, then glides away, heading west. It feels like a benediction.

All right, I'll drive west. Route 28A snakes around curve after curve. There are several fishing gates here that I haven't explored, but the forest nearby has been heavily logged. There are mud-wheeled skidders and piles of timber. The earth feels raw and disturbed. I pass roadside signs: BUSH-KILL ROD & GUN CLUB, REPEAL THE S.A.F.E. ACT, MAKE AMERICA GREAT AGAIN. The Ashokan's Wild West.

I pause by the Boiceville bridge, watching the sparkling creek tumble. Percussion and melody, water on rocks.

At Bread Alone, I order a salad with farro, beets, and ricotta salata from a barista with fading magenta hair, cat-eye glasses, and wings tattooed over both elbows, punk angel. The lunch crowd is younger and tanner than the breakfast crowd at the Pineview. I see Nordic clogs, Tevas, and Vans. The speakers play indie folk of the wispiest kind; there are sriracha bottles.

My salad is excellent, but I don't linger. The sky's clouding up, and if I'm going to see the res from every direction, I need to stop somewhere on Route 28, to the north.

I drive through the Outsider Art Belt—the larger-than-life kitschy Indian statues built in the '30s by French expat Emile Brunel, and Steve

Heller's Fabulous Furniture store, surrounded by welded robots, space-ships, and art cars—and park at a gate. The entry path is a well-groomed dirt road that seems to go on and on, paralleling Route 28 on a long down-hill slant. I've gone most of a mile through meadow and marsh (loose-strife, jewelweed, monarch butterflies), crossed some overgrown railroad tracks, and hiked through a stand of tall pines before I reach the water.

It's turbid and gray, churning fast as it flows from the creek. The mountains look choppy here too: a true wilderness beach. It feels a bit *too* far. The wind's coming up and gray storm clouds are rolling in; I can't stop thinking of bears. But I've come all this way, so I pick my way over the rocky beach, passing another sculptural driftwood and rock installation. Whoever is building these things gets around. Or maybe it's not the same person. Maybe everybody who walks these wild beaches gets struck with the urge to make art, to leave something behind.

I walk back on a carpet of rust-colored, fragrant pine needles, then wend my way uphill to the sound of truck traffic.

Quick pit stop at Olive's Country Store, home of the Faux Fishing License. Then I drive to the Reservoir Inn, on the eastern end of the Asho-kan, where I'm meeting a posse of friends for a celebratory dinner: Jana Martin, Lisa Phillips, Teresa Giordano, Sarah and Geoff Harden, Susan Krawitz and Bruce Davenport. I show them my manuscript box of typed notebook entries, and we raise a toast. I'm drinking something called Bad-Ass Pear Cider, which tastes a lot better than you might expect.

The plan was a sunset walk on the West Hurley Dike Road, but by the time my friends pick up the check—thanks, guys!—it's already dark. We caravan to the dike anyway, gibbous moon rising through scudding clouds. Moon-drunk, we reel out alongside the guardrail, flicking our flashlights at passing trucks so we won't wind up roadkill. Half our num-ber head home, but Sarah, Geoff, Lisa, and I drive down to the Frying Pan, where we can actually walk.

There are skid marks along Spillway Road, black rubber forensics. Right before the last turn, a red fox streaks across the road, shoulder to shoulder, its tail a wild brush.

We set out in moonlight so bright and so blue that we cast long shad-ows over the pavement. No flashlights this time, and no trucks. Just us and the night. There's a hair-tossing wind, and a stink of rotting dead fish near the start of the path that underscores the sensation of wildness. Everyone keeps exclaiming about how cool it is walking at night. We're a group of four friends, but it feels romantic.

We walk most of the way to the weir bridge before we turn back. I'm more than a little footsore—I must have walked ten or twelve miles today, on pavement, dirt roads, and rock beaches. But still, when my friends say goodnight, I drive back to the Olivebridge parking lot, closing the circle that started at dawn.

The wind has come up, and I don't walk out far. I stand gazing at mountains and moon-silvered water. *I did it*, I think, basking in weary triumph.

As I leave the parking lot, I nearly run over a porcupine, thick bodied and low to the ground as it waddles across the road. It's black and remarkably shiny, dragging its dense coat of quills like a toddler in chain mail. There's still so much I've never seen.

Day 367. **September 15, 6:40 PM**

September 15, the same day I set out for an evening walk that turned into a year. The wheel of the seasons has turned, and it's suddenly fall. Flashes of gold and red leaves on the roadside. A sign at the hardscrabble farm: PLEASE STOP KILLING MY CHICKENS—DRIVE SLOWLY!

I do. And keep driving slowly across the weir bridge, where the setting sun gilds the water in magic-hour light.

Tonight's walk is not on, but *above* the reservoir. I had visions of ending my reservoir year at the crest of Ashokan High Point or Overlook Mountain, but my feet are still aching from yesterday's multiple walks, so

I'm getting my eagle's eye view from the top of Ohayo Mountain Road. At the foot of its hill sits the Glenford Church. Hijacked by its congregation and moved onto higher ground by yoked oxen just before the Ashokan began to fill up, it's now an art and performance space.

Ohayo Mountain's narrow hairpin-turn climb is improbably crowded with cars, and I suspect I'm not the only person who chose this steep route for its sunset potential. When I get to the top, I park next to a Sotheby's Realty sign and set off down a spur road that traces the top of the ridge.

The view is astounding. The sky is pale rose, and the reservoir's peacock blue stretches for miles in either direction, cradled by mountains. The sunlit Shawangunk Ridge is its backdrop, with Catskill peaks looming, majestic and green, at both ends. I can see intricate puzzle patterns of coves and peninsulas, the sun-gilded wedge of Kenozia Lake. But I'm seeing it all past a foreground of rich people's driveways and wraparound decks. Even when I pause next to an overgrown meadow filled with dry thistle and yellowing milkweed, I can smell lighter fluid and hickory smoke from somebody's barbecue. I'm too far away.

Is the Sunset Man down there tonight? Where's my heron?

That disconnect layers an autumnal bittersweet onto yesterday's I-did-it triumph. I'm not on the ground anymore; I'm looking back over this place I've been intimate with for a year. I feel I should conjure some end-of-the-road hard-won wisdom. But nothing has ended. I've circled around. One more turning, that's all. And it's all middle anyway, isn't it? This long stretch of pathway between birth and dying. The shards of each moment, each day, that become our mosaic. The moments that shimmer, the details that glint.

I don't like being up at this distance. I want to be *there*, in the thick of it, part of the picture.

I get back in my car. As I round the first hairpin curve, I see why I had to come up here tonight. An enormous full moon levitates through a whisper-pastel sky, perfectly framed between trees. I don't gasp, I shout, "Oohhh!" My veins flush with beauty. I'm fully alive. And I'm on my way home.

Afterword

THESE WALKS took place just a few years ago, and the time I recorded already seems quaint. Later that fall, an unthinkable candidate entered the White House. At first the Ashokan seemed like a place to escape the miasma of dread and rage that enveloped me daily. But there were changes there too, and some of them echoed the darkness I felt.

The StressCrete poles along the pathway—installed after 9/11 but left vacant for years—now bristle with spotlights and surveillance cameras. A swath of tall pines on the rise was clear-cut, with stumps and tossed limbs left to rot on a patch of scarred earth near the monument to reservoir architect J. Waldo Smith. There's more logging along the perimeter, some to clear parking lots for a recreational rail trail along the north shore, some seemingly just to sell timber.

Last winter I witnessed a late-night arrest on the weir bridge, the perp handcuffed facedown on cold rain-slick pavement. A few months later, two DEP cops questioned me on the same bridge for stepping out of my parked car to snap a quick photo (I got off with a warning, but trespassing fines have increased). I watched two more cops drive onto the Driftwood Cove beach to pick up a couple strolling down by the water without fishing poles.

The year I spent walking these shores unsurveilled seems like a throwback to a paradise lost—a paradise built on the shoulders of earlier losses. Things changed. They'll keep changing. Things always do.

This is a truth I learned from my reservoir year. How else did it change me?

I'm calmer. I found an oasis, a daily routine. In the same way I once used to walk my dog, I walk myself. I've learned that the days I resist going out are exactly the days when I need it the most. I lost some, not all, of the "pregnancy weight" I'd carried for twenty years. My eyes opened wider; I pay more attention to details. I can find more constellations in the night sky. I recognize more plants and birdcalls, the flight silhouettes of different raptors. I'm better at guessing how soon it will rain, what kinds of clouds will yield what kind of sunset. I've learned that dawn, sunset, and twilight unfold over time. The practice of learning to notice goes on and on. It's connected me to this particular place, to the cycle of seasons, and to the earth we all share.

Mindful walking is a meditation, a spiritual practice in the nondeity sense of the word (or, if you prefer, in the world-as-god sense). Weather and light are a skeptic's catechism; a walk every day is a way to count beads. The more times you repeat the same ritual, the deeper it takes you. And a year's worth of walks is not such a big deal. Dog walkers and morning joggers have daily practices that go on for decades. The difference, perhaps, is in writing it down.

When I started this project, I had no idea what the year would bring, how easy or hard it would be to keep my vow. Anything could have happened. This is what did, what I noticed each day in this beautiful place of deep water, wild mountains, and sky, layered over a valley that once held twelve towns. It was one particular year's worth of cycles; a different year would have yielded a different book.

Just after I finished my reservoir year, my father tripped over his bedroom slippers and fell. He fractured his pelvis, tailbone, and left arm. He spent three months flat on his back in a hospital bed, wrestling painkiller hallucinations and fighting his way back to life, while my brothers and I took turns staying with Mom in their New York apartment. When Papa came home in a wheelchair, now fully retired, my parents moved upstate full time, and I wheeled him along the Ashokan walkway. He relearned how to walk after weeks of intensive physical therapy, pushing a Rollator walker that mirrored Mom's. The res was his favorite place to practice. When he finally made it as far as the first bench, he sat on it for a long time, staring out at the view before telling my mother, "This is a wonderful place."

The following fall, Mom had her own medical crisis when an emergency pacemaker implant left her unable to walk. Months later, when she'd regained enough strength to get into a wheelchair and car with the help of an aide, we drove her to the reservoir. "Oh!" she exclaimed as she surveyed its shores. "I never thought I'd get to see this again."

My reservoir year was a treasure, a gift that keeps giving. I didn't know it at the time, but that sweet span of days from one September to the next was the only year I could have fulfilled the commitment I made to myself, a restorative pause between wearing the mantles of caregiving mother and caregiving daughter. The Ashokan landscape is a part of me now, a deep well of peace I return to in times of stress and hold in reserve for the times I'll go back there to grieve; a reservoir in every sense of the word.

I still walk there often, though not every day. The public-access walkway from Olivebridge to the Frying Pan now has a new sister, the Ashokan Rail Trail. Opened in October 2019, the eleven-and-a-half-mile former railroad bed traces the reservoir's north shore from West Hurley to Boiceville, granting thousands of visitors access to breathtaking views that were once inaccessible. It seems churlish, while walking its broad ADA-compliant surface amid happy throngs of bicyclists, strollers, and leashed dogs (now legal), to yearn for the days when I stumbled across these same coves by myself, graced by herons and flickers and the odd porcupine skull. There are still many acres ungroomed, many well-hidden beaches where I've never wandered. I look forward to finding them in my own time.

My reservoir walks are a treat now. I skip sleet storms gladly; I don't scrawl down notes, though I do take photos on Maya's old iPhone with a similar dogged obsession. I no longer bend my travel schedule in knots so I won't miss a day on the res. But one evening last fall, when I took the train back from New York, the sky over the Hudson was heavy with sculptural clouds. A shaft of sunlight sliced through like the beacon, and I was seized with the sense that there was something I had to see at the Ashokan, the don't-ask-questions-just-go kind of instinct I've learned to obey.

As I drove, the sky flooded with color, flame against charcoal, lilac, and pink. A throwdown of rain hit the windshield, then stopped.

By the time I arrived, the sun had set and a black mass of storm clouds was building. I scanned the beach: no bald eagles, no bears. I crossed to the opposite guardrail and looked down the hill. A six-point buck was grazing, heavy headed with testosterone. He looked up at me, tossing his rack, then arched his back and leapt into the woods.

Was that what I was supposed to see? I walked on.

A young woman was sitting alone on the stone bench, bent over a sketchpad. The line of her jaw seemed familiar. I wondered what she was drawing but didn't want to invade her space. Then I realized she was doing something I've never seen anyone do on the reservoir: writing.

She looked up and said simply, "Hello." In that instant, I knew why she seemed so familiar: she reminded me of myself. A much younger self, with that same spiky mix of defiance, friendliness, privacy. But she was a young woman *now*, swathed in chic layers, scarf wrapped around honey-blonde hair, round blue eyes, forearm tattoos. She didn't look anything like me.

I nodded a smile and kept walking. The storm cloud did not drop its rain. I heard but did not see the heron, its rusted-gate honk. I crossed the Lemon Squeeze bridge and stopped at the foot of the rise, gazing at the horizon as dusk fell, drinking in the familiar contours of peaks and reflection. My gathering place. The landscape that refills my soul.

I started back, wondering if I'd wind up in the young woman's notebook, as she would in mine. But the stone bench was empty. That girl had moved on.

Olivebridge, New York, 2019

Acknowledgments

THE WORLD OF NATURE is full of marvelous plural nouns: a murmuration of starlings, a pride of lions, an exaltation of larks. I'd like to invent such a word for the wonderful flock that surrounded me during the making of this book. Thanks and hosannas to:

Sergei Pshenitsyn and Sebastian Stuart, who put me up to this.

My intrepid and generous agent, Susie Cohen, who found me an ideal home at Syracuse University Press. Peg Solic, my lovely editor, and her hardworking colleagues Meghan Cafarelli, Mona Hamlin, Vicky Lane, Nora Luey, Kay Steinmetz, and Lynn Wilcox.

The artists whose insight, vision, and love of this landscape make this book glow: Kate McGloughlin (cover painting), Will Lytle (reservoir map and line drawings), and Carol Zaloom (hand-colored linocuts). I cherish your work, and you. Thanks also to photographer Dion Ogust and Wiley Davis at Catskill Art & Office Supply.

The writers and friends who offered invaluable insights and patient support every step of the way: Laura Rose, Mark St. Germain, Zachary Sklar, Mary Louise Wilson, John Bowers, Jana Martin, Robert Burke Warren, Lisa A. Phillips, Teresa Giordano, Nelly Reifler, Beverly Donofrio, Susan Krawitz, Lissa Kiernan, Gail Straub, Paul Russell, Amitava Kumar, Laurie Alberts, David Van Biema, David Smilow, Sigrid Heath, Mary Gallagher, Nicole Quinn, Sarah Chodoff, Geoff Harden, Alan Amtzis, Galen Green, Judie Stahl, Carol Goodman, Joan Burroughs, Catskills Living Treasure Leslie T. Sharpe, zen proofreader Mikhail Horowitz, and so many more.

The audiences at the Golden Notebook bookstore, Word Café, Next Year's Words, Poetry Barn, Lydia's Literary Dinner Salon, Writers in the Mountains, and Unitarian Universalist Congregation of the Catskills, who listened to excerpts from this work in progress; Maureen Cummins, who printed one in her beautiful letterpress journal *Tinker Street*.

Nan Tepper Design and ace photography duo Franco Vogt and Lucia Reale-Vogt for my beautiful website.

The Omega Institute, the Breakers hotel, the Stone Ridge Library, the Olive Free Library, the libraries at Vassar College and the College of New Jersey, and the Malden Seismic Retreat for inspiration, blessed silence, and room to write.

My family, always. You are in these pages and in my heart.

The wonderful team that cares for my parents: Ruth Rich, Lynette Keator, Pauline Mukhozo, Oksana and Miroslava Reznikova, Joan Paneto, and Aaron Smith.

Everyone who walked with me during my reservoir year.

The good people of the Esopus Valley, the living and the dead.

You are my murmuration, my pride, my exaltation. This book is for you.

Suggested Reading

On the Ashokan Reservoir and Catskills Region

Burroughs, John. *Afloat and Afoot*. Chichester, NY: Silver Hollow Audio, 2015. A lovely recording of two classic John Burroughs essays, "Pepacton: A Summer Voyage," narrated by Brett Barry, and "The Heart of the Southern Catskills," narrated by Rolland Smith. Includes expert commentaries by Diane Galusha and Bill Birns.

Burroughs, John. *Signs and Seasons*. New York: The Barnes & Noble Library of Essential Reading, 2008. Originally published in 1886, this essay collection is a delightful introduction to the celebrated naturalist and bard of the Catskills.

Carey, Tobe. *Deep Water*. Glenford, NY: Willow Media, 2005. Documentary film using archival photographs and interviews to tell the story of the Ashokan Reservoir and the communities it displaced.

Evers, Alf. *The Catskills: From Wilderness to Woodstock*. New York: Overlook Press, 1982. The seminal history of the Catskills region by a master historian and writer.

Galusha, Diane. *Liquid Assets: A History of New York City's Water System*. Fleischmanns, NY: Purple Mountain Press, 1999. The contentious history, logistics, and politics of creating the Catskill reservoir system and aqueducts that bring water to New York City.

McGloughlin, Kate. *Requiem for Ashokan: The Story Told in Landscape*. Olivebridge, NY: Davis Corners Press, 2017. An artist's chapbook of prints and poems about the Ashokan Reservoir's impact on its community, including the artist's ancestors.

Sharpe, Leslie T. *The Quarry Fox and Other Critters of the Wild Catskills*. New York: Overlook Press, 2017. A rich intermingling of personal narrative and keen observation of the Catskills' animals, birds, and insect life by a seasoned naturalist.

Steuding, Bob. *The Last of the Handmade Dams*. Fleischmanns, NY: Purple Mountain Press, 1985. An invaluable chronicle of the Ashokan's construction in the early twentieth century.

Straub, Gail. *The Ashokan Way: Landscape's Path into Consciousness*. Pawcatuck, CT: Homebound Publications, 2018. This collection of meditative personal essays explores the Ashokan's landscape as metaphor, inspiration, and spiritual mentor.

On Walking and Nature

Dillard, Annie. *Pilgrim at Tinker Creek*. New York: Harper Perennial, 2007. An incandescent personal account of a year spent observing nature in Virginia's Roanoke Valley.

Hanh, Thich Nhat. *How to Walk*. Berkeley: Parallax Press, 2015. Microessays on walking and mindfulness by a renowned teacher of Zen.

Horowitz, Alexandra. *On Looking: Eleven Walks with Expert Eyes*. New York: Scribner, 2013. The bestselling author of *Inside of a Dog* explores her Manhattan neighborhood with a rotating cast of specialists.

Moor, Robert. *On Trails: An Exploration*. New York: Simon & Schuster, 2017. This *New York Times* bestseller blends personal history of through-hiking the Appalachian and other notable trails with a journalist's insights on the history, construction, and meaning of trails.

Perkins, Michael and Nixon, Will. *Walking Woodstock: Journeys into the Wild Heart of America's Most Famous Small Town*. Woodstock, NY: Bushwhack Books, 2009. Two writer friends walk the back roads and mountain paths of Woodstock, New York.

Solnit, Rebecca. *Wanderlust: A History of Walking*. London: Granta Publications, 2014. An intellectually stimulating collection of personal and historical essays.

Thoreau, Henry David. *Walking*. Orlando: Value Classic Reprints, 2016. First delivered as a lecture in 1851, this seminal essay predates Thoreau's better-known *Walden; or, Life in the Woods*.

About the Author

Nina Shengold's books include the novel *Clearcut* (Anchor Books), *River of Words: Portraits of Hudson Valley Writers* (SUNY Press, with photographer Jennifer May), and fourteen theatre anthologies for Vintage Books and Viking Penguin, many coedited with Eric Lane. She won the Writers Guild Award for her teleplay *Labor of Love* and the ABC Playwright Award for *Homesteaders*. Her plays are published by Playscripts, Broadway Play Publishing, and Samuel French; *War at Home: Students Respond to 9/11*, written with Nicole Quinn and the Rondout Valley High School Drama Club, has been produced around the world. Shengold has profiled more than 150 writers for *Chronogram*, *Poets & Writers*, and *Vassar Quarterly*. She's a founding member of the theatre company Actors & Writers, author series Word Café, and Hudson Valley Writers Resist. A graduate of Wesleyan University, Shengold has taught at Manhattanville College and the University of Maine, and currently teaches creative writing at Vassar College. She was born in Brooklyn, grew up in New Jersey, escaped to Alaska, and now lives and works in the foothills of New York's Catskill Mountains.

About the Artists

Will Lytle grew up a stone's throw from the Ashokan Reservoir. He wrote and illustrated the 2019 picture book *Little One and the Water* in collaboration with Catskill Waters and the Ashokan Watershed Stream Management Program. His meticulous line drawings also appear on the cover of Clark Strand and Perdita Finn's *The Way of the Rose* and in Strand's *Waking Up to the Dark* (Spiegel & Grau), in limited-edition comics, and on storefronts, signs, and mural walls throughout the region, including the Catskill Pines, Phoenicia Flea, Woodstock General Supply, O+ Festival, Keegan Ales, Overlook Mountain Bikes, and the Golden Notebook Bookstore.

Kate McGloughlin is a celebrated painter and printmaker who lives and maintains a successful studio in Olivebridge, New York. Included in over seventy exhibitions, she is the winner of more than a dozen notable awards for achievement, and her work is included in permanent collections in four museums. She is president emeritus of the Woodstock School of Art, where she also teaches Landscape Painting and Printmaking. *Requiem for Ashokan: The Story Told in Landscape*, her multimedia exhibition of paintings, prints, text, and spoken word, premiered at the Woodstock Artists Association & Museum in June 2017; was exhibited at the Center for Contemporary Printmaking in Norwalk, Connecticut, in March

2019; and is the subject of her book of the same title. McGloughlin is a twelfth-generation resident of Ulster County, New York. www.katemcgloughlin.com.

Carol Zaloom lives and works in Saugerties, New York. Largely self-taught, she honed her skills at the Woodstock School of Art. As a linocut printmaker she has exhibited in galleries throughout New York state, with solo shows at Rensselaer Polytechnic Institute in Troy and Donskoj Gallery in Kingston. Her illustration work has appeared in many national publications, including *Sky and Telescope, Yankee*, and the magazines of the National Federation of Teachers. Her cover illustrations have appeared on books for Random House, Harper Collins, David R. Godine, and multiple independent publishers. Some of her work was translated into granite and iron and appears in the Catbird Playground in Carl Schurz Park, next to Gracie Mansion in New York City. She was awarded three Certificates of Design Excellence by *Print* magazine.